Studies in Literature and Criticism 1

EGOISM AND SELF-DISCOVERY IN THE VICTORIAN NOVEL

EGOISM AND SELF-DISCOVERY IN THE VICTORIAN NOVEL

Studies in the Ordeal of Knowledge
in the Nineteenth Century

JOHN HALPERIN
University of Southern California

Introduction By
Walter Allen

BURT FRANKLIN, Publisher
NEW YORK

Published by Burt Franklin, Publishers, 235 E. 44th St., N.Y. 10017
Copyright © 1974, Lenox Hill Publishing & Distribution Corporation.

Library of Congress Cataloging in Publication Data

Halperin, John, 1941-
    Egoism and self-discovery in the Victorian novel.

    (Studies in literature and criticism, 1)
    Bibliography: p.
    1. English fiction—19th century—History and criticism.
I. Title.
PR871.H3 1974   823'.8'0935   73-19510
ISBN 0-8337-5485-8

For My Mother

whose love of life and literature
has been a constant inspiration

Acknowledgments

It is a great pleasure to be able to thank most particularly Professor Walter Allen of the New University of Ulster, Professor A. Walton Litz of Princeton University, Professor Dorothea Krook of Tel-Aviv University, and Professor Alan Warren Friedman of the University of Texas, all of whom read this book in manuscript and made many invaluable suggestions for its improvement. To them I am deeply grateful for many kindnesses and excellent critical advice. Professor William Templeman of the University of Southern California also read sections of this study, and I should like to thank him for suggesting a number of sensible changes.

I am also indebted, for constant encouragement and kind advice, to Professors Alfred Kazin and Judah Stampfer of the State University of New York at Stony Brook, Professor J. Hillis Miller of Yale University, Professor Max F. Schulz of the University of Southern California, and Professor Irving H. Buchen of Fairleigh Dickinson University. To the late Irving Ribner I owe a debt of gratitude and inspiration which no words of friendship can express.

Parts of the first, fourth, and seventh chapters of this book appeared in altered form in *The Language of Meditation: Four Studies in Nineteenth-Century Fiction,* and I am grateful to the book's publisher, Arthur H. Stockwell, Ltd., for permission to incorporate some of the material published there into sections of the present study. A portion of Chapter 2 was presented, also in altered form, as a paper entitled "The Dramatic Structure of *Jane Eyre*" at the Northeast Modern Language Association conference at Skidmore College, Saratoga Springs, New York, in April 1972. And a portion of my discussion of criticism of Henry James in the appended Bibliographical Note originally appeared in altered form as part of my Afterword to a Meridian Books/Popular Library paperback edition of *The Golden Bowl* (1972); I wish to thank the World Publishing Company of New York for permission to use some of that material here.

i

The preparation of the manuscript of this book for the press was facilitated in part by a grant from the Graduate School of the State University of New York at Stony Brook, for which I am grateful, and by the help of Miss Joy Yagman, Mrs. Lillyan Yagman, and Mrs. Lillian Silkworth, for which I am also very grateful.

Contents

Foreword

The purpose of this book is to identify and elucidate a theme common, in my view, in nineteenth-century fiction, and especially in the Victorian novel, and to compare and contrast authorial treatment of and perspective upon this theme as a means of discovering similarities and differences among the authors in question. The particular theme, as the title of this study suggests, is that of the moral and pyschological expansion of protagonists who begin in self-absorption and move, through the course of a tortuous ordeal of education, to more complete self-knowledge. This movement from blinding subjectivism through moral suffering to a more relatively self-denying objectivity varies in its minutiae from novelist to novelist, but the theme remains, I believe, a paramount one in the fiction of the period. Since to deal with all Victorian novels in this study would be patently impossible, and since in any case I have already expressed my views of a number of nineteenth-century novels in an earlier book (*The Language of Meditation: Four Studies in Nineteenth-Century Fiction,* published in England in 1973), I shall be considering in these pages a highly selective number of novels by selected major Victorian novelists—Thackeray, Charlotte Brontë, Trollope, Dickens, George Eliot, Meredith, and Hardy. The Victorian novelists, however, were of course inevitably products of a tradition which itself did not end when they stopped writing, and so to provide some balance and continuity I have also included in this volume some discussion of both Jane Austen and Henry James, whose themes and techniques connect them in a number of important ways to the Victorian novelists.

Due to the multiplication of texts, passages from novels quoted in the course of this study are referred to only by book or chapter number, whichever is appropriate. References appear in parentheses or brackets just before or just after quoted matter of substantive length or importance. I do not mean the absence of footnotes to suggest either that I am not indebted to the work of others or that I am ignorant of it. The Acknowledgments express some of my indebtedness, and a brief bibliographical essay appears at the end of this study as an appendix. My emphasis, however, is on a reading of the Victorian novel in its own context rather than in those of historical criticism or more modern trends in interpretation, and therefore I have experimented to the extent that works by other critics and scholars are not drawn upon specifically in my discussions of particular novels. The appendix does include, however, a brief listing of works by others which have influenced in various ways my approach to and understanding of the novels examined in this study.

J. H.
Lee, Massachusetts
August 1973

INTRODUCTION

It comes as something of a shock to realize that in one's lifetime one has seen the map of English literature changed so radically as to suggest that the terrain itself has been riven by an earthquake. Yet that does not much exaggerate what has happened within fifty years. I recall that when I was an undergraduate in an English university during the early Thirties I took for the final examination for my degree as bachelor of arts with honours in English a special paper in Victorian literature. I soaked myself in Carlyle, Ruskin, Mill, Arnold and Pater, but what strikes me now as extraordinary is that I did not read a single novel, nor was I expected to. It was as though Dickens, George Eliot, the Brontës had never written.

The fact is, in universities at least, the novel had yet to achieve respectability. No need to stress the contrast with today, when the novel appears to reign supreme, and Dickens, George Eliot, Thackeray and the Brontës *are,* at any rate in some eyes, the nineteenth century. One can date the beginning of the change pretty accurately. Wilson's essay "The Two Scrooges" appeared in 1942: almost everything stems from that; and within ten years the revaluation of nineteenth-century fiction was well under way, and there are no signs yet of its coming to an end.

But still, despite the work of the critics and scholars, of Leavis, the Tillotsons, Booth, Ray, Haight, to name only a few, until recently the great Victorians were critically still at a disadvantage. They had been followed by James, the great rebuker, among other things, and it was he who by his practice and precept had shaped our ideas of the novel. We were faced with what seemed a paradox. No denying the greatness of the Victorians as novelists, as creators, but weren't they deficient in art, weren't they, by Jamesian standards, perhaps naive? Well, within the past few years that particular paradox has been resolved. A great imaginative writer who is not at the same time a great artist is a contradiction in terms; whatever

vii

else they may be, novelists of the calibre of Dickens and George Eliot are not naive; and, incidentally, weren't the same kind of charges of deficiency in art levelled against them made in earlier days against Shakespeare? And then Professor Frye has shown us that literary categories are not so simple as some of us thought. More precisely, the word "novel" is no more than a convenient label for many disparate forms of fiction.

So we no longer have to make a case for the Victorians as artists, and one consequence of this is to confer on the critic of Victorian fiction greater freedom than he has had in the past. He need no longer let himself be impeded by irrelevancies but can devote himself to the task at hand. Which brings me to *Egoism and Self-Discovery in the Victorian Novel*. John Halperin's book stands high among the critical writing of the past decade on the Victorian novel. He has isolated, and addresses himself to, one of its great central themes, "that of the moral and psychological expansion of protagonists who begin in self-absorption and move, through the course of a tortuous ordeal of education, to more complete knowledge." He is not the first to have recognised the theme as characteristic of the age, but I cannot think of anyone who has studied it in closer detail; and in doing so he brings out the relations that exist between half a dozen major novelists. I am the more convinced of the truth of Professor Halperin's thesis because, though there are good reasons, literary and social, why the theme is not predominant in contemporary fiction, the fact remains that it has by no means entirely disappeared. When we read, say, Angus Wilson's *The Middle Age of Mrs. Eliot* or the *Children of Violence* sequence of Doris Lessing we find ourselves forced back, for our criteria of criticism, to George Eliot. And something like the theme can, I think, be found in some of the novels of William Golding, for all his apparent difference as a novelist from both the Victorians and Mr. Wilson and Mrs. Lessing.

Specifically, it seems to me, what Professor Halperin has done, in terms of the nineteenth-century English novel, is to have given us chapter and verse for, and brought by close reading to full definition, Lionel Trilling's famous statement:

For our time the most effective agent of the moral imagination has been the novel of the last two hundred years. It was never, either aesthetically or morally, a perfect form and its faults and failures can be quickly enumerated. But its greatness and its practical usefulness lay in its unremitting work of involving the reader himself in the moral life, inviting him to put his own motives under examination, suggesting that reality is not as his conventional education has led him to see it. It taught us, as no other genre ever did, the extent of human variety and the value of this variety. It was the literary form to which the emotions of understanding and forgiveness were indigenous, as if by the definition of the form itself.

In other words, Professor Halperin brings out the reasons why the nineteenth-century novels he has chosen to discuss remain the delight of the common reader and why, also, they have become an essential part of English studies.

I do not always agree with him; or perhaps I should say that some prejudices have proved too stubborn to allow me to be persuaded. In my time, I have tried to do my best by Meredith and have worked hard on him, but I suspect I am too much of an Englishman of my generation to find him readable. But apart from this, how persuasive Professor Halperin is! It is the sign of a good critic—indeed it is the definition of one—that he can show you what you have missed in a book before. For this, enthusiasm is needed as well as learning, sensibility and perception. Professor Halperin has all these qualities. I know that as a teacher and as a writer I shall be referring to his book constantly, so scrupulous and so just are his examinations of what he admirably calls the ordeal of knowledge. And he has warmed my heart because he shows, by his examples, the all-importance of character in the novel, something that novelists themselves have always known but critics sometimes doubted.

In particular, I know that Professor Halperin has expanded my knowledge and appreciation of Charlotte Brontë and Hardy. And there is something else. It is impossible to read his book without realising how seminal Jane Austen is in our fiction. Of course one has always known this, it has become a commonplace of criticism. But by isolating the theme that is predominantly hers and demonstrating the treatment of it in the work of half a dozen other novelists, he succeeds in bringing it home more clearly, more arrestingly, than I recall its being done before. At times I am tempted to revolt against her supremacy, for the same reason as the Athenians revolted against Aristides: they grew bored, you remember, at having constantly to hear him called "the Just." Professor Halperin has cured me of that.

In my view, *Egoism and Self-Discovery in the Victorian Novel* will be read with profit and pleasure by all students of nineteenth-century fiction; and it is written with such humanity and with such a notable lack of jargon that there is no reason why it should not delight the common reader, on whom, in the end, the continuing life of any novel depends.

WALTER ALLEN
London, August 1973

A man should be proud of suffering. All suffering is a reminder of our high estate.

—Novalis

They knew that as a man he was worthless, but nevertheless they loved him. I think the secret of it was chiefly in this,—that he seemed to think so little of himself. . . . Every man to himself is the centre of the whole world,—the axle on which it all turns. All knowledge is but his own perception of the things around him. All love, and care for others, and solicitude for the world's welfare, are but his own feelings as to the world's wants and the world's merits.

—Trollope, *Can You Forgive Her?*

At the same time I confess I never see the *leading* interest of any human hazard but in a consciousness (on the part of the moved and moving creature) subject to fine intensification and wide enlargement.

—Henry James, preface to *The Princess Casamassima*

In the spontaneous realization of the self man unites himself anew with the world—with man, nature, and himself.

—Erich Fromm, *Escape from Freedom*

'We have two lives . . . the life we learn with and the life we live with after that. Suffering is what brings us toward happiness.'

—Bernard Malamud, *The Natural*

'I don't see where good is to spring from, if it is not out of that evil suffering . How can one build a better self unless on the ruins of the old?'

—John Fowles, *The French Lieutenant's Woman*

THE VICTORIAN NOVEL AND JANE AUSTEN

JANE AUSTEN (1775-1817)
National Portrait Gallery, London.

Chapter One

The Victorian Novel
and Jane Austen

The theme of education is a radical one in most literatures. Homer and Joyce are equally concerned with appearance and reality, with what is real and what is not, with what is good and what is not. Characters who experience the ordeal of learning in order to make these distinctions dominate the works of many of the authors of all nations. And so it should not be surprising to find that in the Victorian novel such characters abound.

And yet they do more than merely abound. The ordeal of the individual who begins in ignorance due to self-absorption and ends in sympathetic comprehension of others as a result of the dissipation of egoism and the growth of self-knowledge is a concern found so often in the Victorian novel as to make any sentient student of the fiction of the period aware of its striking omnipresence. It seems that here—at this time and in this *genre*—writers especially saw their fictional personages in terms of a developmental formula. Some of them, like George Eliot and George Meredith, actually put into writing specific formulae for the ways in which they viewed the moral growth of all people of sensibility. Many of the other Victorian novelists saw the organic process of human development in much the same ways but never defined the particular stages of its process outside of their fiction. And yet most of the Victorian novelists, whether their theories were enunciated or not, were apt to see human moral growth in many of the same ways—ways which it is the purpose of this study to identify and describe.

The formula for the psychic development of fictional personages varies from author to author, for each of the writers, as might be expected, has his or her own perspective on the world; moral education means something different to each. And yet there is at least a superficial similarity among these writers as far as the psychic stages through which their characters pass is concerned. In virtually all of the novels under consideration in this study, a major protagonist begins in egoism or some related stage of self-absorption, a condition whose major results are likely to be both deficient self-understanding and blindness to the real natures of other people. Through a series of educational jolts to the ego and thus to the self-perspective, the character begins to doubt his bases for judging himself and others, and eventually attains to a state of relative self-consciousness, which takes the form of a new lack of self-confidence and the revision of previously unshakable opinions of himself and others. This leads to the third and final stage of character-development—that of self-discovery, in which the educational process reaches its climax in a new perspective on self and a correspondingly clearer vision and understanding of others. George Eliot tended to think of most people as going through stages of egoism and despair on the way to what she calls "moral vision" and ultimate sympathy for others: these steps, for her, were the constitutive elements of the ordeal of human education. Meredith saw human moral development in somewhat similar terms and labelled its stages those of blood, brain, and spirit (egoism, rationality, and love). Many of the other Victorian novelists, without expressing themselves so specifically, constructed similar ordeals for their protagonists. And yet it should be emphasized once again that while the psychological growth of these Victorian protagonists is often similar in direction, the structure of their experiences, the conclusions drawn from them, and the perspectives emphasized as a result of them are not always the same—are, in fact, often quite different. It is the purpose of this study to point out these similarities and differences, and to draw out of a consideration of them some conclusions about each writer's view of humanity's potential for moral growth.

I

Jane Austen is not a Victorian writer, and yet her novels anticipate many of the concerns of the Victorians. Her work was looked back upon by some subsequent nineteenth-century writers as a model, and most of them tended to repeat her synthesis of the eighteenth-century novel's battle between elaborate plotting and growing interest in the psychological development of protagonists. One might say that the specific formula governing many Victorian novels, which I have defined as the ordeal leading from egoism to self-discovery, actually begins with the novels of Jane Austen—specifically with her two best novels, *Pride and Prejudice* and *Emma*.

Jane Austen's interest in the psychology of imaginary characters is not the only link between her work and that of her nineteenth-century descendants. Like the Victorian novelists and Henry James, Jane Austen has intense moral preoccupations, often with money; *Persuasion,* for example, is as much a novel about money as *Our Mutual Friend, The Way We Live Now, Silas Marner,* or *The Portrait of A Lady.* Jane Austen, like the later nineteenth-century novelists, is essentially a novelist of manners, concerned as she is with manners as a reflection of morals; and thus her novels, like those of many of the Victorian novelists and James, are set preponderantly in drawing-rooms and studies—inside houses rather than outside of them. Like her literary heirs, Jane Austen is fond of using the Cinderella motif, as one can see, for example, from *Mansfield Park*, as well as *Jane Eyre, Bleak House, The Mill on the Floss, The Ordeal of Richard Feverel,* and, to take just one example from James, *The Wings of the Dove.* In terms of technique there are of course a number of other similarities between Jane Austen's fiction and that which came after her in the nineteenth century. Jane Austen, for example, preferred the indirection of dramatization in order to preserve some "illusion of reality" in her novels. She sought for economy of composition and attempted to root out of her novels whatever failed to contribute to the dominant thematic concerns. James's dictum in his preface to *The Ambassadors* that fiction is composed of scenes and preparations for scenes—and that whatever is not "scene" is "picture"—is a critical principle applied as easily to *Emma* as to *Daniel Deronda* or *The Egoist* or *The Golden Bowl*. In Jane Austen's novels, as in many of those by later nineteenth-century writers, language is an index to character—how people express themselves helps us to determine what kind of people they are (Mr. Collins in *Pride and Prejudice,* Mrs. Gamp in *Martin Chuzzlewit,* Mrs. Poyser in *Adam Bede,* Dr. Middleton in *The Egoist*, Mrs. Lowder in *The Wings of the Dove*). In many of these novels the point of view is limited for the most part to that of a "central consciousness," and thus the theme of the protagonist's education becomes doubly important. Jane Austen's Willoughbys and Middletons significantly reappear, perhaps more than in name only, in *The Egoist,* and the subjects of her novels generally are not wholly different from those of Thackeray, Trollope, George Eliot, Meredith and James. In method and range of interest she is more like James, it may be, than she is like any of the others, and this may well be what prompted Virginia Woolf to write that, had Jane Austen lived longer, she would have been a forerunner not only of James but of Proust as well. Thus Jane Austen's ties to later writers, Victorian as well as modern, are both strong and perhaps beyond unravelling.

II

In *Pride and Prejudice* (1813), Elizabeth Bennet's movement from blind prejudice to objective vision occupies the center of thematic focus. Elizabeth's pride in what she feels is her own unassailably good judgment yields mid-way through the novel to her despair at having been so wrong about Wickham and Darcy, which in turn leads her finally to a clearer understanding of her own nature and those of others, principally Darcy's. The ordeal of her education in values begins in egoism (self-conceit) and moves through a declining series of stages of self-absorption to ultimate self-discovery and a clearer view of the world. The novel's continuously sustained dramatic irony underlines for us again and again the specific process Elizabeth is going through: the various phases of her journey are well-marked. Taking two human beings who have both pride and prejudices, Jane Austen follows them through a series of defeats to their egos until, finally, the discordant elements are harmonized into the synthesis of a perfect marriage. Darcy too undergoes an education in values but his ordeal is mostly offstage. When Elizabeth has changed sufficiently to recognize his merits, she finds that many of the things about him which she had objected to have been purged in and by himself as well.

Elizabeth's ordeal is always before us, often commented on or alluded to ironically through the words spoken by the characters themselves. Early in the novel, for example, Elizabeth accuses her sister Jane of a weakness even more applicable to herself: " 'With *your* good sense, to be so honestly blind to the follies and nonsense of others!' " They have been debating the merits of Mr. Bingley, and Jane sees him for what he is—sensible, good-humored, and kind. Elizabeth hints that any man so well-disposed toward others must be lacking in intelligence, and the debate is on. Jane Austen patently takes Jane's side here, and remarks through her narrator just after the sentence quoted above that one of Elizabeth's cardinal qualities at this stage of development is "a judgment too unassailed by any attention to herself." Elizabeth's faulty vision results largely from lack of self-knowledge. In the very next chapter (I,v) Mary Bennet, that budding pedant whose speeches are often treated comically, nevertheless makes an important statement about pride itself:

'Pride . . . is a very common failing . . . .[H]uman nature is particularly prone to it, and . . . there are very few of us who do not cherish a feeling of self-complacency on the score of some quality or the other, real or imaginary. Vanity and pride are different things, though the words are often used synonymously. A person may be proud without being vain. Pride relates more

to our opinion of ourselves, vanity to what we would
have others think of us.'

This remarkable statement is no less important merely
because it is a textbook lecture delivered, ludicrously enough,
by a child whose self-conceit is already developing apace. It
applies specifically to Elizabeth, to whom it is addressed.
Elizabeth is indeed complacent about her own good judgment, in this case a quality quite imaginary. She has a little
vanity and a great deal of pride; she cares a little for what
others may think of her, but it is her own high opinion of
herself and her supposedly good sense and keen perception
which generate the essential egoism of her perspectives upon
herself and others.

Everywhere, the irony of Elizabeth's self-ignorance is
emphasized, though most often subtly. She tells Charlotte
Lucas that Jane cannot possibly know Bingley's character
sufficiently well after seeing him once at his own house and
dining with him in company four times. She herself, of
course, has Darcy in the iron-clad mold of her own prejudice
after seeing him twice. First impressions may be misleading
her sister, but not, of course, herself. Darcy has pronounced
his disdain for the women in the room at the Netherfield ball;
she was in the room at the time, therefore he has insulted her
and she must dislike him. Her prejudice against him
consistently blinds her to reality. When Darcy seems to be
noticing her above the other women in Mr. Bingley's drawing-
room, Elizabeth attributes it to "something about her more
wrong and reprehensible, according to his ideas of right, than
in any other person present" [I, x]. This is a mistake she makes
several times, and it is a mistake resulting not from humility
but from its opposite—pride, disdain, a prejudice sufficient to
make her unwilling, as the narrator says, "to care for his
approbation." The unconscious irony of Elizabeth's rather
fatuous pronouncements is given greater emphasis in a long
conversation she has with Darcy at Netherfield (I,xi). They
speak of vanity and pride—the subjects of Mary Bennet's
lecture—and Elizabeth accuses Darcy of believing himself
without fault. He confesses to a resentful temper: " 'My good

opinion once lost, is lost for ever.' " Elizabeth replies: " '*That*
is a failing indeed!... Implacable resentment *is* a shade in a
character.' " Her own implacable resentment against Darcy
broadens in the early chapters of the novel to allow her to think
as badly of him as possible; it is an attitude born of an
unshakable faith in her own powers of perception and
judgment and of "implacable resentment"—injured
vanity—resulting from his critical opinion of local women, of
whom she is one. Darcy seems partly to understand these
elements of Elizabeth's character, and tells her at the end of the
chapter that her great defect is the propensity "'wilfully to
misunderstand' " people—a very perspicacious comment
indeed. Elizabeth's early dislike of Darcy is as much willed as it
is spontaneous, and indeed she seems to revel in her dislike.
She cultivates her resentment at every possible opportunity as
a further kind of ego-gratification, and later on in the novel
discovers that she has done so so openly that her family and
friends find it difficult to believe that she is not marrying Darcy
for his money.

In Volume I, Chapter xvi, therefore, Elizabeth eagerly
accepts everything Wickham tells her about Darcy, and feeds
the fuel of her dislike for him with more misconceptions
about his character. She is too self-absorbed to see her own
irrationality or Wickham's lack of disinterestedness. Jane,
who Elizabeth feels is too kind-hearted to see the truth about
anybody, points out to Elizabeth (I,xvii) the folly of believing
everything that Wickham has said about Darcy: " 'It is
impossible. No man of common humanity, no man who had
any value for his character, could be capable of [behaving as
Wickham has said]. Can his most intimate friends be so
excessively deceived in him?' " Elizabeth replies: " 'I beg your
pardon; one knows exactly what to think,' " and she says a
little further on that she " ' is determined to hate' " Darcy.
Here, perhaps, is the apex of her egoistic pride in her own
powers of judgment and her blindness to her own real nature
and those of others.

At the Netherfield ball (I,xviii) the topic of discussion
between Elizabeth and Darcy moves from pride to prejudice.

Elizabeth asks him if he ever allows himself " 'to be blinded by prejudice,' " and when he replies that he hopes not, she retorts: " 'It is particularly incumbent on those who never change their opinion, to be secure of judging properly at first.' " This statement, in its stiff didacticism, sounds like something Mary Bennet might utter, but of course it is as valid in principle as Mary's lecture on pride and vanity and is made even more interesting by the obvious self-reflexive irony. Elizabeth does not know herself sufficiently well as yet to see that she is guilty of the crime she imputes by reference to Darcy. Volume I ends with Elizabeth's blind prejudice at its peak.

Later, discussing with Jane the marriage of Charlotte Lucas and Mr. Collins, Elizabeth is given another hint about the quality of her judgment. She feels injured by Charlotte's ready acceptance of Mr. Collins almost immediately after the latter's vain proposal to Elizabeth herself. Jane replies that often one feels injured without sufficient cause: " 'It is very often nothing but our own vanity that deceives us.' " It is Elizabeth's stultifying self-confidence that has blinded her to the real nature of things. Then, when Jane complains that Mr. Bingley has not the outward trappings of a man in love, Elizabeth says: " 'Is not general incivility the very essence of love?' " Were she capable of applying this sentiment to her own situation, Darcy's declaration several chapters further on would not be such a surprise.

To the last moment before Darcy's declaration Elizabeth has no idea how foolishly she has been acting. She assumes all along that Wickham is a good man, that Darcy is a villain, and that she herself sees them both clearly and accurately. Thus when Darcy tells her that he loves her (II,xi) "Elizabeth's astonishment was beyond expression." Such a possibility, clear to the reader for some time, has never occurred to her, too busy as she has been faulting Darcy for various imagined crimes. She rejects him rather acrimoniously, charging him with "abominable pride." He *is* a proud man, but he is also a good man; when Elizabeth begins to see this, she also begins to see herself and her own character more fully. She reads his letter "with a strong prejudice against everything he might say." The letter convinces her, finally, that part of what he says must be true. If part, then all, and Elizabeth is shocked to discover that she has completely misjudged two men. Her illusions about herself explode in a crescendo of self-discovery:

> 'How despicably have I acted!' she cried; 'I, who have prided myself on my discernment! I, who have valued myself on my abilities! who have often disdained the generous candour of my sister, and gratified my vanity in useless or blameable distrust. How humiliating is this discovery! yet, how just a humiliation! Had I been in love, I could not have been more wretchedly blind. But vanity, not love, has been my folly. Pleased with the preference of one, and offended by the neglect of the other, on the very beginning of our acquaintance, I have courted prepossession and ignorance, and driven reason away, where either were concerned. Till this moment I never knew myself.' (II,xiii)

Elizabeth finally sees that she has been prejudiced and blind in her relations with Wickham and Darcy—prejudiced in favor of Wickham because he has flattered her and against Darcy because, at least until just recently, he has not. She sees now that her supposedly unassailable judgment has been faulty and that her vision of things has been clouded by vanity and pride. Recognizing these things within herself, she can now begin to perceive the fallibilities of her own nature more fully, and in doing so she will objectify her vision and judgment of others. This is the center of her self-discovery: " 'Till this moment I never knew myself.' "

The ordeal of suffering for the blindness caused by her egoism, that necessary stage between self-absorption and final fulfillment, now begins in earnest for Elizabeth. She broods at length on her mistakes and acknowledges her folly to Jane, saying regretfully that she " 'meant to be uncommonly clever in taking so decided a dislike' " to Darcy without any apparent reason. She further acknowledges that her dislike of him was at least partly a result of ego-gratification: " 'It is such a spur to one's genius, such an opening for wit, to have a dislike of that kind.' " When Jane observes how unfortunate it is that Elizabeth has expressed herself so forcefully and clearly to Darcy about Wickham, Elizabeth replies that " 'the misfortune of speaking with bitterness is a most natural consequence of the prejudices I had been encouraging.' " Volume II ends on this note of self-recrimination—a long distance from the end of Volume I, at which time Elizabeth's blind folly was at its height.

Elizabeth's enlightenment intensifies during her visit with the Gardiners to Pemberley (III,i). She has already been convinced that Darcy is no villain, but now she hears from Mrs. Reynolds, Darcy's housekeeper, that he is a good-tempered man as well. That he was nothing of the sort "had been her firmest opinion," and this prejudice too must go the way of the others. " 'Can this be Mr. Darcy?' " she asks herself, and once again must bow to the more illuminated perspective of another. Darcy then appears unexpectedly upon the scene, and Elizabeth, expecting him to be brusque after their last meeting in Kent, is further surprised to encounter his affability and obvious delight in seeing her again, and she wonders how to account for it: " 'Why is he so altered? From what can it proceed? It cannot be for *me*—it cannot be for *my* sake that his manners are thus softened . . . It is impossible that he should still love me.' " Darcy has certainly become much more gracious in manner, but he is not so substantially altered as Elizabeth thinks—it is partly that she sees him differently now. Her perception is finer. On one subject, however, she remains deceived: he is still in love with her, and she is unable to see that this is the case. Where she overestimated herself and her powers of judgment before, she now underestimates herself, feeling that Darcy cannot be in love with her after their last parting in Kent. (In *Emma,* it will become evident, recognition of previous conceit also results temporarily in another kind of distortion—the devaluation of one's powers of attraction.)

Later, reflecting further upon Darcy's good will, Elizabeth begins to feel grateful to him, but she continues to misjudge him to some extent. The unfortunate affair between

Lydia and Wickham leads her to think of what she would want in a husband, and she discovers more fully now that Darcy "was exactly the man who, in disposition and talents, would most suit her. His understanding and temper, though unlike her own, would have answered all her wishes" [III,viii]. Darcy has indeed mellowed somewhat, but he is not as totally changed as Elizabeth thinks—she merely sees him more objectively now. And yet she continues to make mistakes. Having admitted to herself that Darcy would now suit her, she speculates on his probable reaction to such news (III,viii): "What a triumph for him . . . could he know that the proposals which she had proudly spurned only four months ago, would now have been gladly and gratefully received!" Darcy, of course, is not the sort of man to gloat over the love of a woman, as we discover several chapters later. Unsure of himself in matters of the heart, he is instead overjoyed to learn that Elizabeth has changed her mind. She begins in these later chapters to appreciate the generosity of his nature, but as yet she does not see into its depths. When Mrs. Gardiner informs her of Darcy's crucial role in the salvation of what is left of Lydia's honor after the elopement with Wickham, however, Elizabeth finally begins to appreciate Darcy's character for what it is: "Oh! how heartily did she grieve over every ungracious sensation she had ever encouraged, every saucy speech she had ever directed towards him. For herself, she was humbled, but she was proud of him" [III,ix]. These are Elizabeth's final convulsive moments of discovery. She now sees Darcy clearly and fully, primarily because she has already learned to know herself. The novel's last chapters recount the final happy results of Elizabeth's moral development.

Lady Catherine's amazing behavior merely confirms Elizabeth's growing conviction that Darcy and his aunt are not in fact alike after all, although she cannot help wondering if Lady Catherine's arguments against their engagement might appear more sensible to Darcy than to herself. He, of course, destroys her last vestiges of doubt by proposing again, asking if she still feels about him as she did several months previously. Elizabeth replies immediately (III,xvi) that "her sentiments had undergone so material a change since the period to which he alluded" that she is now ready to accept him with "gratitude and pleasure." The only moments of anxiety still before her come when she must convince her father of her love for Darcy—that it is not Darcy's money that has made her accept him: "How earnestly did she then wish that her former opinions had been more reasonable, her expressions more moderate!" After this last pang of self-accusation (III,xvii), the novel ends on a note of perfect happiness and accommodation.

In learning to know herself more fully, Elizabeth's blind egoism is dissipated. Self-regard becomes objective perception, the faculty of judging others correctly in fact as well as in conviction.

III

In *Emma* (1816) there are fewer moral categories than in Jane Austen's earlier novels. That is to say, instead of using different personages to embody different traits of character (pride, prejudice, sense, sensibility, and so on), Jane Austen combines all the contradictions, inconsistencies, weaknesses and strengths of the human psyche within one character—Emma herself. All of Jane Austen's other novels are named for places or concepts—this is the only one named for the protagonist, for in this novel more than in any of the others it is the psychological development of the protagonist herself that is paramount. (Elizabeth's development is of course central, but in *Pride and Prejudice* Jane Austen is also very much concerned with the nature of the two transgressions of the title.) Emma's mind is the primary moral battleground of Jane Austen's story, and it is always at the center of the novel. We have virtually total and continuous access to that mind, while the voice of the novel's omniscient narrator enables us to view it from a perspective of objectivity brought about through the possession of knowledge wider than that of the heroine herself. This is the major source of the novel's ubiquitous dramatic irony. When Emma's understanding of herself and of others catches up with the narrator's and the reader's, deep in the novel, the irony disappears and the novel can end, as does *Pride and Prejudice*, in the synthesis of perfect marriage (actually there are three of them).

Emma has many of the same defects of character as Elizabeth Bennet, but Emma's is a richer and more interesting personality. Emma too has a great deal of confidence in her own powers of judgment and perception. She too is an egoist, preoccupied with her own view of things and unable to see accurately very far beyond herself. Unlike Elizabeth, however, she has little common sense, she is not terribly witty, and she is an awful snob. But she is neither materialistic nor dull. She is a loving and loyal daughter, sister, and friend—compassionate, intelligent and beautiful.

The novel tells the story of Emma's acquisition of common sense and self-comprehension. Beginning in blind selfishness, she manipulates others to suit herself until she discovers what it is that really suits her—and then her self-absorption melts in the illumination of herself to herself. Once again, what the novel describes is the heroine's ordeal of education, the process of her own self-discovery. Emma's education develops in three distinct movements corresponding to the alternating presences in the novel of the three most important male protagonists—Elton, Churchill, and Knightley. She learns more and more about herself through her successive collisions with them, moving in the process through the stages of self-absorption, despair, and self-knowledge.

On the novel's first page we are introduced to Emma Woodhouse: "The real evils indeed of Emma's situation were the power of having rather too much her own way and a disposition to think a little too well of herself. . . . The danger, however, was at present . . . unperceived. . . ." It is the combination of Emma's trust in her own powers of perception and judgment and her ability, because of her "situation," of being able to do as she pleases, which brings a series of disasters down upon her, disasters forming part of her moral education and ultimately enabling her to see both herself and her world more clearly.

Emma's folly takes the paramount form of attempting to play God the Matchmaker. She calls it "the greatest amusement in the world" and boasts that she has been partly responsible for the marriage of her governess, Miss Taylor, and her prosperous neighbor, Mr. Weston. Mr. Knightley, whose function throughout the first two-thirds of the novel is that of a sort of choric deflator, tells her that she has simply " 'made a lucky guess' " and that more harm than good comes of interfering in other people's affairs. " 'Emma never thinks of herself if she can do good to others,' " replies Emma's silly father, Mr. Woodhouse, "understanding but in part." And Emma tells Mr. Knightley that she must " 'look about for a wife' " for Mr. Elton, Highbury's young and fashionable clergyman. Mr. Knightley warns her again to leave Mr. Elton to choose for himself, and the first chapter ends here—Emma's folly and Mr. Knightley's common sense both already well-defined by contrast.

Emma's newly formed friendship with Harriet Smith ultimately brings out the worst in both of them. Harriet's dependence and admiration flatter Emma's vanity, and she determines to "form" Harriet into something Harriet simply is not—a well-bred, sentient, intelligent young lady. Harriet is good-tempered but bovine. For Emma, transforming Harriet into a lady who will be accepted and even courted by her superiors is a challenge to her own self-esteem, and she starts playing with Harriet as with a new toy. She begins by separating Harriet from her respectable friends the Martins: "she would detach her from her bad acquaintance and introduce her into good society; she would form her opinions and her manners. It would be an interesting . . . undertaking, highly becoming her own situation in life, her leisure, and powers" [I,iii]. Emma decides to fill her "leisure" hours by playing God, by interfering in the lives of other people specifically in the way Mr. Knightley has warned her against.

Her vanity requires a loyal parasite who may be shaped in her own image—remade, capable of being "summoned at any time for a walk" or for conversation or for a lesson in decorum or values.

Robert Martin finally proposes to Harriet, and Emma's first battle in behalf of her new friend is to separate her from the Martins so that Harriet will not "be required to sink herself forever." Emma's secret resolution is to marry Harriet off to the fastidious Mr. Elton. Were Emma less of an egoist she would of course see the danger and futility of such machinations. But her interest in people at this stage of her development exists only to the extent that they relate to herself—only insofar as they can be manipulated for amusement and advantage. Her pride in her own judgment, the vanity of her self-perspective, will lead first to disappointment and then ultimately to increased understanding. Now, however, she is still in the very first stages of her ordeal of knowledge.

Mr. Knightley, in a subsequent conversation with Mrs. Weston (I,v), diagnoses Emma's malady perspicaciously. Emma, he says, is unable to subject her " 'fancy' " to her " 'understanding,' " by which he means that Emma's rational powers are less active than her imaginative ones. To be always in the midst of one's own imagination is the height of self-indulgence. Mr. Knightley goes on to say that Emma's association with Harriet will be " 'hourly flattery. How can Emma imagine she has anything to learn herself while Harriet is presenting such a delightful inferiority?' " This choice comment is succeeded by several chapters in which Emma does her best to make Mr. Elton fall in love with Harriet, and thinks she has succeeded. Mr. Elton's attentions to Hartfield, of course, are aimed at its heiress, but Emma's interest in the great game she is playing blinds her to this truth, and she assures Harriet that Mr. Elton will propose to her shortly. Harriet has enough sense to be sceptical, and speaks of the Martins. Emma replies that she would necessarily have had to give up Harriet's acquaintance had Harriet kept up her friendship with the Martins: " 'I could not have visited Mrs.

Robert Martin of Abbey-Mill Farm. Now I am secure of you forever.' " As usual she is thinking of herself, and of others only as they relate (or do not relate) to herself.

In her blind self-absorption, Emma fancies Mr. Elton more in love with Harriet than ever; she pays no attention to Mr. Knightley, who warns her (I,viii) that Mr. Elton will never " 'make an imprudent match. He knows the value of a good income as well as anybody. . . . He will act rationally.' " Emma assures Mr. Knightley that she has " 'done with matchmaking' " and only wants to keep Harriet as a companion, but when he is gone she is patently unrepentant: "she still thought herself a better judge of such a point of female right and refinement than he could be," and she tells herself that Mr. Elton is no more "prudent" than anyone else. Emma's confidence in her own judgment and her propensity to attempt the direction of others' affairs are continually emphasized in these early chapters. Her fancy, her own egoistic pursuits, hold dominion over common sense, and in fact the narrator comments (I,ix) to the effect that Emma finds it "much pleasanter to let her imagination range and work at Harriet's fortune than to be labouring, to enlarge her comprehension or exercise it on sober facts. . . ." The enforced enlargement of her comprehension occupies much of the rest of the novel.

Mr. Elton continues to pay court at Hartfield, and Emma assures Harriet that she is his object. She keeps thrusting the puzzled Mr. Elton at Harriet, and begins to feel "the glory of having schemed successfully." Mr. Knightley continues to warn Emma that her judgment of others is faulty: " 'If you were as much guided by nature in your estimate of men and women, and as little under the power of fancy and whim in your dealings with them, as you are where . . . children are concerned, we might always think alike' " [I, xii]. Once again it is Emma's "fancy," not her rational faculties, which is emphasized. Even John Knightley, understanding the situation at a glance, warns Emma that Mr. Elton is after her and not Harriet. Emma, of course, is paying no attention, is rather "amusing herself in the consideration of the blunders which often arise from a partial knowledge of circumstances, of the mistakes which people of high pretensions to judgment are forever falling into . . ." [I,xiii] .

Emma's education begins in earnest in a closed carriage while she is returning from a dinner party one evening at the Westons (I,xv). There Mr. Elton proposes marriage to her. She is shocked; isn't he in love with Harriet Smith? " 'Good Heaven!' cried Mr. Elton ... 'I never thought of Miss Smith in the course of my existence.' " Emma is incredulous—has he never thought seriously of Harriet? Says Mr. Elton: " 'I need not so totally despair of an equal alliance as to be addressing myself to Miss Smith!' " Emma tells him petulantly that she is not aware of any "very great inequality" between himself and Harriet, and they part coldly. The prophecies of the Knightley brothers have been fulfilled. Mr. Elton, who *is* a prudent man, has indeed set his sights on the heiress of Hartfield. Emma's blundering has brought about what can only be great disappointment to Harriet and embarrassment to herself. She goes home to meditate on the situation, and undergoes for the first time a convulsive reassessment of herself in relation to other people (I,xvi). Her sustained self-confrontation lasts well into the night and represents a dawning of self-awareness, a first step in the process of the exorcism of egoism, which is necessarily painful. To herself she uses such words as "pain," "humiliation," "blunder," "deception," "confusion," and "mortification." She blames herself for having "persuaded Harriet into liking" Mr. Elton. She remembers now how the Knightleys had warned her of her folly, and "blushed to think how much truer a knowledge of Mr. Elton's character had been there shown than any she had reached herself." Here is her first admission that her own judgment has been faulty. Emma now acknowledges to herself that her past courtesy and attention to Mr. Elton may well logically explain his mistake: "If *she* had so misinterpreted his feelings, she had little right to wonder that *he*, with self-interest to blind him, should have mistaken hers." Emma too has been blinded by self-interest—a selfish desire to promote the claims of her friend, whom she has been using as a proxy, as an extension of herself, as a shield against the necessity of becoming involved in a serious attachment. Emma now begins to see, just a little, the arrogance of interference in the personal affairs of others: "It was foolish, it was wrong, to take so active a part in bringing any two people together. It was advertising too far, assuming too much, making light of what ought to be serious—a trick of what ought to be simple. She was quite concerned and ashamed, and resolved to do such things no more" [I,xvi]. She is not, however, substantially cured, for the next moment she is considering William Cox as a possible successor to Harriet's affections. Emma finally goes to bed "with nothing settled but the conviction of her having blundered most dreadfully," and without firmly committing herself to changing her ways. The overthrow of all she had been planning is sufficiently upsetting to lead her into only a few moments of self-searching, to shake only for a short time her fully developed self-confidence, her complaisance about her understanding of others.

The Harriet-Elton affair, the climax of which closes Volume I, has nevertheless opened Emma's eyes at least somewhat to her own nature—has taught her to put a little less reliance on her judgment of others and in her confidence in herself. The ordeal of her education has begun, if only tenuously; it is an ordeal that will lead her eventually to more complete self-knowledge.

The second stage of Emma's ordeal encompasses the relationships between Emma herself and Frank Churchill, Jane Fairfax, Mr. Knightley, and once again Harriet Smith. It begins with Emma's ingeniously surmising a clandestine relationship between Jane and her friend Mr. Dixon, her anticipation of meeting and perhaps falling in love with Churchill, and renewed plans for Harriet's future. Harriet, meanwhile, has been wanting to visit the Martins, so Emma takes her to them in her carriage, leaves her for fourteen minutes with people she had recently stayed with for six weeks, and then goes off with her. It is an act of uncommon rudeness and arrogance, but Emma rationalizes: "it must be done, or what would become of Harriet? . . . How could she have done otherwise? Impossible! She could not repent" [II,v]. It seems, then, that Emma is going down the same road she has just recently sworn to abandon.

Early in the second volume Frank Churchill appears on the scene, and Emma fancies that perhaps she may fall in love with him. He is secretly engaged to Jane Fairfax, a fact which, as it becomes more obvious, nevertheless manages to escape Emma completely. For she is working on another project. After deciding that she cannot fall in love with Churchill herself she marks him out for Harriet, a mistake in judgment even greater than her misjudgment of Mr. Elton. For Churchill is even further above Harriet than Mr. Elton, and even if he were not already engaged to Jane Fairfax he clearly would have no interest in an illegitimate pauper. To complicate matters still more, Harriet is falling in love not with Churchill but with Mr. Knightley. Emma has finally managed to convince her that no one is too good for her, and she picks a man to love who, though kinder than Mr. Elton, is even farther beyond her reach. These, in rough outline, are the events of the next tangle of circumstances in the novel, and Emma's continued misunderstanding and mismanagement of them contribute toward her education.

Emma fancies Churchill in love with her, to be "saved only by her own indifference." In her own defense, it must be pointed out that Churchill does in fact pretend to be courting her to avoid detection of his engagement to Jane, the publication of which would get him disinherited by his rich aunt. Emma, however, is completely taken in, though never seriously in love with him. Mr. Knightley, who is obviously jealous of Churchill and of Emma's possible regard for him, says he is a trifling and silly young man, which is an understatement of magnificent proportions. Emma replies: " 'folly is not always folly. It depends upon the character of those who handle it.' " Emma obviously means this to be self-reflexive at least to some extent, and continues to make excuses to Mr. Knightley for her meddling in the affairs of others. But Jane Austen means us to see that folly is always folly, and always will be.

At the Coles's party Emma finds herself comparing Harriet with Jane Fairfax: "Jane Fairfax did look and move superior, but Emma suspected she might have been glad to change feelings with Harriet, very glad to have purchased the mortification of having loved—yes, of having loved even Mr. Elton in vain—by the surrender of all the dangerous pleasure of knowing herself beloved by the husband of her friend" [II,viii]. Here Emma's folly reaches a new height of ridiculousness. Jane loves, but not in vain, and has no reason to want to change places with Harriet. Her love is not for a married man but for a very eligible young bachelor, to whom she is already engaged. That imagination which Emma had once promised herself to control is running away with her judgment once again. The irony is underscored a few moments later when Mrs. Weston tells Emma that she suspects an attachment between Jane and Mr. Knightley. Emma replies: " 'My dear Mrs. Weston, do not take to matchmaking. You do it very ill.' " And from this pinnacle of wisdom, Emma continues to bombard herself with false notions of what her acquaintances are up to, edging as far away from the truth as she had been in the Elton affair.

Two events now occur which seem to abet Emma's plan to bring Harriet and Churchill together. First, Mr. Elton marries, and Harriet is obliged to cease thinking of him altogether. And second, Churchill inadvertently "saves" Harriet from a band of gypsies and delivers her safe and sound to Hartfield, where Emma rapturously indulges her feeling that "circumstances had been at work to make them peculiarly interesting to each other. . . ." Emma encourages Harriet to believe that she might marry the man who has been so kind to her. Harriet assumes that Emma is referring to Mr. Knightley, who had asked Harriet to dance during the ball at the Crown when no one else would, and she is elated. They name no names, and the conversation continues in this ambiguous way. At the end of it, Emma tells Harriet that she is " 'determined against all interference,' " and that " 'more wonderful things have taken place; there have been matches of greater disparity. . . . Your raising your thoughts to him is a mark of good taste which I shall always know how to value' " [II,iv]. Emma's "interference," in this case, is limited to conversation, but it is to prove just as disastrous as her more active exertion on Harriet's behalf in the Elton affair—for Harriet now thinks that she has Emma's sanction to think of Mr. Knightley as a possible spouse, and of course she is doomed to be disappointed again. Emma, who assumes that the "he" they have been talking about is Frank Churchill, still does not see that Churchill's affections are engaged elsewhere, though the signs of it have become more and more obvious. She even fancies, during the outing to Box Hill, that Churchill has Harriet in mind when he outlines the particulars he should want a wife of his to possess.

Emma, then, is still a victim of conceited self-confidence. The latter stages of her education, when they come, will come quickly and convulsively. The novel's final movement begins with Mr. Knightley's attempt to warn Emma that Churchill and Jane obviously have an understanding of some sort. She rejects his statement, resorting once again to an invocation of her own superior perception and judgment: " 'There is no admiration between them, I do assure you. . . . They are as far from any attachment or admiration for one another as any two beings in the world can be. That is, I *presume* it to be so on her side, and I can answer for its being so on his. I will answer for the gentleman's indifference' " [III,v]. Emma is not stupid; she is merely self-deceived. One of the primary forms her egoism takes is the assumption that her understanding of things is more acute than that of others. On the contrary—like most people, she is capable of being deceived by appearances, making mistakes in judgment, perceiving incorrectly. Her comprehension of her own real nature must involve the understanding that she is more wont to display imagination than sober common sense. The major event of the novel's last volume is the final dissipation of Emma's self-deception and her discovery of her real self—of her real desires and defects.

Soon after the Box Hill outing comes the news of Mrs. Churchill's death and with it the disclosure of Frank's engagement to Jane Fairfax. Emma wonders at Harriet's lack of emotion, at Churchill's behavior, and at her own obtuseness. Though she remains under the illusion that Harriet is attached to Churchill, she at least begins genuinely to see how foolishly she has been behaving:

> She felt completely guilty of having encouraged what she might have repressed. She might have prevented the indulgence and increase of such sentiments. Her influence would have been enough. And now she was very conscious that she ought to have prevented them. She felt that she had been risking her friend's happiness on most insufficient grounds. Common sense would have directed her to tell Harriet that she must not allow herself to think of him, and that there were five hundred chances to one against his ever caring for her. 'But with common sense,' she added, 'I am afraid I have had little to do.' (III,xi)

Emma has finally begun seriously to understand the destructiveness of her folly. But she is in for still another revelation about herself, one even more important.

Soon after the news about Churchill and Jane Fairfax is known in Highbury, Harriet reveals to Emma that she is in love with Mr. Knightley. She would not venture to say such a thing unless she were sure of Emma's approval and encouragement. She would think it a presumption if Emma had not told her that more wonderful things had happened, that matches of even greater disparity had been made. The moment of total revelation is at hand, and Emma, realizing that she has been blind to still one more truth, sits down once again to meditate. Her convulsive self-discovery takes up close to two chapters in the novel, and begins with an honest evaluation of her feelings about a possible marriage between Harriet and Mr. Knightley:

> A few minutes were sufficient for making her acquainted with her own heart. A mind like hers, once opening to suspicion, made rapid progress; she touched, she admitted, she acknowledged, the whole truth. Why was it

so much worse that Harriet should be in love with Mr.
Knightley than with Frank Churchill? Why was the evil
so dreadfully increased by Harriet's having some hope
of return? It darted through her with the speed of an
arrow that Mr. Knightley must marry no one but
herself!

Her own conduct, as well as her own heart, was
before her in the same few minutes. She saw it all with a
clearness which had never blessed her before. How im-
properly had she been acting by Harriet! How inconsiderate, how indelicate, how irrational, how unfeeling,
had been her conduct! What blindness, what madness
had led her on! It struck her with dreadful force, and she
was ready to give to it every bad name in the world.
(III,xi)

At last, Emma is becoming familiar with herself—with her
own nature and needs. Her vision, no longer obstructed by
the barriers of egoism and fancy, is now clearer. Like
Elizabeth Bennet, Emma finally sees herself in relation to
others with total clarity in a moment of deep personal adversity—sees the folly of her self-absorption, the selfishness of
her imagination, the weakness of her own judgment and the
strength of her own desires. Emma's self-discovery, however,
does not end here. Rather, it goes on with even more intensity. Her mind, says the narrator, "was in all the perturbation
that such a development of self . . . such a confusion of
sudden and perplexing emotions, must create." Emma's
"self" is being "developed" in a crucible of suffering brought
about through the conceit of "fancy."

As Harriet is about to leave, Emma asks her if Mr.
Knightley's kindness to her might not be in behalf of his
friend Mr. Martin. Harriet replies spiritedly: " 'I hope I know
better now than to care for Mr. Martin or to be suspected of
it.' " She says that she never would have thought of Mr.
Knightley at all except for Emma herself: " 'now I seem to
feel that I may deserve him; and that if he does choose me, it
will not be anything so very wonderful.' " Needless to say,
Harriet's comments now occasion "bitter feelings" in Emma,
the more so since Emma is now more fully aware of her own
unsavory part in the whole business. While she knows that

she has not specifically encouraged Harriet to pursue Mr.
Knightley, she also knows that her lively imagination, her
penchant for matchmaking, and her general meddling in
other peoples' lives have all contributed to the presently
threatening state of affairs. As Harriet goes, Emma says to
herself in shame and despair: " 'Oh, God! That I had never
seen her!' "

The misery that results from egoism and precedes moral
vision and fulfillment now dominates Emma. Her ongoing
self-revelation continues both to haunt her and to illuminate
further reaches of herself to herself. Like Isabel Archer in *The
Portrait of A Lady*, she meditates far into the night:

> How to understand it all! How to understand the decep-
> tions she had been thus practicing on herself and living
> under! The blunders, the blindness of her own head and
> heart! . . . She perceived that she had acted most weak-
> ly; that she had been imposed on by others in a most
> mortifying degree; that she had been imposing on herself
> in a degree yet more mortifying; that she was wretched
> and should probably find this day but the beginning of
> wretchedness.
>   To understand, thoroughly understand, her own
> heart was the first endeavour. . . . She saw that there
> never had been a time when she did not consider Mr.
> Knightley as infinitely . . . superior or when his regard
> for her had not been infinitely the most dear. She saw
> that in persuading herself, in fancying, in acting to the
> contrary, she had been entirely under a delusion, totally
> ignorant of her own heart. . . . This was the knowledge
> of herself, on the first question of inquiry, which she
> reached; and without being long in reaching it. She was
> most sorrowfully indignant, ashamed of every sensation
> but the one revealed to her—her affection for Mr.
> Knightley. Every other part of her mind was disgusting.
> (III,xi)

Deceptions, blunders, blindness, weakness—what can these
add up to but wretchedness and shame? Emma, in the convul-
sion of her self-discovery, knows the misery of the egoist. The
emphasis here is on the movement from ignorance of self to
knowledge of self, as the language of the passage makes clear.
Like Elizabeth Bennet, Emma has not understood herself un-

til real adversity brings on self-revelation; and like Elizabeth's illumination, hers is expressed in terms of *vision:* she now "sees" what she has not seen before. The self-absorption of egoism has as a major symptom a perception of things which is blocked or twisted by selfish desires and preoccupations. Emma's ignorance of her own heart has been the chief result of the delusions brought on by excessive fancy. Thus self-discovery, at least in one sense, is the intensely realized increase of one's store of self-knowledge. The cultivation of the art of vision is a painful, because self-revealing, process, and so the movement from self-absorption to self-understanding inevitably involves wretchedness and despair along the way.

The last part of Emma's extended retrospective meditation is largely a final series of trenchant self-reproaches:

> With insufferable vanity had she believed herself in the secret of everybody's feelings, with unpardonable arrogance proposed to arrange everybody's destiny. She was proved to have been universally mistaken, and she had not quite done nothing—for she had done mischief. She had brought evil on Harriet, on herself, and, she too much feared, on Mr. Knightley . . . Who had been at pains to give Harriet notions of self-consequence but herself? Who but herself had taught her that she was to elevate herself if possible, and that her claims were great to a high worldly establishment? If Harriet, from being humble, were grown vain, it was her doing too. (III,xi)

Here Emma recognizes the specific components of her egoism: the vanity and arrogance of her belief in her powers of understanding others and of manipulating them into a pattern she both approves and desires. Her new self-knowledge seems to work in two ways here. Her ignorance of the human heart has been both a personal and a general ignorance, and her realization of this illuminates both herself and others to herself. Understanding of herself helps prepare the way for understanding of others, and that new understanding of others in turn assists the more complete understanding of her own heart. The dissipation of egoism and acquisition of real vision, then, depends on a virtually symbiotic relationship between self-knowledge and a more generally acute perception of exterior reality.

At the end of Emma's meditation, Jane Austen's narrator summarizes Emma's newly perceived situation: "Till now that she was threatened with its loss, Emma had never known how much of her happiness depended on being first with Mr. Knightley, first in interest and affection. Satisfied that it was so, and feeling it her due, she had enjoyed it without reflection, and only in the dread of being supplanted found how inexpressibly important it had been" [III,xii]. (The wording here inevitably recalls Elizabeth Bennet's climactic self-revelation: " 'Till this moment I never knew myself.' ") Emma, like many others, is a victim of mediated desire; she does not consciously realize what it is that she wants until she discovers that somebody else wants it. Her understanding of her feeling for Mr. Knightley is the most important result of her self-discovery and is the resolution toward which many of the novel's seemingly cacophonous events have been leading. A paramount concomitant of self-knowledge is the discovery of the state of one's own genuine *feelings* (not fancies).

Emma now makes several resolutions. As long as her father is alive, she will not marry Mr. Knightley—even should he ask her to do so. She will watch Mr. Knightley carefully to see if Harriet's love for him is reciprocated. She will cultivate more assiduously the friendship of Jane Fairfax, who, as Mr. Knightley has always told her, is a more fitting companion and friend for her than Harriet Smith. And she immerses herself generally "in the resolution of her own better conduct, and the hope that however inferior in spirit and gaiety might be the following and every future winter of her life to the past, it would yet find her more rational, more acquainted with herself, and leave her less to regret when it were gone" [III,xii]. The fruits of rational self-exploration have finally been acknowledged to be more valuable and viable than those of the imagination, and so Emma resolves to become better "acquainted with herself."

The next day Mr. Knightley comes to call, and she assumes from his lack of cheerfulness that he has been communicating to his brother, who would be sure to disapprove of it, his plan to marry Harriet. His low spirits are in actuality the result of his feeling the need to comfort Emma after the revelation of the Jane Fairfax - Frank Churchill engagement. Emma, of course, does not need that sort of consolation, and she tells him so almost immediately: " 'My blindness to what was going on led me to act by them [Jane and Frank] in a way that I must always be ashamed of, and I was very foolishly tempted to say and do many things which may well lay me open to unpleasant conjectures, but I have no other reason to regret that I was not in the secret earlier' " [III,xiii]. Mr. Knightley has believed all along that she is in love with Frank Churchill, and seems incredulous. Emma explains that Churchill merely flattered her vanity and bamboozled her intuition: " 'It was his object to blind all about him; and no one, I am sure, could be more effectually blinded . . . [than] one who sets up as I do for Understanding.' " Knightley is pensive, and Emma assumes that he is trying to find a gentle way to break to her the news of his engagement to Harriet. In this assumption, Emma underestimates herself for the first time. Like Elizabeth Bennet's thoughts of Darcy in the latter pages of *Pride and Prejudice*, Emma's assumption now is that her sustained folly earlier in her relationship with Mr. Knightley must prohibit any present love between them. In this, Emma has been deceiving herself once again—she has been blinded again by her own feelings, but now in a more understandable and less self-indulgent way. So that when Mr. Knightley proceeds to propose to her, Emma is shocked once again—this time, of course, pleasantly. No longer is she willing to thrust her friend into her place in a foolish paroxysm of sentiment and fancy. She sees

> that Harriet's hope had been entirely groundless, a mistake, a delusion, as complete a delusion as any of her own. . . . As to any of that heroism of sentiment which might have prompted her to entreat him to transfer his affection from herself to Harriet as infinitely the most

worthy of the two—or even the more simple sublimity of resolving to refuse him at once and forever, without vouchsafing any motive because he could not marry them both, Emma had it not. She felt for Harriet with pain and contrition; but no flight of generosity run mad, opposing all that could be probable or reasonable, entered her brain. She had led her friend astray, and it would be a reproach to her forever; but her judgment was as strong as her feelings, and as strong as it had ever been before, in reprobating any such alliance for him as most unequal and degrading. Her way was clear. . . . (III,xiii)

Now that Emma's judgment has in fact caught up with and even surmounted her imagination ("her judgment was as strong as her feelings"), it is unlikely that she will ever be so self-deceived again. In her pain and contrition she has no more delusions. "Reasonable" at last, her perception is now focused and thus her "way" is "clear." She has discovered who and what she is; arrogance and vanity have been both exorcised and expiated, and the ordeal of her education has been completed in a new intensity of vision and sympathetic understanding. The fulfillment of a happy marriage is her ultimate reward.

The novel's last few pages merely tie together a few loose ends, for the story of Emma's self-discovery has been told. Mr. Knightley, commenting on Frank Churchill's long letter to Mrs. Weston, which attempts to explain his previous duplicity, says to Emma: " 'Mystery, finesse—how they pervert the understanding! My Emma, does not everything serve to prove more and more the beauty of truth and sincerity in all our dealings with each other?' Emma agreed to it, with a blush of sensibility" [III,xv]. And when Jane Fairfax tells Emma when and where she is to be married, Emma replies (III,xvi): " 'Thank you, thank you. This is just what I wanted to be assured of. Oh! If you knew how much I love everything that is decided and open!' " The virtues of honesty and common sense are emphasized in the novel's last chapters; imaginative and secret interpretation of the behavior of others is debunked at every turn—especially by the repentant Emma herself. News comes, at the end, that Harriet is engaged to marry Mr. Martin, and Emma expresses her approbation to Mr. Knightley. He, of course, is surprised: " 'You are materially changed since we talked on this subject before.' " Emma replies that she had been a fool and that it would now be a "great pleasure" for her to know Robert Martin. She resolves henceforth to conceal none of her true feelings from Mr. Knightley: "The disguise, equivocation, mystery, so hateful to her to practise, might soon be over." For Emma, the pains of education are almost over; only its fruits lie ahead.

IV

Both Elizabeth and Emma have the facts necessary for making rational and sensible judgments of people and situations, but both assemble their facts erroneously as a result of egoism. Both impose outward upon reality a shadow of their own making and blind themselves to the real nature of things. As their egoism is dissipated in the wake of increased knowledge and more objective perception, they learn more not only about the nature of reality but about themselves as well; and this new self-knowledge leads in turn to an even more perceptive assessment of exterior reality. Both Elizabeth and Emma, during the ordeal of education, move from fancy to common sense, from self-absorption to sympathetic moral vision. The importance of this movement is emphasized continuously by Jane Austen, who sees in it the seeds of spiritual salvation. As she says (through Edmund Bertram) in *Mansfield Park* (III,16), " 'The most valuable knowledge we could any of us acquire [is] the knowledge of ourselves . . . .' "

The specific pattern and its meaning varies somewhat among the Victorian novelists, but the general movement is the same. For Thackeray, Charlotte Brontë, Trollope, Dickens, George Eliot, Meredith and Hardy—and Henry James as well—the movement is generally that from egoism and self-absorption through pain and misery to self-discovery and fuller vision. While it is not the province of this study to prove "influence," it is a fact nevertheless that all of the major Victorian novelists at least read Jane Austen. Some of them acknowledged their admiration (Charlotte Brontë detested her novels and Dickens and Hardy say little about them—these are the major exceptions; James is not always complimentary to her, as in his essay "The Lesson of Balzac," but he obviously learned a great deal from her). One finds that many of the grounds of concern which Jane Austen staked out for the novel are taken over, sometimes more obsessively, by her successors.

WILLIAM MAKEPEACE THACKERAY (1811-1863)
National Portrait Gallery, London

Chapter Two

Thackeray, Charlotte Brontë, and Trollope

Thackeray's *Vanity Fair* (1847-48) tells the story of two kinds of egoism: conscious and unconscious selfishness. The novel, of course, is a general indictment of many things—most inclusively, the way early nineteenth-century Englishmen lived. Virtually all of the characters who people this novel exemplify to some degree the vanity of narrow and short-sighted human wishes. To bring his lesson home specifically, however, Thackeray tells the story of two selfish women—one of whom is always conscious of what she is doing, the other usually unconscious. One of Thackeray's most important theses seems to be that both strains of egoism are equally—or at least nearly equally—destructive and harmful. His exemplars of these two strains of egoism are Becky Sharp and Amelia Sedley. Becky has been anatomized so often by critics that by now she is nearly shredded. Surely she is one of the most delightful villains in fiction—delightful because Thackeray, like Shakespeare in *Richard III*, makes his villain totally self-conscious and aware and lets him take the audience into his confidence and manipulate it into a position almost of neutrality. Becky, like Richard III, fully admits her infamy and that she is out to deflate and despoil the Establishment; and since we are not particularly attached to the Establishment in either instance, we watch the villain operate with fascination and even with some degree of admiration. Becky is out for all that she can get from the fools and knaves of Vanity Fair, and at whatever cost to others: this constitutes her conscious selfishness, her egoism. For her, there can be no climactic self-discovery; she is fully aware of her own nature from the beginning of the novel. These things are fairly apparent to most readers, and I will not attempt to rehearse them again. My concern is with the other, more subtle strain of egoism here, the unconscious selfishness of Amelia Sedley.

For Becky, self-discovery is both impossible and unnecessary, for, as I have said, there never seems to be a time
when she does not know who she is, what she has done, or
what she is doing. For Amelia, however, who is usually not
aware of her egoism, self-discovery is necessary before her
selfishness can be dissipated. Becky's nature has long been
recognized by Thackeray's critics, many of whom ignore
Amelia because she is by far the duller of the two
protagonists. It is of course a critical commonplace by now
that Amelia is Thackeray's ironic caricature of the traditional
heroine of fiction up to his time. She has the usual beauty and
the usual chastity; Thackeray stresses her insipidity, her lack
of feeling, and above all her stupidity, in the course of his
satiric (though sometimes sympathetic) portrait. But Amelia,
I think, represents for Thackeray more than an attack on
conventional ideas of heroism; she also represents another
strain of villainy—less pronounced, less conscious than
Becky's, but just as virulent and just as destructive. Amelia's
selfishness has no less paralyzing an effect on others merely
because she does not understand its nature or her own; on the
contrary, it is directly or indirectly responsible for a great
deal of misery in the novel. Toward the end of *Vanity Fair*,
Amelia comes to understand the nature of her selfishness, discovers her own needs and desires, and opens the way for
herself to enjoy a useful and fruitful existence.

It is part of the genius of Amelia's portrait that she seems
to be one of the least selfish characters in the novel. She is
self-sacrificing, humble, forgiving, and kind. It is easy to fall
into Thackeray's trap—to sympathize with a guileless, simple
creature such as Amelia—to suspend our powers of judgment
and to pity her ignorance of the world. But her stupidity,
while innocent, is neither passive nor neutral. It takes the
form of an unconscious selfishness—unconscious because she
is stupid—which encroaches destructively on the lives of
several other people. Amelia's unconscious self-absorption
encourages the treachery of Becky and George, compounds
the misery of her destitute parents, dangerously colors the upbringing of her son, and is indirectly responsible for the death

of her brother. Above all, and most importantly, it almost ruins the life of the novel's only admirable character. Dobbin, of course, is a "spooney" and should have deflated Amelia long before he does so, and thus some readers may choose to think that he is not admirable after all. But in the created world of Thackeray's novel, he is the only character who manages to combine generosity and selflessness with intelligence and strength. And yet throughout *Vanity Fair*—almost to the end of it—his happiness is continually being annihilated by Amelia's selfishness: "She wished to give him nothing, but that he should give her all" [66]. This is the essence of Amelia's egoism, the story of her half of the novel.

Thackeray introduces Amelia to us in the first chapter as patently unheroic: she is "silly," she is "stupid," and "had twelve intimate and bosom friends out of the twenty-four young ladies" at Miss Pinkerton's school. In succeeding chapters she "prudently," to use Thackeray's ironic adverb, encourages Becky's designs on her brother Jos, letting her one-sided friendship with Becky blind her to more substantial concerns. Amelia's solipsism is anticipated in Thackeray's description, a few pages later, of her feelings for George Osborne, which approach the ridiculous. Thackeray calls her "imprudent," "idolatrous," and "silly," discusses her effusively "blind devotion" to the worthless George, and then comments very soberly that "poor Emmy had not a well-regulated mind." He goes on to underscore the myopic idolatry of Amelia's attachment by making us better acquainted with the object of her adoration, who is of course himself the epitome of selfishness and conceit. He is disloyal, pompous, and arrogant. He lights his cigars with Amelia's letters. He agrees with Amelia that he is "one of the most gallant and brilliant men in the empire." He is, as Becky says late in the novel, a "selfish humbug," a "low-bred cockney-dandy," a "padded booby" without "wit," "manners," or "heart" [67]. Amelia's self-imposed blindness is comprised in large measure of her failure to see George's real nature, her misplaced and self-destructive adoration of him, and the long-lasting disastrous effects on others of her self-indulgence. While Becky's egoism is a concomitant of a conscious nature—unscrupulous, clever, and sentient—Amelia's is a concomitant of stupidity. But it is neither less destructive nor more excusable than Becky's, and therefore it is of equal importance in the novel.

Amelia's complacency is barely touched by the financial disaster which overtakes her parents. As her father becomes more and more gloomy day after day, Amelia, says Thackeray, remains "absorbed still in one selfish, tender thought, and quite regardless of all the world besides. . . ." The adjective "selfish" is one that will be applied to her again and again throughout the novel. It is the essence of her egoism. It is manifested in what, a few pages later, Thackeray describes as her "crime of loving wrongly, too violently, against reason." Certainly the act of loving itself is not usually a selfish one. But when loving the wrong person is combined with total disregard for everything and everyone else, when self-indulgence is combined with total blindness, then selfishness is virtually inevitable. Thus Amelia at this point is little inclined to sympathize with her parents' troubles. While their world collapses around them, she sits at the window watching for George, failing to see either that it is Dobbin who forces his friend to honor his commitment to her against the elder Mr. Osborne's opposition, or that Dobbin, who is infinitely the better of the two, loves her much more sincerely and deeply than George does—if George loves her at all. Instead, as always, Amelia judges only by surfaces. Her shallowness, which is responsible for her worship of George, is also responsible for her early attitude toward Dobbin: "Little Amelia . . . had rather a mean opinion of her husband's friend, Captain Dobbin. He lisped—he was very plain and homely-looking: and exceedingly awkward and ungainly. She liked him for his attachment to her husband (to be sure there was very little merit in that), and she thought George was most generous and kind in extending his friendship to his brother officer" [25]. Dobbin, of course, remains clumsy and plain, and so Amelia continues to regard him with in-

difference throughout much of the novel, unaware that the
few pleasures she manages to retain after George's death are
largely the result of Dobbin's generosity. Her judgment of
others, like almost everything else about her, is a form of
vacuous self-indulgence, which in turn is a function of her
moral stupidity.

George, as I have noted, must be forced by Dobbin to
keep to his engagement with Amelia, and his long absences
from her just after their marriage give her, occasionally,
pause for thought—or rather what Thackeray calls "selfish
brooding": "Did she own to herself how different the real
man was from that superb young hero whom she had
worshipped? It requires many, many years—and a man must
be very bad indeed—before a woman's pride and vanity will
let her own to such a confession" [26]. Amelia's "pride"
and "vanity" have blinded her to George's real nature and to
the seriousness of his flirtation with Becky just after his
marriage to Amelia. Amelia suspects something, but not
enough—and because she continually misjudges both
George's character and Becky's she makes it possible for
them to move toward an affair which would have destroyed
two marriages (Becky has by this time married Rawdon
Crawley) but for Napoleon's timely advance into Belgium.
She does not realize the seriousness of the affair, of course,
until many years later. Almost everyone around her is involved in deceit and duplicity of some kind; and since Amelia
"took her opinions from those people who surrounded her"
it is not surprising that her own shallowness prevents her
from seeing things and people as they really are. On the few
occasions when George, feeling guilty, pays her any attention, she is blankly worshipful.

After George's death in the Battle of Waterloo, Amelia
transfers her violent affections to her young son, who is
almost ruined for life thereby. He becomes, as he grows older,
spoiled, self-indulgent, and selfish, like both of his parents.
Amelia, of course, has no idea of how poorly off her husband
had left her (he had been disinherited by his father) or that
Dobbin is supporting her, her son, and her parents. In her

leisure hours she worships the memory of her sainted husband. When the trumped-up news of Dobbin's alleged marriage in India reaches her, however, we have the first indication that perhaps her pride, her possessiveness, her penchant for controlling as far as possible the men she knows, may be disappointedly frustrated. Her reaction to the news is the first suggestion in the novel that she considers Dobbin more than a useful servant. But, as in Emma's case, a more genuine blow to her self-esteem is necessary before she can first begin to see the true state of her feelings:

> Amelia said 'Oh!' Amelia was very *very* happy indeed. But she supposed Glorvina [Dobbin's supposed fiancée] could not be like her old acquaintance, who was most kind—but—but she was very happy indeed. And by some impulse, of which I cannot explain the meaning, she took George in her arms and kissed him with an extraordinary tenderness. Her eyes were quite moist when she put the child down; and she scarcely spoke a word during the whole of the drive—though she was so very happy indeed. (38)

Thackeray makes it clear in this section of the novel that Amelia, perhaps unconsciously, regards Dobbin's existence as a support for and extension of her own; she fears that her dominating power over him will be demolished. Thus the irony of passages such as this one: "She was glad to be able to own and feel how warmly and gratefully she regarded him—and as for the idea of being jealous of Glorvina, (Glorvina, indeed!) Amelia would have scouted it, if an angel from heaven had hinted it to her" [42]. The congratulatory letter she writes to Dobbin (43), filled with italics, is a masterpiece of psychological revelation, pretending as it does only calm solicitude, and hiding, quite obviously, resentment and disappointment. Thackeray pointedly refers to it as "protesting throughout as to the extreme satisfaction of the writer." Dobbin sees only its surface protestations, calls Amelia "a stone," and reflects upon her "selfishness" and her imperviousness to "fidelity," "constant truth and passion," and "warmth."

Amelia's worship of her dead husband, as I have said, is transferred to her young son; and under the circumstances of such idolatry, Georgy begins to develop his parents' tendencies—conceit, imperviousness, and selfishness. He is, however, basically honest where his father was not, and so he is ultimately receptive to the moral influence of Dobbin later in the novel. When Georgy reaches school-age and leaves his mother cheerfully every morning, Amelia's reaction is to be hurt by his cheerfulness. She is "repentant" for being so "selfish as to wish her own son to be unhappy," but she cannot help herself. As Georgy tugs harder and harder at the maternal strings, she redoubles her worship of him; and her unenlightened sentimentality, as much as ever, bars any objective view of the world and her proper place in it. She is almost totally subjective and self-indulgent. When she is finally forced, because of the inescapable financial needs of her family, to give Georgy up to his paternal grandfather, she views the situation, as she views almost everything else, in terms of its effect upon herself and her attachment to the memory of her husband: "She must give him up; and then—and then she would go to George; and they would watch over the child, and wait for him until he came to them in Heaven" [50]. Certainly Amelia's situation is pitiable. Her reaction to it, however, is not one to create additional sympathy. Thackeray describes her during this period of her life in terms of one effusive burst of self-indulgence after another. Her desire to be with George in heaven, waiting for their son to join them, is an exceedingly strange manifestation of motherhood.

Georgy, of course, is delighted at the prospect of going to live with his rich grandfather: "In two days he . . . adopted a slight imperious air and patronizing manner. He was born to command, his mother thinks, as his father was before him" [50]. Amelia does not see, however, how really like his father he is in his arrogance and thoughtlessness. Her early influence upon him, combined with his grandfather's indulgence, almost ruins the boy: "If he had been a Prince Royal he could not have been better brought up to think well of himself." (Georgy, however, is still young enough to be redeemable.) When Mrs. Sedley dies, toward the end of this section of the novel (that is, before the return of Dobbin and Jos from India), Amelia momentarily wishes once again to be dead as well, a sentiment which Thackeray unhesitatingly labels as "selfish" and which, he says, is a result of her "selfish, guilty love" for her husband and son.

Dobbin and Jos now return from India, and Amelia's fortunes are considerably improved. Her tormenting of Dobbin is unabated; it is clear that she is unwilling to give up her tyranny over him:

> 'I've another arrival to announce,' he said, after a pause.
> 'Mrs. Dobbin?' Amelia said, making a movement back—Why didn't he speak? (58)

She talks to him incessantly about Georgy, even though she can see, as everyone else sees, that he is still in love with her. At one point she shows him a brief essay Georgy has written, appropriately enough, "On Selfishness"—that theme which is so central to this novel. Georgy's essay, a masterpiece of ironic unselfconsciousness, says in part: " 'Of all the vices which degrade the human character, Selfishness is the most odious and contemptible. An undue love of self leads to the most monstrous crimes, and occasions the greatest misfortunes both in *States* and *Families*. . . A selfish man will impoverish his family and often bring them to ruin. . . . We are not to consult our own interest and ambition, but . . . consider the interests of others as well as our own' " [58]. Georgy's essay, which also pompously quotes the *Iliad,* is an important statement, for it both identifies the vice most of the personages in *Vanity Fair* are guilty of and demonstrates the contest in which that vice is practiced—that is, in ignorance of the true state of one's motives. Like Mary Bennet's peroration on pride, it is expressed in innocence, yet aptly. The dramatic irony is further underscored by Amelia's reaction to the essay. All she perceives in it is Georgy's precociousness: " 'Think of him writing such a hand, and quoting Greek too, at his age. . . .' " Amelia, as usual, sees only the surfaces of things; she is incapable of reading either herself or anyone else in depth.

The novel's last hundred or so pages tell the story of Dobbin's ultimate success in his long and weary courtship of Amelia. His reunion with her, however, does not begin promisingly. Both her brother and her friend Mary Clapp suggest that perhaps she will soon be married again. Amelia, however, continues to indulge her monomania: "a woman who had been married to such an angel . . . could never think of any other union." Thinking over what she has finally recognized as Dobbin's love for her, she is coldly and cruelly rational: "She would give him that friendly regard, which so much excellence and fidelity merited; she would treat him with perfect cordiality and frankness until he made his proposals: and *then* it would be time enough for her to speak, and to put an end to hopes which never could be realized" [59]. Amelia, in a word, is leading Dobbin on to disappointment, and here she is doing it consciously. Sympathy is overpowered by self-indulgence. Having made her decision she is more at ease, and Thackeray goes out of his way to underscore her perversity: "She slept, therefore, very soundly that evening . . . and was more than ordinarily happy. . . ."

Another instance of Amelia's egoistic self-absorption occurs shortly thereafter. A chance remark of Dobbin's enlightens her on the subject of the old piano she has been treasuring for years as one of George's few presents to her. She now discovers, as the reader has known all along, that this kindness, like most of those she received during her short married life, was also of Dobbin's doing. Does she thank him for the piano, or comment upon his generosity and thoughtfulness? Of course not. Instead, once again, she retreats behind further self-indulgence: "It was not George's gift. It was valueless now. The next time that old Sedley asked her to play, she said it was shockingly out of tune, that she had a headache, that she couldn't play" [59].

Dobbin now undertakes Georgy's formation. He takes him to the theater, and the boy says he will not sit in the pit with Dobbin—only in a box. But when Dobbin goes down to the pit alone, Georgy realizes how ridiculous he is being and joins Dobbin there. Amelia's reaction is typical: "How charmed she was when she heard of this instance of George's goodness!" Thackeray's condemnation of Amelia's thoughtlessness, as usual, is somewhat mitigated by irony, but it is patently there. When, shortly thereafter, both Mr. Sedley and Mr. Osborne die and Amelia discovers that Dobbin's money had been maintaining her and her child for some years, she is still unable to get the better of her monomania: "gratitude was all that she had to pay back for such admirable devotion and benefits—only gratitude! If she thought of any other return, the image of George stood up out of the grave, and said, 'You are mine, and mine only, now and for ever' " [61]. George, of course, would never say anything like this—dead or alive. But Amelia's self-absorption remains impenetrable. Thackeray comments, however, to the effect that Amelia "had never met a gentleman in her life until the present moment" and that her "tastes" and her "intelligence" have never really had a chance to be "educated." And yet he undercuts this half-hearted defense of her a few sentences later by emphasizing once again the shallowness of her perception, the failure in her of any independent judgment or objectivity: "Dobbin certainly had very large hands and feet, which the two George Osbornes used to caricature and laugh at, and their jeers and laughter perhaps led poor Emmy astray as to his worth" [62]. After all his devotion and sacrifice, Dobbin is still viewed by Amelia in terms of a juvenile image of him she had formed many years earlier. Why can she doubt his "worth"? Only because her self-absorption gets in the way of a more complete appreciation of his character.

Amelia's last mistake is both the most destructive thing she does and the means of her salvation from the abyss of solipsism. I refer to her taking in Becky during the sojourn at Pumpernickel. Amelia chooses to be bamboozled once again, and the outcome is both good and bad—good in that it results in Becky's ultimate pricking of Amelia's bubble, bad because it throws Becky in the way of Jos once again. Becky winds up, later on, murdering him (more or less) for some in-surance money, and thus Amelia is at least partly responsible for the death of her brother.

Before Becky's revelation to Amelia of George Osborne's real character, however, Amelia continues her high-handed treatment of Dobbin. One manifestation of her egoism is her desire to possess him totally—to regard him merely as an extension of herself, to take his loyalty for granted: "This woman had a way of tyrannizing over Major Dobbin . . . and she ordered him about, and patted him, and made him fetch and carry just as if he was a great New-foundland dog" [66]. But when Dobbin, arguing against the invitation to Becky to join their group, reminds Amelia that Becky was not always her friend (that is, that she flirted with George openly in Brussels before the Waterloo cam-paign), it is as if his many years of loyalty and generosity to her had never been. She calls him cruel, vows never to forgive him, and addresses one last ridiculous platitude to her dead husband: " 'You were pure—Oh yes, you were pure, my saint in heaven!' " When Becky arrives to stay, Amelia, demonstrating incredible ignorance of the identity of her true friends, welcomes her effusively and rebuffs Dobbin. This is perhaps Amelia's worst moment, and also the last time we see her so completely at the mercy of her own subjectivity. She works up her anger against Dobbin, says Thackeray, for "private reasons of her own"; "the pitiless little woman had found a pretext, and determined to be free" of Dobbin's long-standing courtship. She wants to keep his attention and loyal-ty but to avoid having to return his love. And so she tells Dobbin, incredibly enough, that she will never forgive him for "insulting" George's memory, hoping that in this way she will never have to extend herself to him: "She wished to give him nothing, but that he should give her all" [66]. This, as I have said, is Thackeray's most unqualified state-ment of Amelia's egoism, her desire to possess but not to give. It is at this point that Dobbin makes to her the famous speech dissolving the chain by which she has bound him to herself for so many years. In it he tells her what we have

known all along—that she is incapable of responding to any
genuine disinterested love, that she herself has only a "little
feeble remnant of love" to give, and that she is an un-
generous, self-indulgent woman. Becky, overhearing their
conversation, is impressed both by Dobbin's "noble heart"
and by "how shamefully that woman plays with it," and she
resolves to enlighten Amelia. As for Amelia, Thackeray comments sarcastically: "had she not done her duty? She had her
picture of George for a consolation."

In the novel's last pages, Becky chides Amelia for
behaving so cruelly to Dobbin, and Amelia responds by saying that her conduct was dictated "only by the purest
religious principles," that when one is once married to an
"angel" one is "married for ever," that she cannot forget
George. In response, Becky finally unloads on her once and
for all; calling Amelia "silly," "heartless," and "ungrateful,"
Becky at last tells her the whole truth:

> 'Couldn't forget *him*!' cried out Becky, 'that selfish hum-
> bug, that low-bred cockney-dandy, that padded booby,
> who had neither wit, nor manners, nor heart, and was
> no more to be compared to your friend . . . than you
> are to Queen Elizabeth! Why, the man was weary of
> you, and would have jilted you, but that Dobbin forced
> him to keep his word. He owned it to me. He never cared
> for you. He used to sneer about you to me, time after
> time; and made love to me the week after he married you!'
> (67)

Amelia, of course, cannot believe this until Becky produces
the note George wrote to her on the night of the Duke of
Richmond's ball, and then she must believe it. It is a final
stroke of irony that Amelia is enlightened by her unscrupulous friend, who is also an egoist but who nevertheless
is honest enough to hate misplaced sentimentality and admire the merit of the man who is her enemy and whom
Amelia has been too self-absorbed to appreciate. The revelation, at any rate, finally produces the emetic Amelia has been
in need of all along (67): "Who shall analyse [her] tears,
and say whether they were sweet or bitter? Was she most
grieved, because the idol of her life was tumbled down and

shivered at her feet; or indignant that her love had been so despised; or glad because the barrier was removed which modesty had placed between her and a new, a real affection?" She is now free to love wholly and generously; the impulse toward solipsistic self-indulgence has been exorcised (very suddenly, it is true), and thus she can call Dobbin back to her. Neither Amelia nor Dobbin can ever be wholly free of the past, however, and perhaps this is why at the end of the novel we are told that Dobbin is fonder of his new daughter than of his wife. Amelia herself has become a "tender little parasite" clinging round a "rugged old oak." Her former selfishness, though expiated, has inevitably colored the familial relationships of her new life.

Amelia's ordeal, then, is her education in values, an education in the course of which she learns, finally, to eschew selfishness and superficiality. In this, at least, she is not unlike the heroines of *Pride and Prejudice* and *Emma*. She ultimately discovers that her judgment and comprehension of others have been faulty—have, in fact, been based on subjective needs and wish-fulfillment; and this new self-knowledge ultimately enables her to acknowledge her real needs and desires and to find a place in Vanity Fair wherein she can at least enjoy her natural talents as a wife and a mother. She is still intellectually shallow, but her moral ineptitude is diminished as more of the realities of human life reach her. She has come home to herself.

II

Charlotte Brontë admired Thackeray and dedicated the second edition of her finest novel, *Jane Eyre* (1847), to him. Thus it may be more than a coincidence that, even though only the early chapters of *Vanity Fair* had been published as she was writing *Jane Eyre*, her novel, like his, is concerned with two kinds of egoism. *Jane Eyre* is a novel of didactic dichotomies and contrasts, and the most important dichotomy found in the book is that between an egoism capable of being discovered and thus redeemed, and a totally

CHARLOTTE BRONTË (1816-1855)
National Portrait Gallery, London

unreflective egoism incapable of being discovered. The first belongs to Edward Rochester, the second to St. John Rivers. Rochester's egoism is a result of feeling without reason, a rampant possessiveness yearning for love without marriage, gratification without commitment. Jane herself becomes the instrument of his self-discovery late in the novel. St. John's egoism reverses the equation. It results from reason without feeling, a rampant possessiveness desirous of marriage without love, duty without commitment. He remains unaware of his true nature as long as we see him; for him there is no self-discovery.

It is necessary to recognize the importance of both forms of egoism; that is what the novel is about. Feeling, the novel says, is as incomplete without reason as reason is without feeling. Marriage and love are necessarily symbiotic, as are duty on the one hand and principled commitment on the other. Each of these things—feeling, reason, love, marriage, duty, principle—is incomplete alone. Since "we are born to strive and endure" (27), these things do not come together easily; they must be worked at, waited for. This reading of the story explains why the last third of the novel, so often castigated as the mere intervention of gratuitous coincidence, is included. The Moor House chapters do not only represent a convenient interlude during which Bertha Rochester and Jane's rich uncle can die and prepare the way for her re-entrance into Rochester's life. These chapters also balance and comment upon earlier parts of the novel, just as in *Wuthering Heights*, written at the same time and in the same house, the second half of the story comments upon and elucidates the meaning of the first half. We understand Rochester's egoism and Jane's behavior more fully after reading about her collision with St. John Rivers, just as we understand St. John's errors more fully by seeing them in the context of Rochester's, already committed. Without this balancing, it would perhaps be possible to see Jane as capricious and unfeeling, in the one case almost ruining a man's life because of inordinately high principles and in the other confounding a basically principled man with his lack of sensuality. But love and duty, reason and feeling, must be united, and it is the function of these two studies in egoism to point these things out—to Jane, and therefore to us. I do not mean to suggest that Rochester and Rivers are the only egoists in this novel, for there are many others (the Reeds, the Brocklehursts, the Ingrams, etc.); but the novel is structured on these two contrasting forms of egoism, one of which culminates in self-discovery and the other in an ambitious commitment to God. It seems as if, somehow, one cannot know himself fully and love God fully at the same time; if so, Charlotte Brontë may be arguing for a relatively literal form of truth: knowledge of the real nature of this world and of the human species inhabiting it. When Rochester thanks God at the end of the novel it is for the restoration of Jane and the return of bodily comfort. St. John's final words, in the form of a letter to Jane, speak of spiritual comfort and the glory of death in a spiritual war. It seems obvious that Charlotte Brontë looks upon this latter perspective with a somewhat jaundiced eye, as the language of the later parts of the novel makes clear. In the discovery of his God, St. John fails to discover himself, to see himself as he truly is. For Charlotte Brontë, self-knowledge is an important quality—it is what Jane Eyre has and what most of the others lack; it enables her to choose and act both correctly and morally. Rochester's behavior is understandable, even sympathetic—but it is not morally correct, at least for Charlotte Brontë. St. John's behavior is moral, at least in an abstract sense, but it is neither correct nor sympathetic. What governs the behavior of each of the three is the amount of self-knowledge each possesses, and thus the movement away from the constricting subjectivity of egoism and toward self-knowledge—or the failure to exorcise egoism and discover the self—is the central issue here. One must strive *to* endure.

In the early chapters, Rochester is haughty and hard:

> Mr. Rochester must have been aware of the entrance of Mrs. Fairfax and myself, but it appeared he was not in the mood to notice us, for he never lifted his head as we approached . . . 'Let Miss Eyre be seated,'

he said: and there was something in the forced stiff bow, in the impatient yet formal tone, which seemed further to express, 'what the deuce is it to me whether Miss Eyre be there or not?' (13)

He begins by ordering her to come and go, harshly and without grace (" 'I am used to say "Do this" and it is done: I cannot alter my customary habits for one new inmate' "), and by acknowledging her existence with "frigid" bows.

The egoist, as Meredith says, clothes himself at everyone else's expense, and when Jane tries, after getting to know him better, to preach repentance for past excesses to Rochester, he tells her that he has " 'a right to get pleasure out of life: and I *will* get it, cost what it may.' " Rochester is "proud, sardonic, harsh," and Jane understands that his intermittent kindness to her "was balanced by unjust severity to many others." His nature is again and again compared, indirectly but unmistakably, to Jane's, which constantly errs on the side of humility and self-deprecation—as when, having considered the possibility that Rochester might be falling in love with her, Jane rejects the idea for what she believes is its patent impossibility and makes herself perform penance as a punishment for absurdity.

Rochester, however, is of course falling in love with her after all, and goes to some lengths to probe the depths of her nature. His impersonation of a gypsy fortune-teller in Chapter 19 is merely a form of self-gratification at the expense of others. Still another is his harping to Jane on his supposed forthcoming marriage to Blanche Ingram (" 'she's an extensive armful . . . one can't have too much of such a very excellent thing as my beautiful Blanche. . . .' "), and his constant reminders to Jane that she will have to leave Thornfield after the marriage and that they will be hundreds of miles apart (23). He admits to her later how selfish his motives were: " 'I feigned courtship of Miss Ingram, because I wished to render you as madly in love with me as I was with you; and I knew jealousy would be the best ally . . . for the furtherance of that end' " [24].

We have a foreshadowing in these chapers of the moral issue that is soon to divide Rochester and Jane. He says to her at one point: " 'For the world's judgment—I wash my hands thereof. For man's opinion—I defy it' " [23]. She warns him that she will " 'not stand . . . an inch in the stead of a seraglio,' " but he continues to treat her "as a sultan might" and to give her things as if she were "a slave his gold and gems had enriched." Such language underlines Rochester's possessiveness, his penchant for regarding her merely as an extension of himself, totally dependent upon his whim and mood. And she in turn castigates him for his pride and his passion for ownership. He continually tries to "see" into her, to get past exteriors and apprehend her soul so that he can possess it. And Jane, though she loves him, warns him again and again that he can never possess her completely until they become part of one another in marriage. And so Rochester arranges the marriage ceremony that is so memorably aborted.

When it is revealed that Rochester has a living wife and thus cannot marry Jane, he further demonstrates his selfishness by making several savage verbal attacks upon the poor madwoman who is his wife. Jane denounces him for the malignancy of his attack on the helpless Bertha. But Rochester replies that he hates her not because she is mad but because her existence prevents him from marrying Jane herself. We can understand and sympathize with Rochester's sentiment, but Charlotte Brontë also means us to see once again, in the self-pity rather than compassion with which he views his wife, his overpowering urge toward self-gratification. This urge also makes him propose to Jane that she become his mistress and live with him in France. She argues that love without marriage, self-indulgence without commitment, feeling without reason, is immoral and improper, and she refuses. When Rochester says in despair that she is condemning him to wretchedness, she replies: " 'I no more assign this fate to you than I grasp at it for myself. We were born to strive and endure—you as well as I: do so' " [27] . He has offered her only what he himself wants—self-gratification in the form of indulgence without commitment, possession without principle. Jane realizes that he cannot be argued back into rationality, and so, following her dictum that we are born to strive and to endure, she leaves Thornfield secretly and starts the journey which ends, some days later, at Moor House. Thus concludes this movement of the novel. When Jane finally arrives, tired and hungry, on the Rivers's doorstep, the next movement begins—a movement interesting both in itself and as a commentary on and further elucidation of what the story of Jane's relationship to Rochester means. That meaning becomes clearer the better we get to know St. John Rivers.

St. John, unlike Rochester, is cool and unimpassioned, except in his devotion to God and to his missionary work. Jane's initial impression of him is that he is more like "a statue [than] a man," that he is a "hard" man who is nevertheless both "restless" and "eager" within. He uses his eyes to plumb the depths of others' natures without "revealing his own," a "combination of keenness and reserve . . . more calculated to embarrass than to encourage." He too wishes to possess without giving. Despite his zealousness and conscientiousness in the service of God, he is not, Jane thinks, at peace either with himself or with the God he serves. Physical nature merely makes him gloomier: "he . . . did not appear to enjoy that mental serenity, that inward content, which should be the reward of every sincere Christian and practical philanthropist" [30]. It becomes clearer as St. John is more fully revealed to us that his "missions" in and around Morton are a matter more of duty than of love, for St. John loves only one thing—and that is personal advancement in the service of his God. His asceticism is really a virulent strain of ambition; the primary form his egoism takes is in the self-advancement he pictures to himself as the reward of his earthly labors. He is willing to sacrifice everything and everybody to his ambition; he too is willing to clothe himself at the expense of others. It seems that he not only wants to get to heaven—he wants an orchestra seat there: " 'the more arid and unreclaimed the soil where the Christian labourer's task of tillage is appointed him—the scantier the meed, his toil brings—the higher the honour' " [30]. Missionary work, in St. John's system, is not only a good thing in itself—it is also calculated to be the most expeditious means of securing a pre-eminent place in heaven. He will allow nothing to stand in his way—will, indeed, trample over as many others as necessary in order to take his seat. The soil of India is as "arid" and "unreclaimed" as one could ask, and so it is in that direction that St. John bends his cold eye.

Jane accepts a position as mistress of a school for poor girls, and when in her new and humble surroundings she stops to meditate on the lot she reluctantly exchanged for the present one, she concludes (31): "Yes, I feel . . . that I was right when I adhered to principle and law, and scorned and crushed the insane promptings of a frenzied moment. God directed me to a correct choice: I thank His providence for the guidance!" "Principle" and "law" were her answers to Rochester, and "love" and "feeling" are soon to be her answers to St. John Rivers. All four are necessary, for Charlotte Brontë, in any marriage, and God will again direct the protagonist "to a correct choice."

St. John visits Jane often in her new abode. He is, as she sees, "inexorable as death," a man who wants and needs devotion but gives nothing of himself; he "locks every feeling and pang within—expresses, confesses, imparts nothing." He has nothing but contempt for the "delirium and delusion" of the pleasures of this life, and measures his conversations with his pocket-watch so that they will not last too long. When Jane urges him to give up his missionary work and marry the willing Miss Oliver, he tells her that he can never relinquish, as he puts it, " 'My foundation laid on earth for a mansion in heaven. . . .' " He tells her that he is " 'a cold hard man' "; " 'my ambition is unlimited; my desire to rise higher, to do more than others, insatiable' " [32]. St. John is aware of this strain of his egoism; however, he is not aware, ultimately, of how completely his egoism has deprived his nature of charity, sympathy, and compassion. He says to Jane that " 'Reason, and not Feeling, is my guide,' " which is correct, but he never sees, as we finally do, what this means in terms of personal and immediate human existence. Both reason and feeling are necessary for a man to be whole. Rochester's feelings dominated his nature; St. John's reason dominates his. Neither man is complete until and unless he has both—a state of grace the Christian St. John can never achieve due to spiritual blindness but which the pagan and physically blind Rochester can and does achieve by the end of the novel.

Charlotte Brontë's language, the more St. John is revealed to us, suggests that, in his incapacity to feel, St. John is an incomplete man. No passage in any of her novels more perfectly expresses her horror of mindless asceticism than that in Chapter 33 of *Jane Eyre* in which Jane closely examines St. John's face during a visit he makes to her in the schoolroom: "I began to fear his wits were touched. If he were insane, however, his was a very cool and collected insanity: I had never seen that handsome-featured face of his look more like chiselled marble than it did just now, as he put aside his snow-wet hair from his forehead and let the firelight shine free on his pale brow and cheek as pale. . . ." St. John is monumentally unsympathetic and detached, a consummate egoist both in his self-regard and in his lack of empathy.

When St. John informs Jane that she is the heiress of twenty thousand pounds, she tells him that she will divide it four ways between herself and her cousins. St. John replies that she may keep it all with a clear conscience. Jane says: " 'With me . . . it is fully as much a matter of feeling as of conscience: I must indulge my feelings. . . .' " Both principle and feeling are necessary for Jane; she cannot imagine a life totally devoid of either. For St. John, feelings, at least human feelings, are basically irrelevant. "The humanities and amenities of life had no attractions for him—its peaceful enjoyments no charm. Literally, he lived only to *aspire* . . . He would never rest; nor approve of others resting round him" [34]. He sits at the fireside of Moor House, "a cold cumbrous column, gloomy and out of place." St. John's inhumanity, his total lack of warmth and feeling, distinguishes him from the hot-tempered and impulsive Rochester. Where Rochester lacked any guiding principles, St. John lacks all fellow-feeling. Charlotte Brontë's point is that Jane needs both, and it is toward this synthesis that she is moving. Rochester's egoism is in his self-indulgent contempt for the world and its standards of behavior. St. John's egoism lies in his monomaniac desire for self-fulfillment at whatever cost to others. We are soon to view a repentant and changed Rochester. St. John, however, can never change, any more than marble can become plastic.

Chapter 34 contains one of the novel's pivotal scenes—that in which St. John proposes to Jane that she accompany him to India. His proposal, which is also a proposal of marriage, leads ultimately to the climactic moment of the story—that in which Jane "hears" Rochester's voice and decides to return to him. St. John's invitation to Jane is made in terms typically unemotional and without fervor: " 'Jane, come with me to India: come as my helpmeet and fellow-labourer . . . you are formed for labour, not for love. . . . I claim you—not for my pleasure, but for my Sovereign's service.' " Now it is marriage without love that is being offered to Jane, just as Rochester had offered her love without marriage. The idea of love or any personal relationship seems absent from St. John's conception of marriage.

In his egoism, St. John has asked for the total possession of another human being, but he is unwilling to surrender himself to such possession. He would revere Jane on "principle" but could not love her. And so Jane, refusing to submit to the hypocrisy of a marriage ceremony, tells St. John that she will go with him only if they do *not* marry—a direct reversal of her answer to Rochester, wherein she refused to accompany him to France unless they were married, which was then impossible. A meaningful human relationship for her cannot consist entirely of either dutifulness or self-gratification. St. John seems as blind to this principle as Rochester had been—and in fact St. John, unlike Rochester, never really understands Jane's attitude. Her proposal to accompany him unwed as his assistant in the missionary work he plans meets

immediate opposition: " 'either our union must be consecrated and sealed by marriage, or it cannot exist: practical
obstacles oppose themselves to any other plan.' " Jane sees
these obstacles, but to her what is even more important is
"that we did not love each other as man and wife should; and
therefore . . . we ought not to marry." But St. John is adamant, and it becomes clearer the more he insists that his interest in Jane is primarily proprietary: " 'I . . . do not want a
sister; a sister might any day be taken from me. I want a wife:
the sole helpmeet I can influence efficiently in life, and retain
absolutely till death' " [34]. Such crass egoism stuns Jane,
and she "shudders" as St. John goes on to explain that he
must "mate" a "missionary" for a practical reason: he will
need help in India. She tells St. John that if she were to go
with him she would devote all of her energies to missionary
work but that she could never be so totally a possession of his
as he would wish—she cannot give up all of herself. (The
spectre of marriage without love reveals to Jane, as it often
reveals to George Meredith's characters, the necessity, in
Clara Middleton's words, of "recesses in my mind which
would be only mine.") St. John, who seems throughout
Chapter 34 to be having trouble distinguishing between
himself and his heavenly "Master," replies: " 'Do you think
God will be satisfied with half an oblation? Will he accept a
mutilated sacrifice? It is the cause of God I advocate: it is under His standard I enlist you. I cannot accept on His behalf a
divided allegiance: it must be entire.' " Without love, such
complete submission is impossible for Jane. She tells him: " 'I
will give my heart to God. . . . *You* do not want it.' " St. John
is puzzled but not impeded by her outburst; he replies that
marriage would provide for them the "impetus" necessary for
their missionary "efforts." Jane tells him once again that she
will go with him as a helper, " 'but not as your wife; I cannot
marry you and become part of you.' " St. John answers her
coldly: " 'A part of me you must become . . . otherwise the
bargain is void.' " Her value for him is only as an extension of
himself, a possession to be used to gain ends both practical

and personal. He cannot separate his proposal of marriage and his all-consuming ambition.

Jane tells him, finally, that she can feel nothing for him beyond loyalty, fraternity, and respect. He says that these are the only things he wants from her for the time being, and that " 'love would follow upon marriage to render the union right . . . .' " Jane replies: " 'I scorn your idea of love . . . . I scorn the counterfeit sentiment you offer . . . .' " St. John's final answer to her is the height of arrogance and insensitivity (34): " 'if you reject my offer of marriage, it is not me you deny, but God. Through my means, He opens to you a noble career; as my wife only can you enter upon it. Refuse to be my wife, and you limit yourself forever to a track of selfish ease and barren obscurity. Tremble lest in that case you should be numbered among those who have denied the faith, and are worse than infidels!' " For St. John, who speaks effortlessly here about selfishness, her denial of him as a husband is equivalent to denial of "the faith." His egoism is a combination of arrogance, self-delusion, and lack of sympathy. At the end of their interview, Jane reflects upon his "iron . . . austere and despotic nature," which always "expected submission," and his "cool, inflexible judgment," which always expected acquiescence and which had detected in her "feelings and views in which it [had] no power to sympathise." Ignoring the dictates of personal feeling, he had wished "to coerce [her] into obedience."

After this scene St. John treats Jane even more coldly, becoming in her presence "no longer flesh, but marble," as if "his heart had really been a matter of stone or metal." Jane calls him "icy" once again and likens his displeasure with her to "the fall of the avalanche" and "the breaking up of the frozen sea." It is St. John's lack of all human feeling, so important to Jane, that the language emphasizes again and again. When Jane reproaches him for "hating" her, he seems surprised and tells her that " 'it is the duty of man to forgive his fellow, even until seventy-and-seven times.' " This is the answer he makes to the woman to whom a short time ago he had proposed marriage. And St. John, ironically and perhaps unconsciously, has notably shortened the forgiveness period. According to St. Matthew it should be until four-hundred and ninety times (seventy *times* seven times). But the monomaniac fixation of St. John's spiritual ambition blinds him both to the spirit and the letter of Christian charity.

In Chapter 35 Jane explains to Diana Rivers why she cannot marry St. John: " 'his sole idea in proposing to me is to procure a fitting fellow-labourer in his Indian toils . . . it is not himself but his office he wishes to mate. He has told me I am formed for labour—not for love. . . . If I am not formed for love, it follows that I am not formed for marriage. Would it not be strange . . . to be chained for life to a man who regarded one but as a useful tool?' " This is precisely the way in which St. John regards her. Jane, of course, is very much formed for love; she is a loving person, but St. John is incapable of receiving love or of giving it. Jane, therefore, will not marry him. She tells Diana (Chapter 35): ' "He would not want me to love him; and if I showed the feeling, he would make me sensible that it was a superfluity unrequired by him. . . . He forgets, pitilessly, the feelings and claims of little people, in pursuing his own large views.' " Here is an accurate distillation of St. John's egoism.

St. John makes one final attempt to persuade Jane to marry him. In the process he seems to confuse once again marriage to himself with marriage to God: " 'If I listened to human pride, I should say no more to you of marriage with me; but I listen to my duty, and keep steadily in view my first aim—to do all things to the glory of God. My Master was long-suffering: so will I be. I cannot give you up to perdition as a vessel of wrath: repent—resolve; while there is yet time' " [35]. For St. John, who thinks he is eschewing "human pride," denial of himself is a denial of duty to God. For Jane it is simply a denial of a loveless marriage—but she has a final moment of wavering. St. John, like a "pastor" or a "guardian angel," lays his hand upon her head, and for a few seconds Jane puts "love out of the question and thinks only of duty." But, as with Rochester's proposal, her time of temptation is very short indeed: "I was almost as hard beset by St.

John now as I had been once before, in a different way, by another. I was a fool both times. To have yielded then would have been an error of principle; to have yielded now would have been an error of judgment" [35]. Jane recognizes immediately the crux of the moral issue. To live as Rochester's mistress would have been sacrificing principle to expedience; to live as St. John's wife would be sacrificing judgment to a metaphysical idea of duty in which she does not really believe. Each side of the equation is incomplete without the other, and Jane must resist coercion on both sides until the figure can be made whole. Since her experience of both sides of the equation is just now complete, the figure can be made whole, and thus it is at this precise moment that Jane "hears" Rochester's cry: this is the beginning of synthesis.

This event, which has often been scoffed at by even the most sympathetic of readers, is more easily explained thematically than physiologically. In the first place, the book's intellectual argument now demands some sort of reconciliation, as I have just suggested. Also, Jane and Rochester, throughout the earlier parts of the novel, have been very close to one another spiritually—close enough to read one another's mind, to intuit deeper sentiments, to develop an intense psychological sympathy. Their minds are characterized in several passages as being virtually inseparable. Thus the fact that Jane hears Rochester's cry at the exact moment when, as it turns out, he shouted for her at a distance of many miles, is not so startling after all. One could characterize this event simply as one part of a human mind speaking to another part. In addition, Rochester, now wifeless, blind, and repentant, has recognized his past sins and his need for the conventional relationship of marriage with Jane. Since Jane is ready, after her battle with St. John, to be a real wife to a man she genuinely loves, a meeting of their minds is now logical. Mutual commitment and spiritual harmony between them have become possible no matter what Rochester's condition, which is unknown to Jane, might be. Thus he shouts and she hears him—a physical impossibility but, for Charlotte Brontë, the symbolic and logical result of the development of her protagonists. They are only recreating physically a spiritual condition.

When Jane finds Rochester at Ferndean, it is clear that, unlike St. John Rivers, he has learned something about himself. For Rochester, having Jane " 'about my hand and chair—to wait on me as a kind little nurse' " is no longer enough. She has taught him that there must be a commitment with love, and his most immediate desire, now that he can do so, is to marry her. He had once asked her to eschew principle and become his mistress; Rochester now says: " 'All the melody on earth is concentrated in my Jane's tongue to my ear . . . all the sunshine I can feel is in her presence.' " Rochester has become dependent upon her; unlike St. John, he both loves and needs her. His literal blindness, which, like that of Oedipus, or Gloucester in *King Lear*, may perhaps be considered both an ironic result of the lateness of his new and deeper "sight" and a kind of symbolic castration for his former immorality, begins to abate as their relationship nears perfection. Rochester, in his blindness, has seen the truth: " 'I want a wife. . . . Never mind the fine clothes and jewels now: all that is not worth a fillip.' " It is the substance of marriage that is important to him now—not merely its trappings. Jane says to him: " 'I love you better now, when I can really be useful to you, than I did in your state of proud independence.' " For her, love and duty are inseparable. Rochester's reply is the most important expression of the discovery he has made about his own nature:

> 'my heart swells with gratitude to the beneficent God of this earth just now. He sees not as man sees, but far clearer: judges not as man judges, but far more wisely. I did wrong: I would have sullied my innocent flower—breathed guilt on its purity: the Omnipotent snatched it from me. I, in my stiff-necked rebellion, almost cursed the dispensation: instead of bending to the decree, I defied it. Divine justice pursued its course; disasters came thick on me. . . . Of late . . . I began to see and acknowledge the hand of God in my doom. I began to experience remorse, repentance. . . .' (37)

Here is an expression of Christian faith infinitely more sim-

ple, sincere, and moving than any of St. John's utterances.
Rochester has discovered what Jane has always known: that
self-gratification independent of principle—feeling divorced
from judgment—is unacceptable to the world's guardian
spirit. In learning this he has discovered his own blind
selfishness, and the discovery has enabled him to exorcise the
last elements of self-absorption. God and Jane have conquered his egoism, and thus Rochester and Jane are able,
finally, to "meet in spirit," as he says. And so, as Jane says at
the end of the novel, "I am my husband's life as fully as he is
mine. No woman was ever nearer to her mate than I am: ever
more absolutely bone of his bone, and flesh of his flesh. . . .
All my confidence is bestowed on him, as his confidence is
devoted to me; we are precisely suited in character—perfect
concord is the result" [38].

For Charlotte Brontë it is wrong for one person to
try to absorb or possess another entirely; there must be
mutual confidence, commitment, and love. These things were
missing from Jane's earlier relationship with Rochester, and
missing as well, of course, from her one-sided relationship
with St. John Rivers, whose only love was an ambitious love
of God. To love God *alone*, even for the right reasons, is for
Charlotte Brontë a suicidal denial of man and therefore of life
itself.

The last paragraph of the novel, interestingly enough, is
an extract from St. John's final letter to Jane: " 'My Master
. . . has forewarned me. Daily he announces more dis-
tinctly,—"Surely I come quickly!" and hourly I more eagerly
respond,—"Amen; even so come, Lord Jesus!" ' " The
emphasis here is still on personal fulfillment; St. John, to the
end, puts his own spiritual case before all others. For him,
there is no ultimate self-discovery. It is instructive to compare
his final statement with Rochester's (37): " 'I thank my
Maker, that in the midst of judgment he has remembered
mercy. I humbly entreat my redeemer to give me strength to
lead henceforth a purer life than I have done hitherto!' "
Rather than self-proclamation, this is a statement of humility
and acceptance, an embodiment of the realization that man is

insufficient of himself alone, that to strive and to endure means making one's peace with others and that accepting their differences is a necessary prerequisite of love and fulfillment. The Christian St. John, despite his zeal, quite clearly has missed his aim at a state of Grace—heavenly or earth-bound; while the pagan Rochester, physically blind, has acquired moral vision through the self-education of suffering. Thus for Rochester, finally, Jane has "the look of another world" in her face; and it is that world toward which she leads him.

III

In *Framley Parsonage* (1860-61), which virtually overnight made Anthony Trollope famous, the Reverend Mark Robarts, like St. John Rivers, is an ambitious man. Robarts's ambitions, however, are more worldly than Rivers's; his egoism takes the form not so much of spiritual arrogance as of social pragmatism. In his desire for rapid, even premature, clerical advancement, Robarts puts self-gratification ahead of rationality and consideration for his family; he realizes the full extent of his folly only when he is threatened with financial (and thus professional and social) ruin. Unlike Rochester and St. John, he is not naturally an egoist, full of self-confidence and unresponsive to the feelings of others. On the contrary—Robarts is basically compassionate and clearheaded, a loving husband, father, and brother, a faithful and loyal friend, a priest who, if he looks upon the Church primarily as an avenue of advancement (as did so many of his peers in the nineteenth century), nevertheless also believes in the dignity and moral responsibility of his calling. What happens to Robarts in *Framley Parsonage* happens because, for a time, his better instincts are buried under the lure of quick advancement—and the excitement of the chase after it perverts, temporarily, some of these better instincts. While the lurid glow of ambition beckons him on, he forgets that he has a loving wife, two dependent children and a loyal patroness

ANTHONY TROLLOPE (1815-1882)
National Portrait Gallery, London

(Lady Lufton). His egoism is, perhaps, a temporary lapse, but its duration coincides with that particular period of his life treated in the novel, and as such his moral development is very much a part of the general pattern I am attempting to elucidate in this study. Robarts descends to various depths of self-gratification in the course of the novel, only in the end to discover how foolish and inconsiderate he has been—a self-discovery which, we are led to believe, is sufficiently traumatic to make him eschew clerical politics for the rest of his life. As he is only twenty-six, it is safe to predict, finally, that his new wisdom has come upon him early enough to enable him to avoid the snares and delusions of professional ambition at a time when many men are most susceptible to them. The joys of family life and a clear conscience are, for Trollope, infinitely preferable to the pursuit of advancement, inevitable concomitants of which are selfishness, obsequiousness, compromise, and thus, in a basically moral man, guilt and self-doubt. As in most of Trollope's novels, there are several stories, and this is only one of a number of plots; but it is the most important story in *Framley Parsonage,* and its ramifications affect more people directly than any of the others.

Although often aware that his conduct is not entirely unimpeachable, Mark Robarts maps out for himself a course designed to bring him promotion in the church hierarchy. He is already blessed with a good living, a loyal wife, and a beneficent patroness—but, even at the age of twenty-six, he is hungering for more. He is sometimes beset by pangs of guilt, but often manages to suppress them—at least throughout the early sections of the novel. Trollope's introduction of Robarts to us suggests that his "square forehead" denotes "intelligence rather than thought," and indeed Robarts's reflective powers (like Michael Henchard's in *The Mayor of Casterbridge)* are usually exercised after the fact rather than before it. We see his weakness manifested twice in the very first chapter. He allows Lady Lufton to appoint a schoolmistress for the parish who he feels is unqualified; his excuse to his wife for diplomatic non-resistance to the appointment is that " 'If I persist this time, I shall certainly have to yield the next; and then the next may probably be more important.' " And he tells his wife that he is going for a week to Chaldicotes, a notorious Whig center of political intrigue, in order to meet some important and influential people—such as Mr. Harold Smith: " 'I have no doubt that Harold Smith will be in the government some day, and I cannot afford to neglect such a man's acquaintance.' " The principles of a parish clergyman—one appointed by an old Tory family—are apparently being threatened by the aspirations of the ambitious clerical politician.

Yet Robarts is never wholly without a conscience; his saving grace is his constant awareness that his values may perhaps be warped. Thus he can talk of his projected trip to Chaldicotes with equanimity in conversation with his curate Evans, but "Why could he not talk of it in the same tone to Lady Lufton?" Both Lady Lufton and his wife Fanny caution him not to become too intimate with the Chaldicotes men, and particularly to avoid the notoriously impecunious Mr. Sowerby, the member for West Barsetshire—a tool of the great but unprincipled Whig lord the Duke of Omnium, who is a particular and emphatic enemy of the Lufton family. (This is the bachelor uncle of Plantagenet Palliser, Duke of Omnium and chief protagonist of Trollope's later political novels.) But Mark has already become a friend of Mr. Sowerby, who in turn sees in his prosperous new clerical friend another possible source of revenue.

Mark goes off to Chaldicotes not entirely clear of conscience but with a great many rationalizations calculated to set his mind at ease:

> a man in the world must meet all sorts of men; and . . .
> in these days it did not do for a clergyman to be a hermit.
> . . . He did know that Mr. Sowerby was a dangerous
> man; he was aware that he was over head and ears in
> debt, and that he had already entangled young Lord
> Lufton in some pecuniary embarrassment; his con-
> science did tell him that it would be well for him, as one
> of Christ's soldiers, to look out for companions of a

different stamp. But nevertheless he went to
Chaldicotes, not satisfied with himself indeed, but
repeating to himself a great many arguments why he
should be so satisfied. (III)

Robarts, we note here, is fully aware beforehand of Sowerby's character and habits. What happens later, therefore, cannot be attributed to the vicar's innocence, his ignorance of the
true character of his new friend. On the contrary, he knows
that character well enough but pays little attention to the
dangers.

The perceptive Miss Dunstable says to him in the
Chaldicotes drawing-room that she thinks " 'it ought to be
the happiest life that a man can lead, that of a parish
clergyman, with a wife and family and a sufficient income.' "
Robarts says that it is, and then asks himself if he is really
"satisfied at all points. He had all these things of which Miss
Dunstable spoke, and yet he had told his wife, the other day,
that he could not afford to neglect the acquaintance of a rising politician like Harold Smith" [III]. The implication of
this exchange seems to be that Robarts really does have
everything that ought to make him happy but simply does not
realize it. His ambition has warped his perception, and he is
following a course designed to bring only unhappiness to
himself and his family. In his self-absorption he is unable to
see the folly of his behavior. Trollope says at the end of the
third chapter: "I will not degrade him by calling him a tuft-
hunter; but he undoubtedly had a feeling that the paths most
pleasant for a clergyman's feet were those which were
trodden by the great ones of the earth." This seems to be an
odd way for a clergyman to think, and Trollope, although he
is no ascetic and does not comment directly, means us to understand this. An invitation to Gatherum Castle now comes
to Mark from Mr. Fothergill, the Duke of Omnium's man of
business, and the clergyman's ambitious nature is highly
gratified. He says he will not go, but we know that he
will—despite some misgivings and his knowledge that
Gatherum is the hangout of the fastest set among the Whig
politicians and hangers-on.

In Chapter IV, "A Matter of Conscience," Trollope momentarily plays the devil's advocate with notable lack of conviction.

> [A]mbition is a great vice . . . if the ambition of the man be with reference to his own advancement, and not to the advancement of others. But then, how many of us are there who are not ambitious in this vicious manner? And there is nothing viler than the desire to know great people—people of great rank, I should say; nothing worse than the hunting of titles and worshipping of wealth. We all know this, and say it every day of our lives. But presuming that a way into the society of Park Lane was open to us, and a way also into that of Bedford Row, how many of us are there who would prefer Bedford Row because it is so vile to worship wealth and title?
>
> I am led into these rather trite remarks by the necessity of putting forward some sort of excuse for the frame of mind in which the Rev. Mark Robarts awoke on the morning after his arrive at Chaldicotes.

Trollope, here in clearly Thackerayan tones, defines Robarts's lapse from grace. His ambition, like that of St. John Rivers, is not for the advancement of others but rather for the advancement of himself. This quasi-ironic expression of the superior popularity of wealth over poverty, which might well have been lifted from *Vanity Fair*, does not hide the author's disapproval of Robarts's behavior, which is emphasized by the mention of the clerical title in the last sentence. Robarts's egoism takes the form of a desire for personal advancement without proper consideration of the moral compromises necessary for such advancement. In the case of a clergyman, such a mistake is doubly unfortunate. What Robarts must discover before he can exorcise his devil is that his life can be complete and fulfilling without such advancement and that a clear conscience can be restored to him only when such ambition is abrogated. As yet, however, he understands none of these things. On the contrary: "he felt that he was different from other parsons,—more fitted by nature for intimacy with great persons, more urbane, more polished, and more richly endowed with modern clerical well-to-do aptitudes" [IV]. Robarts's self-conceit is here made manifest; it is always himself about whom he thinks.

> Of whom generally did prime ministers and official bigwigs think it expedient to make bishops and deans? Was it not, as a rule, of those clergymen who had shown themselves able to perform their clerical duties efficiently, and able also to take their place with ease in high society? He was very well off certainly at Framley; but he could never hope for anything beyond Framley, if he allowed himself to regard Lady Lufton as a bugbear. . . . Perhaps it might be more prudent for him to return home. But . . . it behoved him as a man and priest to break through that Framley thraldom. . . . (IV)

Robarts, in his self-indulgent consideration of the duties of "a man and priest," seems to have lost sight of his duties as a minister of God on earth, an omission Trollope's audience plainly is meant to understand. And it is also meant to understand that Robarts owes more to Lady Lufton than he has been giving. She awarded him the Framley living and also found his excellent wife for him. And yet he is able to rationalize her into a "bugbear" and believes he is being held back professionally by the "thraldom" of her influence.

Mark's exercise in self-deception culminates when Mr. Fothergill renews the Duke's invitation to visit Gatherum Castle: "What could a young flattered fool of a parson do, but say that he would go?" Robarts, of course, feels that to decline would be to interrupt the progress of his own advancement. He does not see that the Omnium interests, as usual, are merely looking after themselves, are trying to establish a political foothold on the Tory soil occupied by Lady Lufton and her dependents. This, at least, is Mr. Fothergill's motive. Meanwhile Sowerby cultivates his intimacy with Robarts in hopes, later on, of getting some money out of him.

Mark, all this time, is dreaming of bishop's palaces. He writes to Fanny to tell her the reason for his extended absence and to ask for some money; the letter, to his credit, is a cornucopia of guilty feelings and obfuscations, and Lady Lufton makes short work of it: " 'he'll find that it's better for him . . . in every way, to stick to his old friends. It will be better for his peace of mind, better for his character as a clergyman, better for his pocket, better for his children and for [his wife],—and better for his eternal welfare' " [V]. And Lady Lufton, of course, is right on all of these counts, as subsequent events prove.

At Chaldicotes Mark spends most of his time trying to rationalize to himself his presence there. It is painful and irksome to him to hear Sowerby refer to Lady Lufton as the "old woman," says Trollope, "till habit made it easy." On a Sunday morning, waiting for the others to get ready for church, Robarts wonders (VII) "whether it was good that he should be waiting there, in painful anxiety, to gallop over a dozen miles in order that he might not be too late with his sermon. . . . He could not afford not to know Harold Smith, and Mr. Sowerby, and the Duke of Omnium. . . . He had to rise in the world. . . . But what pleasure had come to him as yet from these intimacies? How much had he hitherto done towards rising?" His hesitations at this point are the result less of any moral revulsion than of the frustrated desire of seeing some immediate and practical result of his fraternization with the great ones. And yet, as they get to the church late on that Sunday, Robarts does begin to wonder if the price he is paying to know these people is too high (VII): "they made their way up the church as the Absolution was being read, and Mark Robarts felt thoroughly ashamed of himself. If his rising in the world brought him in contact with such things as these, would it not be better for him that he should do without rising?"

At Gatherum Castle Mark sees more of Mr. Sowerby than ever: "Mark . . . could not but feel a certain animosity against Mr. Sowerby—could not but suspect that he was a bad man. Nay, must he not have known that he was very bad? And yet he continued walking with him through the duke's grounds talking about Lord Lufton's affairs . . ." [VIII]. Lufton is Mark's oldest friend and has been swindled by Sowerby out of great sums of money, as everyone suspects and as Lufton himself has told Mark. Even this, however, is insufficient to keep Mark from basking in the regard of the influential member for West Barsetshire; Sowerby's continuing intimacy with him "flattered our young clergyman not a little."

The Gatherum episode ends with Robarts, to oblige Sowerby, signing a bill making himself responsible for four hundred pounds in three months should Sowerby be unable to pay it. There is of course never any question, in our minds or in Sowerby's, about his intention or his ability to meet the bill. Mark Robarts is beginning to pay the price of his folly. He realizes on his way home that he will also be unable to pay the bill when it falls due and berates himself for his ambition:

> Why had he come to this horrid place? Had he not everything at home at Framley which the heart of man could desire? No; the heart of man can desire deaneries—the heart, that is, of the man vicar; and the heart of the man dean can desire bishoprics; and before the eyes of the man bishop does there not loom the transcendental glory of Lambeth? . . . The German student when he first made his bargain with the devil felt an indescribable attraction to his new friend; and such was the case now with Robarts. (IX)

This is only the first of several references to Sowerby as the devil tempting the Faustian Mark Robarts to fall from grace.

Robarts returns to Framley, where his wife and friends welcome him home as if he has had a narrow escape from the Philistines. Mark laughs, but thinks to himself "that he was, in very truth, already 'himself in bonds under Philistian yoke.' " The vicar thinks over the pecuniary mess he has been entangled in by Mr. Sowerby and begins to see "that it would have been better for him to have relinquished altogether the glories of Chaldicotes and Gatherum Castle." In the meantime he rationalizes keeping the transaction a secret from his wife: "Were he to tell her at the present moment . . . the intelligence would frighten her into illness . . . . It would kill her, he said to himself over and over again, were he to tell her of it . . ."[X]. Fanny, of course, is much stronger than he is, but Mark, having made a mistake, makes another one in fearing to share his worries with the one person most likely to relieve his mind and restore his self-confidence. Once again, despite his mental protestations to the contrary, he is only indulging himself. But Mark resolves not to worry; he even argues himself, briefly enough, into a jolly mood:

> A load which would crush a man at first becomes, by habit, not only endurable, but easy and comfortable to the bearer. . . . Mr. Sowerby certainly was a pleasant fellow, and gave a man something in return for his money. . . . Had that gentleman fallen across his clerical friend at the present moment, he might no doubt have gotten from him an acceptance for another four hundred pounds. (XII)

It appears that Mark Robarts, at this stage of his development, has not learned very much from his intercourse with the devil.

Riding to hounds several months later, Mark meets Sowerby again and asks him when he is going to take care of the bill. Sowerby seems to have forgotten all about it, and calls Mark "green" for having endorsed it. Mark is surprised and distressed by his attitude; Sowerby replies: " ' "Sufficient for the day is the evil thereof.' " And away they both went together, parson and member of Parliament." Sowerby's flippant scriptural answer is a further suggestion of how lightly Mark Robarts is wearing his clerical robes. Mark, who has now become a member of that clerical class some Victorians contemptuously referred to as "hunting parsons," resolves once again, after this encounter, to keep the secret of the bill from Fanny. The reward for his patience is Sowerby's request in a letter that he sign another note for five hundred pounds. Doing so, says Sowerby, will extend the deadline for payment of the first bill. Having learned very little from his experiences of the past few months, Robarts signs the second bill.

> What else was he to do? Fool that he was. A man always can do right even though he has done wrong before. But that previous wrong adds so much difficulty to the path—a difficulty which increases in tremendous ratio, till a man at last is choked in his struggling, and is drowned beneath the waters. . . . He put away Sowerby's letter carefully, locking it up from his wife's sight. It was a letter that no parish clergyman should have receiv-

ed. So much he acknowledged to himself. . . . And now again for a few hours this affair made him very miserable. (XII)

Mark's better instincts are still not enough to exorcise the desire to indulge his personal ambitions, and so this further betrayal of his family and, potentially, his reputation, makes him miserable only "for a few hours." Sowerby, in an attempt to confuse hopelessly his financial dealings with Robarts, as he has already done with Lord Lufton, also tries to sell Mark a horse for hunting. The tenor of their intercourse, says Trollope, was such as would suggest that Sowerby was becoming "more and more oblivious of his friend's sacred profession," and might lead one to think that "the vicar himself [was] too frequently oblivious of it also. But no: he was not oblivious of it. He was ever mindful of it; but mindful of it in such a manner that his thoughts on the subject were nowadays always painful" [XIV].

The rather cavalier way in which the vicar now pursues his parish duties finally begins to alarm Lady Lufton, and she puts Mr. Crawley, the pious and impoverished vicar of nearby Hogglestock, up to trying to recall Robarts to a sense of duty. In a brief interview (XV), Crawley tells Mark bluntly that his " 'present mode of life is one that is not befitting a soldier in Christ's army,' " and asks him whether he honestly thinks he is leading " 'such a life as may become a parish clergyman among his parishioners.' " Mark replies: " 'There are but a few of us. . .who could safely answer that question in the affirmative,' " and he sits down after Crawley's departure "to think over his present life."

Unfortunately for Mark, however, it is during this brief period of serious self-examination that his social peregrinations now seem to be beginning to pay a dividend. Through the efforts of Sowerby, Harold Smith, and the Duke of Omnium, Robarts has the prebendal stall at Barchester conferred upon him—a post usually reserved for older men of the Church. Meanwhile, in the course of his renewed intimacy with Sowerby, he has been talked into buying the hunter, and now himself begins to wonder "what his friends

and neighbours would say about him." His fears are sup-
ported when Lord Lufton remarks: " 'the world will of course
tell you that you have paid . . . for this stall at Barchester.' "
Mark's mind conjures up images of "misery and ruin":

> he loathed with his whole soul the position in which he
> found himself placed, and his own folly which had plac-
> ed him there. How could he reconcile it to his conscience
> that he was there in London with Sowerby and Harold
> Smith, petitioning for Church preferment to a man who
> should have been altogether powerless in such a matter,
> buying horses, and arranging about past due bills. He
> did not reconcile it to his conscience. (XIX)

Robarts admits to Lufton that he has been "wrong" and
"outrageously foolish" in his association with Sowerby. He
has an "uneasy night" in London, thinking with "horror and
dismay" of the evils of simony. He seems to be edging toward
self-discovery and reversal of his past behavior—but he is not
there quite yet.

> [T]hat line of conduct which he . . . laid down for himself
> in the first moments of his indignation against Lord Luf-
> ton, by adopting which he would have to encounter
> poverty, and ridicule, and discomfort, the annihilation
> of his high hopes, and the ruin of his ambition—that, he
> said to himself over and over again, would now be the
> best for him. But it is so hard for us to give up our high
> hopes, and willingly encounter poverty, ridicule, and
> discomfort! (XIX)

And so he does not give up the stall; rather, his conversations
with Sowerby during his visit to London "raise" his "spirits."
Sowerby's assurance about the bills he has signed is "very
comforting to him; and, strange to say, he absolutely believed
it." And so he goes home to tell those at Framley of his new
good fortune, proud but not entirely happy, for, as Trollope
says, "The enjoyment of one's own happiness at such wind-
falls depends so much on the free and freely expressed enjoyment of others!" Mark regrets the unpleasantness of his
situation but still has not recognized the depth of his
selfishness. He dislikes to suffer himself but seems incapable
of anticipating fully the "poverty, ridicule, and discomfort"

his ambition may bring down upon his family and friends as a result of his failure to sever his unsavory connections and his acceptance of the stall—which is, more or less, Sowerby's reward to him for the loan (and payment in full for it as well).

When the story returns, over a hundred pages later, to Mark Robarts and his troubles, we learn first that he has decided to sign his name to no other bill in any last-minute attempt to avoid a final catastrophe—such as, for example, the impounding of his furniture and personal effects by the bailiffs for his failure to pay the debt. Sowerby pleads with him to sign another bill in order to put off the execution of the first two. Mark's reply is an indication both of his past naiveté and his present incisiveness:

> 'It seems to me that you have robbed me. That I have been a fool, and worse than a fool, I know well; but . . . I thought that your position in the world would guarantee me from such treatment as this. . . . I wonder whether you ever thought of my wife and children when you were planning this ruin of me! . . . What an ass I have been to be so cozened by a sharper! . . . On no earthly consideration that can be put before me will I again sign my name to any bill in the guise of an acceptance. I have been very weak, and am ashamed of my weakness; but so much strength as that, I hope, is left to me. I have been very wicked, and am ashamed of my wickedness; but so much right principle as that, I hope, remains. I will put my name to no other bill; not for you, not even for myself. . . . What a fool I was. . . .'
> (XXXIII)

Sowerby remonstrates with him, telling him that at least one good result of their friendship was the Barchester stall. But the vanity of Mark's ambition is now totally manifest to him:

> Would that he had [given up the stall]! That was Mark's wish now,—his futile wish. In what a slough of despond had he come to wallow in consequence of his folly on that night at Gatherum Castle! He had then done a silly thing, and was he now to rue it by almost total ruin? He was sickened also with all [of Sowerby's] lies. His very soul was dismayed by the dirt through which he was forced to wade. He had become unconsciously connected with the lowest dregs of mankind, and would

> have to see his name mingled with theirs in the daily
> newspapers. And for what had he done this? Why had
> he thus filed his mind and made himself a disgrace to his
> cloth? In order that he might befriend such a one as Mr.
> Sowerby! (XXXIII)

The language of these two passages emphasizes the progress
of Mark's self-discovery. Mark calls himself a "fool" and an
"ass" and is "ashamed" now of his "weakness" and his
"wickedness." "Wallowing" in a "slough of despond," he
now recognizes his own "folly" and "silliness" and desperate-
ly "rues" his past conduct. He feels "sickened" and
"disgraced" by the "dirt" through which his ambitions have
forced him to "wade." This is the despair which, in any sentient moral being, is both the inevitable result of solipsistic
self-indulgence and the necessary correlative of self-discovery
and newly objective moral vision. Mark is discovering not
only that his egoism has compromised him morally, but also
that his soul has been in danger of pollution and that the
best way to rehabilitate it is to withdraw completely from all
possible sources of corruption. As part of his penance he
finally tells the whole story to Fanny, which of course he
should have done long before: "For there is no folly so great
as keeping one's sorrows hidden." Trollope now departs
from this part of his novel once again, having made it clear
that if Mark's problem has not been solved in practical terms,
at least he now has enough knowledge both of himself and of
the world to avoid future pitfalls of ambition.

When we return to Mark some hundred pages later the
bailiffs' execution is felt to be imminent and the Robartses
are merely waiting for the final public disgrace. Sowerby
writes Mark one more time, urging him to sign a last bill to
avoid the present danger. A good part of Chapter XLII
("Touching Pitch") is devoted to Mark's reaction to the
letter.

> That the man who had written this letter should be his
> friend . . . was a disgrace to him . . . This was the man
> whom he had been so glad to call his friend; for whose
> sake he had been willing to quarrel with Lady Lufton,

and at whose instance he had unconsciously abandoned so many of the best resolutions of his life. . . . He thought also of the manner in which he had been tempted to the house of the Duke of Omnium, and the conviction on his mind at the time that his giving way to that temptation would surely bring him to evil . . . He had lacked the courage to say, 'No,' though he knew at the time how gross was the error he was committing. . . . He had been fond of pleasure and had given way to temptation. . . . The stuff of which his manhood was to be formed had been slow of growth, as it is with many men; and, consequently, when temptation was offered to him he had fallen. But he deeply grieved over his own stumbling. . . . Had it come to that with him that he could not . . . hold up his head with a safe conscience as the pastor of his parish? . . . He was a poor man now—a distressed, poverty-stricken man; but nevertheless he wished with all his heart that he had never become a sharer in the good things of the Barchester chapter.

In this passage Trollope moves at will within and without the mind of his protagonist, giving us Mark's penitential musings alternated with comments of his own. Mark here is rightfully self-accusatory, seeing finally that his association with un-principled politicians was a "temptation" he plainly could have resisted. Because he has finally learned to recognize his own past weaknesses, one feels it unlikely that he will suc-cumb to such temptations again. And because he is still young, one also feels that the lesson has been learned in time for him to lead a more enlightened existence—come what may as a result of the present issue. His "manhood," though "slow of growth," has been "formed."

At the end of this section of the novel, Trollope, with his usual frankness and disregard for what Henry James called the "illusion of reality" in fiction, suggests that Mark Robarts should have remained a parish curate until he was older—that his debts, his hunting, and his fraternizing with those in high places were perhaps inevitable consequences of the catastrophic combination of personal weakness, youth, and increased means. Trollope, though no ascetic,

nevertheless makes it clear that clergymen should not entertain worldly ambitions, and also that men of whatever profession are better off waiting and working for their advancement
than acquiring it too quickly—a typical Trollopian theme
and one undoubtedly familiar to readers of some of his other
novels (particularly the later political novels). Trollope goes
on: "Mark Robarts's mistake was mainly this,—he had
thought to touch pitch and not be defiled. . . .His ass's ears
were tickled, and he learned to fancy that he was intended by
nature for the society of high people" [XLII]. He should have
been satisfied with his parsonage, his wife, and his old
friends, says Trollope, and instead found them dull when
compared with a "more lively life." His ambition, his egoism,
led him away from these things, and thus he was "defiled."
Mark himself says at the end of this chapter: " 'I have learned
a lesson which I hope I may never forget. . . .Of the faults
which a man commits he must bear the punishment.' " This
typically Victorian theme—prominent, for example, in the
novels of Dickens and George Eliot, among others—is one to
which Trollope resorts again and again in his stories. In the
case of Mark Robarts it is specifically tied to the theme of
egoism and self-discovery, an ordeal of education through
which the protagonist must make his way before he can
become a useful member of his community.

The "Philistines" now arrive at the parsonage in the person of the bailiffs, and Mark, ashamed of the ambition that
has made him "carry his head so high above the heads of
neighbouring parsons," hides in his study, fully aware of the
folly of great expectations and of the personal selfishness that
has brought ruin to his household. " 'I wonder . . . that you
can bear to stay in the room with me,' " he says shame-
facedly to his wife. Trollope uses Fanny's open-heartedness,
selflessness, and simple faith as a model for her husband to
follow—one, perhaps, he would have recognized earlier had
his egoism not led him away from home so often (XLIV):
" 'Mark . . . my own . . . dearest husband! who is to be true to
you, if I am not? You shall not turn from me. How can
anything like this make a difference between you and me?' "

When Lord Lufton arrives to save the Robarts's furniture, Mark sees selflessness displayed in his home once again, and is even more ashamed: " 'I have no one to blame but myself.' " Lady Lufton also forgives him—but not until after a final editorial comment: " 'Mr. Robarts's character as a clergyman should have kept him from such troubles, if no other feeling did so.' " Mark's troubles, of course, are largely the result of his having behaved during the last few months more like a politician than a clergyman. When he next meets Lady Lufton his embarrassment over past error does him credit, says Trollope: "no good man who has broken down in his goodness can carry the disgrace of his fall without some look of shame. When a man is able to do that, he ceases to be in any way good" [XLV]. Mark Robarts has not ceased to be good; on the contrary, he is just starting out at it.

Mark's final lash comes from the *Jupiter*, which reports publicly that his "piety and conduct are sadly wanting"; and Trollope comments at the end of the novel once again to the effect that Nemesis never fails to give wickedness its comeuppance: "In this instance the wicked man had been our unfortunate friend Mark Robarts; wicked in that he had wittingly touched pitch, gone to Gatherum Castle, ridden fast mares across the country . . . and fallen very imprudently among the [moneylenders] . . ." [XLVII]. Of the faults which a man commits he must bear the punishment, even when the faults result from bad judgment and selfishness rather than genuine malignancy. Mark Robarts's punishment is the ordeal of his education in values, an ordeal during which time he compromises his principles, alienates his friends, estranges his wife, and suffers great mental anxiety. But, Trollope suggests, he is ultimately a better man for his ordeal for he learns of the vanity of ambition, the destructiveness of egoism, and the advantages of the satisfaction one may feel in being with those with whom he belongs. *Framley Parsonage,* of course, is about other things as well, but it is principally about these things.

Some twenty years later, in *The Duke's Children* (1880), Trollope's favorite character, the Duke of Omnium (nephew of the man who is Duke of Omnium in *Framley Parsonage*), says to his eldest son: " 'A man can never be happy unless his first objects are outside himself. Personal self-indulgence begets a sense of meanness which sticks to a man even when he has got beyond all hope of rescue' " [XXVI]. Mark Roberts's "rescue" consists precisely in this realization that self-indulgence breeds evil and that it is in our feelings for others that salvation lies.

CHARLES DICKENS (1812-1870)
National Portrait Gallery, London

Chapter Three

Dickens

In Dickens's novels, egoism usually takes the form of arrogance—an indifference to the feelings of others or to the ways in which one's own existence may affect them. Sometimes this indifference is a function of self-conceit and sometimes it is the result of a basic lack either of respect for or interest in other people. In Dickens's novels, as in those we have previously examined, characters who have the capacity for self-redemption within them undergo an ordeal of suffering as a prerequisite to the discovery of self and the world which climaxes the movement toward moral vision. It is all, once again, an education in values that the more complex Dickensian protagonists receive.

In some of Dickens's early novels this kind of psychological development is simply not there. The following discussion focuses on three of Dickens's novels in which the psychic evolution of the protagonist is more patently at the center of things.

I

Dombey and Son (1846-48), Dickens's first novel of genuine psychological complexity—in which a character's mind *is* at the center of things—is the story of a man whose existence is so bound up in his own notions and self-importance that he is unable, throughout most of his life, to comprehend and acknowledge the feelings of the other inhabitants of his world. Mr. Dombey's egoism is the egoism of personal arrogance, an arrogance at times so solipsistic as to cut him off completely from those people whose existences—because he is the head of a family, the head of a business, and an influential member of society—are to some extent dependent upon his. His ordeal of bitter loneliness finally ends when he is able to acknowledge his own humanity—when, that is, he realizes that, like everyone else, he needs the love and companionship of other people. Throughout much of his life, however, his inability or un-willingness to be interested, to care, in short to *feel,* reinforces the arrogance of a proud nature, and he resists the en-croachments of a world in which he has no interests beyond purely material and social ones.

Mr. Dombey, however, does have one passionate in-terest when we first encounter him, and that interest is in hav-ing a son who will carry on the business of his shipping house. A potential son is the only thing that interests him, however—and this despite the fact that *Dombey and Son* is primarily about Dombey and daughter. Its title expresses the particular solipsistic obsession of Mr. Dombey's arrogance. For daughters have no importance or value in Mr. Dombey's world; his major interest is in Dombey and Son, for whose future a son is always necessary.

Dombey and Son opens with an account of Dombey's feelings on the occasion of the birth of Son. The capital letter, in the text of the novel and thus here, is no accident; it emphasizes the fact that Dombey is primarily interested in his son not as a son *per se* or as a little human being dependent upon himself, but rather as Son, as the potential other half of his business. The capital letter is used in the novel's first sentence, and appears mockingly through the early pages.

As little Paul comes into the world his mother is in the process of leaving it, but Mr. Dombey, "stern and pom-pous," is too bound up in grand notions of the future of his house to know or care. As his wife lies dying, Mr. Dombey sits next to her thinking about Dombey and Son.

> Those three words conveyed the one idea of Mr. Dombey's life. The earth was made for Dombey and Son to trade in, and the sun and moon were made to give them light. Rivers and seas were formed to float their ships; rainbows gave them promise of fair weather; winds blew for or against their enterprises; stars and planets circled in their orbits to preserve inviolate a system of which they were the centre. Common ab-

breviations took new meanings in his eyes, and had sole reference to them: A.D. had no concern with Anno Domini, but stood for Anno Dombei—and Son. (1)

Mr. Dombey's world revolves around himself and his business. There is no question of his being part of something else—all things are in him. Feelings are unimportant: "Dombey and Son had often dealt in hides, but never in hearts." Florence, his six-year-old daughter, is to him merely a "base coin that couldn't be invested." For Florence, crouching by her mother's deathbed, her father is a metaphorical abstraction, a "stiff white cravat," a "pair of creaking boots and a very loud ticking watch." He has never demonstrated to her in any way a modicum of humanity, and this lack of humanity is underscored throughout the novel by a series of metaphors of which this is the first—metaphors which reduce Mr. Dombey emotionally to the status of an inanimate object. His daughter, thinks Mr. Dombey as his son is getting born, may be "all very well, but this is another matter. This young gentleman has to accomplish a destiny." And thus begins Dombey's attempt to shape son into Son, an undertaking which inevitably is to be frustrated.

The first chapter ends with the death of Mrs. Dombey, for which Mr. Dombey is as "sorry" as he would be to lose something "from among his plate and furniture, and other household possessions." For all his wife's death means to Mr. Dombey is that "the life and progress on which he built such hopes should be endangered in the outset" by the need of a nurse. One is immediately found, and Mr. Dombey, turning around in his easy chair "as one piece, and not as a man with limbs and joints," tells her that when she is no longer needed " 'the child will cease to remember you; and you will cease . . . to remember the child.' " Such a statement betrays both Mr. Dombey's jealousy of others' relationships with his son and his total inability to consider emotional needs or personal relationships in the arena of the world's commerce. He is even capable of thinking that the nurse, Mrs. Toodle, might possibly exchange her own infant for little Paul as a kind of commercial speculation.

Mr. Dombey locks himself in his room for some time to brood over these things. He does not think of comforting his daughter, who is of course heartbroken over her mother's death. He sees Florence so infrequently, observes Susan Nipper, the girl's maid, that he would not know who she was if he met her on the street. Why does he so neglect her now? Because Mr. Dombey, in the silence of his room, sees over and over again the last sad embrace between his wife and his daughter, "which was at once a revelation and a reproach to him . . . He could not forget that he had had no part in it." His pride and perhaps his guilt turn his indifference towards Florence into "uneasiness of an extraordinary kind." She seems to him to have "an innate knowledge" of the ways of sympathy, tenderness, feeling—and this scares him because it is a knowledge he himself is without. She makes him ill at ease, for she combines the uselessness of her femininity with the unfathomable secret of the gift of love; and so she "troubles his peace" in a vague way. He is "afraid that he might come to hate her." He seems to be incapable of acting as a father to her; he is merely her landlord. Her tentative efforts toward comforting him and being comforted by him in return are met with coldness. He is afraid, perhaps, of revealing to her the shallowness of his emotions, especially his indifference to his wife's death. And so he puts her away from him. He cannot respond to tenderness, for he has none himself and does not know what it is; he only responds to those who, "understanding their . . . own position . . . showed a fitting reverence for his . . . and bowed low before him."

Like Sir Austin Feverel in Meredith's *The Ordeal of Richard Feverel,* written a dozen years after *Dombey and Son*, Mr. Dombey wants to be all in all to his son. Like Sir Austin, he attempts to keep all influences but his own away from his son, and like him he is jealous of any "rival or partner in the boy's respect and deference." He wishes to be his son's God, to possess him completely. He cannot sympathize with or tolerate any other kind of relationship, for he has never encountered any himself: "In all his life, he had never made a friend. His cold and distant nature had neither sought

one, nor found one" [5]. In his resolves on the matter of little
Paul's upbringing, he is, says Dickens, "frozen. . .into one
unyielding block." During the description of Paul's
christening party the same sort of imagery is repeated, with
Mr. Dombey's hard, cold stiffness represented as "blighting"
and "freezing" everything around him, Mr. Dombey himself
behaving as if his closest relationship is to the fire irons in his
drawing room. His demeanor depresses the whole party: "He
might have been hung up for sale at a Russian fair as a
specimen of a frozen gentleman." If he feels happy at his son's
christening he is afraid to show it perhaps out of fear that if he
unbends the company will see the true poverty of his other
emotions and feelings. When, shortly after the christening,
Mrs. Toodle is discharged for going to visit her own son and
Florence weeps at her departure, it is "a dagger in the haughty
father's heart, an arrow in his brain" to see her cling to flesh
and blood not her own "and he sitting by," but still he does
nothing to let Florence know that he recognizes her existence.
Again, she makes him uneasy. He fancies that she is somehow
disloyal.

As Paul grows up, Mr. Dombey's primary feeling is that
of impatience—"Impatience for the time to come, when his
visions of their united consequence and grandeur would be
triumphantly realized." He behaves to his son not as a father
but rather as a senior partner—the Dombey of Dombey and
Son. While he apparently does love little Paul in a thoroughly
selfish way, he regards him primarily "as a part of his own
greatness, or (which is the same), of the greatness of Dombey
and Son." The climactic moment of these early pages of the
novel comes in that famous scene in which Paul asks his
father what money is, and what it can do. Mr. Dombey
answers: " 'Money, Paul, can do anything.' " And he tells his
son that "money caused us to be honoured, feared, respected,
courted, and admired, and made us powerful and glorious in
the eyes of all men," and that "it could, very often, even keep
off death, for a long time together" [3]. Little Paul wonders,
" 'Why didn't money save me my mama?' " There is, of
course, no answer to this; and thus ends the first stage of

Paul's growth and education in the house of his father.

Paul's health is delicate, and he is taken to live at Brighton with a Mrs. Pipchin. At the age of six Paul is sent to school, that of the nearby Dr. Blimber. In justifying to Mrs. Pipchin Paul's removal to the school, Mr. Dombey says: " 'There is nothing of change or doubt in the course before my son. His way in life was clear and prepared, and marked out before he existed.' " Like Sir Austin Feverel, Mr. Dombey is unwilling or incapable of taking into account the unpredictableness of nature, both physical and human, and he takes it upon himself to reign over his son's universe. Dr. Blimber's establishment is to Mr. Dombey's liking because it is situated, emotionally speaking, in "the frostiest circumstances. Nature was of no consequence at all." For an unnatural man this is ideal, and so Mr. Dombey takes his son there, telling Paul "exultantly" that " 'This is the way indeed to be Dombey and Son, and have money. You are almost a man already.' " For Mr. Dombey, childhood is merely the necessary prelude to the burdens of manhood—there is no room in it for undirected fun of any sort. And under this regimen little Paul grows old very quickly, becoming more sickly and precociously cynical. Mr. Dombey comes to visit him from time to time, but Paul obviously prefers the company of Florence, who is left near him at Brighton. His son's preference, which is nothing more or less than a natural response to unhidden affection, makes Mr. Dombey dislike his daughter even more.

And now for some pages the novel turns to a consideration of the house of Dombey and Son itself, and the reader is introduced to a number of persons in Mr. Dombey's employ. Chief among them is James Carker, who has gained his preeminence by combining shrewdness with artful and continuous flattery of Mr. Dombey. Any man more sensitive than Mr. Dombey would have seen through Carker long ago, but Mr. Dombey's ego demands constant obsequiousness, and so Carker, whom we see at once to be a dangerous man, supplies it constantly. There are others in his employ whom Mr. Dombey "freezes" as readily at the office as he freezes everyone at home. Among them is Walter Gay, a friend of Florence's, whose "elasticity" and "hopefulness to please" Mr. Dombey takes as "defiance"—and so he sends the young man off to his West Indies office.

Meanwhile Paul, who has been growing more and more "old-fashioned," finally dies in the arms of Florence of some vague disease that could well be, figuratively speaking, old age, a kind of metaphor for the fact that Mr. Dombey has never regarded him as a child at all but rather, as we have seen, as a junior partner. There is no room for boyhood under these circumstances, and so Paul dies young. Once again Florence has committed the unforgiveable sin of being, because of her tenderness and compassion, preferred to her father by the invalid. Mr. Dombey locks himself up in his room for the purpose of self-commiseration, never considering, as before, that he has a daughter who may need consolation too. He "did not even know that she was in the house." He unthinkingly directs the stonemason to carve " 'beloved and only child' " on Paul's tombstone, and has to be reminded that he has another child. When Florence, lonely and heartbroken, comes down to her father's room with the intention of trying to comfort him, his coldness freezes her "into stone," and she is amazed at his expression:

> There was not one touch of tenderness or pity in it. There was not one gleam of interest, parental recognition, or relenting in it. There was a change in it, but not of that kind. The old indifference and cold restraint had given place to something; what, she never thought and did not dare to think, and yet she felt it in its force, and knew it well without a name. . . . Did he see before him the successful rival of his son, in health and life? Did he look upon his own successful rival in that son's affection? Did a mad jealousy and withered pride poison sweet remembrances that should have endeared and made her precious to him? Could it be possible that it was gall to him to look upon her in her beauty and her promise, thinking of his infant boy! (18)

Florence is at this time about thirteen years old.

In his self-imposed solitude, Mr. Dombey broods over many things, not the least of which is little Paul's old question about money and what it could do—"what *could* it do indeed; what had it done?" But "pride easily found its reassurance," and the lapse from certainty is only momentary. For Mr. Dombey the loss of his son is not so much familial as it is material; Paul is the "lost child, who was to have divided with him his riches, and his projects, and his power and allied with whom he was to have shut out all the world as with a double door of gold . . ." [20]. Mr. Dombey resents all of those who took an interest in his son; they are to him would-be thieves who would have liked to creep "into the place wherein he would have lorded it, alone!" Things, including people, take the relation for Mr. Dombey of being owned either by himself or by somebody else. Mr. Dombey, however, has for just an instant doubted the efficacy of money, which is equivalent in him to self-doubt. Yet the failure of sensibility is unmoderated, and once again it is expressed in blind resentment of Florence's existence:

> One child was gone, and one child left. Why was the object of his hope removed instead of her?
> [Her] presence . . . moved him to no reflection but that. She had been unwelcome to him from the first; she was an aggravation of his bitterness now. If his son had been his only child, and the same blow had fallen on him, it would have been heavy to bear, but infinitely lighter than now, when it might have fallen on her (whom he could name lost, or he believed it, without a pang), and had not. (20)

Such an incredible sentiment on the part of a father is largely the result in Mr. Dombey of an emotional void, which is in turn at least partly due to the fact that he has been "so long shut up with himself" and has rarely "overstepped the enchanted circle within which the operations of Dombey and Son were conducted." It is precisely this failure to relate to others, to get away from self, that constitutes Mr. Dombey's egoism. In his monomaniacal materialism he is virtually incapable of sympathetic identification with anyone or anything beyond his own interests. And so he goes off with Major Bagstock on a sort of vacation, the result of which is his acquaintance with Edith Granger, whose own cold pride affects him much more substantially than Florence's tenderness has affected him—for it is arrogance itself, not its possible grounds, that he most admires. He sees Edith as the potential source of another partnership, and perhaps he also sees her as a possible vehicle for the begetting of another Son.

Florence, meanwhile, has characteristically been left alone with the servants to shift for herself as best she can. Wanting to be loved by her father and feeling that she is not, she excuses him to herself on the grounds that he does not know "how much she loved him." Like Catherine Sloper in James's *Washington Square* (1881), Florence concludes that she must in some way be at fault and racks her brain to find a way to please her father—"Strange study for a child, to learn the road to a hard parent's heart!" During a visit to Sir Barnet Skettles and his family she pathetically studies the other children in the house, trying to learn the secret of how to be loved by one's parents.

Mr. Dombey is now pursuing Edith Granger, a proud woman under the thumb of an avaricious mother determined to sell her beautiful daughter to the highest bidder. Mr. Dombey is sufficiently high. Major Bagstock admiringly tells the mother, Mrs. Skewton, that Mr. Dombey " 'is as proud . . . as Lucifer,' " and Mrs. Skewton responds that it is " 'a charming quality,' " reminding her " 'of dearest Edith.' " The impending alliance of these two titanic egos bodes no good for anybody; but Mr. Dombey, "laying himself on a sofa like a man of wood without a hinge or a joint in him," thinks that Edith's arrogance would do justice to his house and determines to marry her. He is not aware that her haughtiness is primarily the defense-mechanism of a sensitive nature horrified at being sold in the marriage market but apparently unable, because of Mrs. Skewton's impecuniousness, to avoid such a consummation. Thus Edith, who is basically a good person, is always at war with herself, determined in her pride never to show by the slightest sign that she is either aware of or pleased by Mr. Dombey's wealth—for this would be an open admission of her having been sold, which she feels, for her mother's sake as well as her own, she cannot acknowledge. Thus she is "frigid and restrained" in Mr. Dombey's company, but, at least for the moment, yielding to him. "Mr. Dombey was . . . proud of his power [over her], and liked to show it"—an ill omen for their married life, indeed. When he finally proposes to her and she accepts, Edith considers it a "purchase" and swears to her mother that she will consent to be "exhibited" by Mr. Dombey but that she will consent to nothing else. And in this way Mr. Dombey prepares to enter into matrimonial bliss once again.

During this time Florence has been waiting for her father to return, turning over in her mind various schemes to win his love. She decides that one way is to observe and emulate those few who are in her father's confidence—one of whom, ironically enough, is the insidious Carker. When Mr. Dombey finally returns with his fiancée to his house and his daughter, Florence takes his hand and puts it to her lips. He withdraws it immediately: "It touched the door in shutting it, with quite as much endearment as it had touched her." Florence is then introduced to the woman who is going to be her new "mama," and weepingly embraces her. It is clear that there is an instant sympathy between Florence and Edith, both of whom are suffering under Mr. Dombey's yoke. Such a mutual attachment, of course, bodes no good for either in the house of a jealous and possessive man.

The marriage-day comes closer, and Mr. Dombey remains secure in his decision to marry Edith Granger: "He had that good reason for sympathy with haughtiness and coldness. . . . It flattered him to picture to himself this proud and stately woman doing the honours of his house, and chilling his guests after his own manner. The dignity of Dombey and Son would be heightened and maintained . . ." [30]. Mr. Dombey, one strongly suspects, secretly nurses the hope of having another son, though he is now in his mid-fifties and planning to marry a woman who secretly dislikes him. Whatever the case, he is still pursued during many moments by the vision of his neglected daughter—sometimes guiltily, more often resentfully. He still considers her a "difficulty," a "disappointment," a "rival": "Florence—always Florence

— turned up so fast, and so confusedly," that he frequently finds it imperative to "escape" from her presence. Florence and Edith, however, who are bound to one another immediately through sympathetic identification, become closer every day.

The wedding-day arrives. Mr. Dombey's primary feeling upon the occasion is that "he is going to confer a great distinction on a lady"; Edith, on the other hand, unwilling to acknowledge that the honor is entirely hers, stands at the altar "disdainful and defiant . . . composed, erect, inscrutable of will, resplendent and majestic . . . yet beating down, and treading on [all] admiration." And so they are married. Mr. Dombey, predictably, is totally unaware of the resentment that his proprietary behavior toward his new wife has excited in her.

When they return from their honeymoon, Florence observes in her father more of an interest in her. Perhaps he has been softened by Edith. Mr. Dombey, however, is more absorbed by the extensive alterations in his house than by those in his daughter, and comments once again to the effect that money can do anything. Edith, of course, always becomes even more haughty and scornful when the subject of money is broached, and Mr. Dombey, though disappointed that she is unwilling to acknowledge the power of his money, nevertheless feels that she is behaving in the main properly: "Mr. Dombey, being a good deal in the statue way himself, was well enough pleased to see his handsome wife immovable and proud and cold." He can respond to and appreciate only the most restrained and decorous behavior.

In Chapter 35 occurs a famous scene which proves to be the undoing of them all. Florence is alone with her father in a room "for the first time within her memory," and Mr. Dombey, who is pretending to doze, is secretly observing her with some interest and even a trace of self-reproach and a mild sense of his own "cruel injustice." He has the passing thought that he had always had "a happy home within his reach" and "had overlooked it in his stiff-necked sullen arrogance. . . . As he looked, she became blended with the child he had loved, and he could hardly separate the two." Perhaps it is his marriage that has softened him; or perhaps, conversely, it is his disappointment in Edith's lack of tenderness; perhaps it is genuine contrition. Whatever the explanation, his new perspective upon his daughter is shortlived. For into the room comes Edith, who, thinking her husband asleep, sits down next to Florence and kisses her tenderly. "He hardly knew his wife. She was so changed. It was not merely that her smile was new to him—though that he had never seen—but her manner, the tone of her voice, the light of her eyes, the interest, the confidence, and winning wish to please, expressed in all—this was not Edith." The old jealousies and resentments now reassert themselves doubly, and Florence is perhaps less loved by her father at this moment than at any other in her life. Florence's mother, her brother, and now her stepmother have all, apparently, preferred her to the head of Dombey and Son, who cannot in his pride bear to come second in anything. He still does not see that tender natures need love to grow on, not money.

The Dombeys now give a housewarming party to show off the new "frosted metal," "scenting flowers," and other paraphernalia of their altered establishment, a party notable for the ways in which the guests are once again "frozen" and generally made uncomfortable. Ice, we are told, is an "unnecessary article in Mr. Dombey's banquets." The guests consider themselves "neglected and aggrieved," and the servants outside compare the party "to a funeral out of mourning, with none of the company remembered in the will." This leads to the first serious argument between husband and wife—though the real cause of it, as we have seen, undoubtedly lies elsewhere. With Carker present, Mr. Dombey complains to his wife that she has behaved badly to their guests. When she asks that he not speak to her in front of his clerk, he warms to the subject, complaining, ironically, that she is too cold and distant with others. He is, of course, used to having his way in everything, and expects her immediate submission. Edith's response is a look of "intense, unutterable, withering scorn" and "ineffable disdain and

haughtiness"—it is a fitting response to his own attitude, and
for once Mr. Dombey feels uncomfortably out-Dombeyed.
He becomes even more resentful, however, as he continues to
see how tender his wife can be with Florence, and he resolves
to do something about it. He sends Carker—a humiliation in
itself, so she feels—to tell Edith that if she continues to make
her preference for Florence so marked the consequences will
be detrimental to both of them—there is even a hint that
Florence may be disinherited. " 'Dombey and Son,' " says
Carker to Edith, " 'know neither time, nor place, nor season,
but bear them all down' "; and he tells her, with only a shade
of irony, that if Mr. Dombey " 'has a fault, it is a lofty stub-
bornness, rooted in that noble pride and sense of power
which belong to him, and which we must all defer to, which is
not assailable like the obstinacy of other characters, and
which grows upon itself from day to day, and year to year' "
[37]. Edith treats him with disdain but is secretly horrified at
her husband's treatment of her and his threat against his
daughter, made primarily to humble his wife. Carker,
meanwhile, who understands Edith's nature fairly well, has
allowed himself to fall in love with her. And so things go until
we encounter a pivotal chapter entitled "Domestic
Relations" (40).

The chapter begins with a lengthy and detailed account
of Mr. Dombey's state of mind, of the balance of various psychological impulses which have accounted for his behavior in
the past and are determining it in the present. It is the sort of
passage which, in its depth of psychological analysis, one
would be unlikely to find, for the most part, in Dickens's
earlier novels. In it we are told that Edith's resistance to "the
imperious asperity of his temper" and "the cold hard armour
of pride in which he lived encased" has only made Mr.
Dombey more resolved to rule over her. While his nature is
such that "deference and concession swell its evil qualities,"
so too does defiance, which even further "enslaves the breast
in which [such a nature] has its throne," making such a man
"as hard a master as the Devil in dark fables." Egoism of Mr.
Dombey's kind, in other words, does not falter when it meets

resistance or scorn; it grows larger in its desire to dominate
the source of such resistance. In his "cold and lofty
arrogance," Mr. Dombey had borne himself like a "removed
Being" towards his first wife: "He had been 'Mr. Dombey'
with her when she first saw him, and he was 'Mr. Dombey'
when she died." He had continually "asserted his greatness"
to her and had "kept his distant seat on the top of his
throne. . . ." He had thought that Edith's pride, on the other
hand, "would have been added to his own—would have
merged into it, and exalted his greatness. He had pictured
himself haughtier than ever, with Edith's haughtiness
subservient to his." In the face of her unexpected defiance, his
pride, rather than withering, "put forth new shoots, became
more concentrated and intense, more gloomy, sullen, irksome,
and unyielding than it had ever been before." Mr. Dombey's
relationship with his wives has not been one of mutual regard
and trust, but rather assertions of superiority in order to
gratify that proud ego directing emotional responses. Such a
need, of course, "is proof against conciliation, love, and confidence! against all gentle sympathy without, all trust, all
tenderness, all soft emotion; but to deep stabs in the self-love,
it is as vulnerable as the bare breast to steel . . ." [40]. Mr.
Dombey lacks "sympathy" and "tenderness" precisely
because the motivating power of his existence is "self-love."
One cannot love one's self better than others and still sympathize with those others and see one's self objectively. And
so Mr. Dombey persists in his persecution of his daughter,
whose only significance for him is that she has made him
"humbled and powerless where he would be most strong."
He blames her for winning the hearts of his wives and his son
where he was unable to do so, and for thriving and growing
beautiful when those "aided by his . . . regard or notice . . .
died." He has dreaded all along that he might come to "hate
her in his heart" someday, and the dreaded moment has now
apparently arrived. Florence has somehow not been sufficiently dutiful or submissive; she and her father have always
been estranged; she has crossed him at every opportunity and
"was leagued against him now"; she softened those who were

hard to him, and "insulted him with an unnatural triumph." Deep down in him "there were mutterings of an awakened feeling in his breast" for her, but he smothers any natural regard for his child "with the rolling sea of pride" and, in an orgy of "self-inflicted torment," he finally decides that he must hate Florence. But the paramount task before him, Mr. Dombey feels, is to humble his wife: "His pride was set upon maintaining his magnificent supremacy, and forcing recognition of it from her. She would have been racked to death, and turned but her haughty glance of calm inflexible disdain upon him, to the last" [40]. But Mr. Dombey resolves "to show her that he was supreme. There must be no will but his." He is particularly infuriated that it is his own device that she has been using against him: "her cold supreme indifference—his own unquestioned attribute usurped—stung him more than any other kind of treatment could have done; and he determined to bend her to his magnificent and stately will." (In his attitude toward his wife, and in his ultimate choice of the dependency of his daughter as a weapon to use against her, Mr. Dombey is not unlike Gilbert Osmond of James's *Portrait*.)

This long series of related passages opening Chapter 40, from which I have quoted only a fraction, is perhaps the clearest statement of Dickens's major theme. The primary source of unhappiness in the world is man's inhumanity, manifested most particularly in the hard-heartedness and lovelessness with which he is capable of treating those most closely associated with him. Like James, Dickens sees fellow-feeling often absent where it is most needed: in familial relationships. For Dickens, man's most heinous crime is the substitution of self-love for love, pride for sympathy, self-indulgence for generosity. In the sin of egoism one can trace the most tragic errors man commits; Mr. Dombey's feeling that "there must be no will but his" is the central expression of his depersonalization, of the triumph of pure ego over *caritas*. It is lack of *feeling* that dehumanizes man, an idea Dickens expresses again and again in various ways throughout his novels. Like Trollope, he sees man's salvation in feeling for others.

Mr. Dombey, having made up his mind to humble his wife, tells her that she is merely one of his "dependents" and must bow to his will. In his "insolence of self-importance" he insists on deference and obedience "before the world," and threatens her with another visit from Carker should she fail to toe the line. As he is about to leave her in all the splendor of his "moral magnificence" Edith stops him, tells him they have both been at fault, and promises to mend her ways if he will do the same. He answers her by saying that he will not "temporize" with her, that she has received his "ultimatum," and that she had better pay attention to it. Edith, horrified and indignant, asks him to leave her room, and with him departs any final chance the doomed pair may have of reconciliation and happiness.

Edith, of course, refuses to change her ways, and so Mr. Dombey visits Carker for the purpose of entrusting him with a message for his wife—the deliverance of which, as Mr. Dombey well knows, will be a humiliation to Edith. He tells Carker: " 'my will is law, and . . . I cannot allow of one exception to the whole rule of my life . . . There is a principle of opposition in Mrs. Dombey that must be eradicated. . . .' " Mr. Dombey's final word to Carker is the most ominous: " 'You will please to tell [Mrs. Dombey] that her show of devotion for my daughter is disagreeable to me. It is likely to be noticed. It is likely to induce people to contrast Mrs. Dombey in her relation towards my daughter with Mrs. Dombey in her relation towards myself. You will have the goodness to let Mrs. Dombey know, plainly, that I object to it . . .' " [42]. His last words to Carker are: " 'What I say is final.' "

The interview between Carker and Edith is a memorable one, for not only does Carker deliver Mr. Dombey's messages, including a warning to Edith not to make any outward show of affection for Florence—he also reveals openly the depth of his hatred for his long-time employer in an attempt to ingratiate himself with Edith. Carker says in part:

'You did not know how exacting and how proud he is, or how he is . . . the slave of his own greatness, and goes yoked to his own triumphal car like a beast of burden, with no idea on earth but that it is behind him and is to be drawn on, over everything and through everything . . . Nobody else is to be considered when he is in question. We who are about him have . . . done our part . . . to confirm him in his way of thinking; but if we had not done so, others would—or they would not have been about him; and it has always been from the beginning the very staple of his life!' (45)

Edith listens and plans accordingly, and Carker returns to work at the shipping house, where he has systematically gotten the affairs of Dombey and Son into such an immense tangle that even Mr. Dombey himself, later on, is unable to fathom them. But his speech to Edith, despite his insidious nature, is a perspicacious distillation of Mr. Dombey's state of mind. Shakespearean in tenor, Carker's language defines eloquently the essential nature of a solipsist, a man who is indeed a "slave of his own greatness" and who is capable of considering no one else as he "goes yoked to his own triumphal car like a beast of burden."

Mr. Dombey, meanwhile, "in the monstrous delusion of his life," is unable to perceive the trouble on the horizon. It is a characteristic failing of the egoist that he is incapable of considering the future because he is so wrapped up in the present—that is, in himself. The feelings of others are foreign to him, and so of course he is unable to discern their thoughts. His life is indeed a delusion. Such an unnatural condition, as I have said, Dickens finds to be the central evil of humanity. In Chapter 47 he is even more explicit about it:

Was Mr. Dombey's master-vice, that ruled him so inexorably, an unnatural characteristic? It might be worthwhile . . . to inquire what Nature is, and how men work to change her, and whether, in the enforced distortion so produced, it is not natural to be unnatural. Coop any son or daughter of our mighty mother within narrow range, and bind the prisoner to one idea, and foster it by servile worship of it on the part of the few timid or designing people standing round, and what is nature to the willing captive who has never risen upon the wings of a free mind . . . to see her in her comprehensive truth! . . . When we shall gather grapes from thorns, and figs from thistles; when fields of grain shall spring up from the offal in the byways of our wicked cities, and roses bloom in the fat churchyards that they cherish—then we may look for natural humanity and find it growing from such seed.

The monomaniacal Mr. Dombey becomes, in a sense, Dickens's metaphor for the dehumanization of man in an increasingly industrial and money-conscious age, a theme reinforced in other sections of this gargantuan novel by passages depicting the new railroads as mechanical monsters of human design bearing down upon a helpless humanity. The relationship between the growth of capitalism and the decline of man is a theme explored often in Dickens's work—most notably, for example, in *Hard Times* (1854), *Little Dorrit* (1855-57), *Great Expectations* (1860-61), and *Our Mutual Friend* (1864-65). But here, a decade before the great dark novels of Dickens's later years began to appear, the novelist seems to anticipate the subsequent direction his imagination was to take with a portrait of a man emasculated by self-importance based entirely on wealth and social position. In this same chapter (47) Dickens defines even more explicitly the kind of nature he is condemning—that which is possessed by people "who never have looked out upon the world of human life around [them, and have no] knowledge of their own relation to it," those who are sufficiently insensitive to be unaware of the "perversion of nature in their own contracted sympathies and estimates. . . ." It is precisely this pattern of self-ignorance and "contracted sympathies" which we have encountered in the novels previously examined. Dickens, who is rarely considered a "psychological" novelist, is none the less interested here in that kind of personality which is unable to comprehend other personalities because of a shrivelling of the spirit into a purely private state of self-regard.

And so Mr. Dombey remains a "chilled spring" in his relations with his wife, while she turns the face of a "marble rock" toward him—and they both, for very different reasons, turn colder to Florence, who begins to think of relationships between parents and their offspring as of a "mere abstraction." The climax to the worsening relations between Mr. Dombey and his wife comes one evening at dinner, with Florence and Carker present throughout much of the scene. Mr. Dombey takes Edith to task for her " 'stubborn disposition' " and the " 'rebellious principle' " within her. Edith retorts that he has made her " 'sacrifice . . . the only gentle feeling and interest' " of her life, which of course is a reference to Florence. Florence again! Mr. Dombey is infuriated, but Edith goes on, telling him that henceforth she " 'will be exhibited to no one as the refractory slave' " he has purchased, and asking him for a separation. Mr. Dombey is astounded (47): " 'Do you know who I am, madam? Do you know what I represent? Did you ever hear of Dombey and Son? People to say that Mr. Dombey—Mr. Dombey!—was separated from his wife? Common people to talk of Mr. Dombey and his domestic affairs!' " Mr. Dombey then turns to Carker and asks him to inform Mrs. Dombey, who it sitting at the same table, that " 'it is not the rule of my life to allow myself to be thwarted by anybody,' " and that " 'if she continues to make this house the scene of contention it has become, I shall consider my daughter responsible in some degree . . . and shall visit her with my severe displeasure' " [47]. Carker, however, now sides with Edith, with whom he hopes to become allied, and asks Mr. Dombey if he is not " 'sacrificing Mrs. Dombey to the preservation' " of his " 'pre-eminent and unassailable position. . . .' " He finally expresses to Mr. Dombey his resentment at being considered " 'an inferior person' " and thus an appropriate agent " 'for the humiliation of Mrs. Dombey.' "

Edith, in her wild desire to hurt and humiliate her husband as fully as possible, agrees to decamp with Carker, whom she also detests. Florence attempts to comfort her father when the news of their escape is known; he responds by striking her: "as he dealt the blow, he told her what Edith was, and bade her follow her, since they had always been in

league." This act, for Florence, finally murders once and for
all "that fond idea to which she had held in spite of him. She
saw his cruelty, neglect, and hatred. . . . She had no father
upon earth, and ran out, orphaned, from his house" [47]. We
see less of Florence after this, for the novel's final emphasis
falls on Mr. Dombey in his new loneliness. But we do know
that Walter Gay has returned from his shipwreck and the
West Indies and that Florence, by now a young lady of seven-
teen, ultimately accepts his proposal of marriage.

Chapter 51 is entitled "Mr. Dombey and the World"
and focuses on that gentleman and the thing that has been,
with so much regard and so little understanding, one of his
major concerns—the "world," the world of finance and
society which has been his milieu. It is this "world" which has
so interested Mr. Dombey throughout his altercations with
Edith, and he is now, ironically enough, left entirely alone
with it. It turns out to be an inadequate companion. Mr.
Dombey is discovering, albeit slowly, that this "world" of his
is an abstraction, that it consists mainly not of people, individuals, but of a state of mind, a way of thinking of things.
He feels lonely, but he does not understand as yet how lonely
he really is. He has no idea where Florence is, but he does not
think that she has left him for good—he has been "too long
shut up in his towering supremacy" for that to occur to him.
He is somewhat humbled but still thinks of himself as the
main attraction of his universe: "the world . . . he believes
has but one purpose for the time, and that, to watch him
eagerly wherever he goes. . . . What the world thinks of him,
how it looks at him, what it sees in him, and what it
says—this is the haunting demon of his mind" [51]. Mr.
Dombey, like Gilbert Osmond in James' *Portrait,* fits exactly
Mary Bennet's definition of vanity—a strain of egoism in
which the world exists only as one's personal audience. Mr.
Dombey remains for a time more worried about the "world"
than his daughter, but nevertheless eventually and slowly "he
is humbled." Lonely and neglected for the first time in his
life, he begins to become "an altered man." He finds that being alone with the "world" is not enough for him—he is miss-

ing something. And so he rouses himself to action, planning as a first step to find his wife and Carker. Still confident in the power of money, he uses it to buy information about the pair—he is almost "a madman in his wounded pride." His most sensitive organ has been touched.

What follows is largely melodrama. Mr. Dombey finds Edith and Carker in Dijon. She escapes, but Carker, in the course of his escape from Mr. Dombey, is killed by a train, the novel's ubiquitous symbol of the dehumanizing power of capitalism. Mr. Dombey returns to his house and to financial ruin, for without Carker's expertise at hand he can now make nothing of the affairs of Dombey and Son. Nor does he now care, apparently, and Dombey and Son fails. Mr. Dombey locks himself in his room at the old mansion, which he is about to lose along with everything else. No one sees him, but the remaining servants say he is melancholy.

In Chapter 59, entitled "Retribution," the auctioneer's men dismantle all the symbols of vanity and pride, and Mr. Dombey's possessions are carted out into the street like so much refuse. And yet Mr. Dombey seems unmoved by any of this. The only question he asks is—finally—where is Florence? He is lonely now: he misses not the "world" but his daughter, and it occurs to him that perhaps his misery is a fitting punishment for his past treatment of her. His moment of self-discovery, of tragic knowledge, is finally at hand:

> that which was his own work, that which he could so easily have wrought into a blessing, and had set himself so steadily for years to form into a curse, that was the sharp grief of his soul . . . He knew, now, what he had done. He knew, now, that he had called down that upon his head which bowed it lower than the heaviest stroke of fortune. He knew, now, what it was to be rejected and deserted—now, when every loving blossom he had withered in his innocent daughter's heart was snowing down in ashes on him . . . He thought, now, that of all around him, she alone had never changed . . . As, one by one, they fell away before his mind—his baby-hope, his wife, his friend, his fortune—Oh how the mist, through which he had seen her, cleared, and showed him her true self! (59)

To know is to see, and Mr. Dombey's ordeal of an education in values has reached its dénouement at last. His final understanding and appreciation of his daughter enables him to see his own conduct clearly for the first time, and in doing so he understands what kind of man he has been. In discovering his daughter he has also discovered himself. His new vision enables him to see how vain his life has been. And so "he let the world go from him freely. As it fell away, he shook it off. . . He had no idea of any one companion in his misery, but the one he had driven away. . . . [H]e always knew she would have been true to him, if he had suffered her . . . He always knew she would have loved him better now than at any other time. . . . He chiefly thought of what might have been and what was not" [59]. He wanders through the empty house, still too proud to ask anyone for help but also too certain that his punishment is just. He weeps when he thinks of the two children he has lost, and even contemplates suicide. It is at this juncture that Florence, having heard of his misfortune, returns to the house of misery to comfort him—and he feels once again, and even more deeply, "all that he had done." Mr. Dombey's final utterance in this climactic chapter demonstrates the ultimate depth and urgency of his contrition: " 'Oh my God, forgive me, for I need it very much!' " And so the junior partner of Dombey and Son turns out to be a daughter after all.

In Chapter 61, "Relenting," we see Mr. Dombey in his final state of grace and enlightenment. He is first plunged into deep remorse, and in fact almost dies of it. Like Pip's in *Great Expectations*, Mr. Dombey's physical illness at the end of the novel is a moral correlative and result of a purging from his system of the last germs of a spiritual infection. After his complete physical and moral recovery, Mr. Dombey is at last fully capable of considering the feelings of others. He now worries constantly about the health of Florence and her family. We see him at the end, "a white-haired gentleman, whose face bears heavy marks of care and suffering; but they are traces of a storm that has passed on forever, and left a clear evening in its track. Ambitious projects trouble him no more.

His only pride is in his daughter and her husband" [62]. He becomes, significantly enough, tremendously fond of his little granddaughter, also named Florence: "He hoards her in his heart. He cannot bear to see a cloud upon her face. He cannot bear to see her sit apart. He fancies that she feels a slight when there is none. He steals away to look at her in her sleep" [62]. And thus the novel ends.

Mr. Dombey's conversion has been sudden but not totally unexpected or unprepared for. As Dickens says of Mr. Dombey in his preface to the novel, "an obstinate nature exists in a perpetual struggle with itself . . . A sense of his injustice is within him all along. The more he represses it, the more unjust he necessarily is. Internal shame and external circumstances" work his conversion, and we are ready for it when it comes. And so Mr. Dombey too moves from egoism to empathy, from blindness to moral vision. There are, of course, a number of other stories in this long and complex novel, but this moral pattern is clearly the novelist's central concern. For in the fable of Dombey and Son, in the story of the rich and proud man humbled into feeling for others through the ordeal of an education in values, Dickens charts the only road to salvation available to an increasingly selfish and materialistic society.

II

The anti-hero who becomes the hero of *A Tale of Two Cities* (1859) also begins in arrogance and indifference. We first meet Sydney Carton at the treason trial of Charles Darnay at the Old Bailey, where he is assisting in the defense. The first few references to him in the text do not mention him by name. He is merely a "wigged gentleman who looked at the ceiling" of the courtroom in sheer boredom. His appearance is "careless and slovenly if not debauched"; we are told that he is a "reckless" version of the more conventional Darnay, whom he resembles. Throughout the trial Carton changes "neither his place nor his attitude," leaning back in his chair "with his gown torn half off him, his untidy wig put on just as it happened to light on his head after its removal, his hands in his pockets, and his eyes on the ceiling . . ." [II,3]. His lounging manner is "so careless as to be almost insolent." He only exerts himself enough to tell Darnay to expect the worst: " 'It's the wisest thing to expect, and the likeliest.' " After helping to get Darnay off, Carton then withdraws back into his studied indifference. After the trial he informs Mr. Lorry, Darnay's banker friend, that he has no real business and should not attend to it if he had any. He smells of port wine, does not appear to be entirely sober, and tells Darnay over dinner that his only desire in life " 'is to forget that I belong to [the world]. It has no good in it for me—except wine like this—nor I for it.' " His one moment of earnestness comes when he asks Darnay whether or not it is " 'worth being tried for one's life, to be the object of . . . sympathy and compassion' " (on the part of Darnay's fiancée, Lucie Manette). Darnay takes this as a reminder that Carton has helped save his life, and thanks him for it. " 'I neither want any thanks, nor merit any,' " is the careless rejoinder. Carton had apparently been alluding to his self-enforced loneliness, and in fact this is more patently clear when he says, a few moments later: " 'I am a disappointed drudge, sir. I care for no man on earth, and no man on earth cares for me' " [II,4]. Like Mr. Dombey, Carton is without a single friend.

In Sydney Carton we find an egoism of a somewhat different strain, an egoism of more careless self-indulgence. Carton is neither ambitious nor avaricious. His tendency to strike poses and attitudes, to regard himself romantically as a lonely and useless outcast, to obfuscate his real desires and interests with a mask of careless indifference—these are the trappings of his self-indulgence. He is constantly conjuring up visions of himself to himself; he spends a good deal of time in front of the mirror. One of the novel's major themes is that of Carton's movement away from self-indulgent arrogance, a movement inspired primarily by the growth of feeling for another human being. For the story of Sydney Carton is essentially the story of a man on whom love and concern for another person have a transforming, even a transfiguring, effect. His self-discovery is a discovery of other people and their importance to him. Again it is feeling for others, beyond one's own narrow concerns, that must be cultivated before the protagonist can escape from his self-constructed shell of subjectivity and its concomitantly blurred moral vision. Self becomes in this novel, both figuratively and literally, sacrificed in the interest of others, but in that way self also becomes both purged of self-regard and immortally ennobled. This is the course mapped out by Dickens for Sydney Carton.

It is some time before he begins on this course, however. We see him as Mr. Stryver's "jackal," as the lawyer who helps another prepare cases but finds the credit for winning them beneath his notice. He is the "idlest and most unpromising of men," a man who drinks too much, considers himself unlucky, and seems not to care how others think of him. He assumes he has fallen quite naturally into his proper "rank" and views with ready indifference Stryver's contention that he has always been "nowhere" and is likely to remain there. Honor, self-denial, ambition, and perseverance are all a "mirage" to him; his usual practice is to drink himself into near oblivion every night and then cry himself to sleep. And such is our introduction to this "man of good abilities and good emotions, incapable of their directed exercise, incapable of his own help and his own happiness, sensible of the blight upon him, and resigning to let it eat him away" [II,5]. Such self-indulgence, whether injurious only to one's self or to others as well, Dickens roundly condemns: for life, he implies, is meaningless unless people can learn to interest themselves in and care for one another. This was a central lesson of *Dombey and Son,* and it is a central one of *A Tale of Two Cities* as well. Humanity will not be safe from itself as long as indulgence of self is put before feeling for others.

Carton's moral conversion is gradual, and it begins with his attendance, sporadic but steady, upon the household of Dr. Manette and his daughter, whom he had met at Darnay's trial. He still lounges and leans, but it is plain that Lucie Manette both interests and moves him—even though he knows that she and Darnay are practically engaged. It is, perhaps, Stryver's behavior that causes Carton's feeling for Lucie to crystallize. Stryver calls him " 'an insensible dog . . . morose . . . silent and sullen and hangdog . . . [without] sensitiveness or delicacy of feeling . . . [or] sense.' " Carton replies that he is simply "incorrigible" and will never change. But when Stryver tells Carton that he intends to ask Miss Manette to marry him, Sydney examines his feelings and discovers that he is not so insensible after all. (As in *Emma*, it is a case of mediated desire.) What he really discovers is that he is in love with Lucie; and although he knows that neither he himself nor Stryver has any chance with her against Darnay, he has now at least some slender reason for living—that is, to help and protect the woman he loves. Stryver's suit, advanced with great self-assurance, of course fails.

When we next encounter Sydney Carton it is in an attitude surprisingly new to himself. Carton requests and is granted a private interview with Lucie, and what follows is central to our understanding and appreciation of his moral development—one of the novel's most important themes. In the past, Carton's frequent visits to Dr. Manette's house had merely impressed the inhabitants thereof with his moodiness and moroseness; "the cloud of caring for nothing which overshadowed him . . . was very rarely pierced by the light within him." Now he begins by telling Lucy, who fears he is not well and begs him to change his way of life, that he can never change: " 'I shall never be better than I am. I shall sink lower and be worse . . . I am like one who died young. All my life might have been' " [II,13]. She replies that the best part of his life is surely still to come and that he could be much worthier of himself. Carton, with "a fixed despair of himself," replies as follows:

> 'Since I knew you, I have been troubled by a remorse
> that I thought would never reproach me again, and have
> heard whispers from old voices impelling me upward,
> that I thought were silent forever. I have had unformed
> ideas of striving afresh, beginning anew, shaking off

sloth and sensuality, and fighting out the abandoned fight. A dream, all a dream, that ends in nothing, and leaves the sleeper where he lay down, but I wish you to know that you inspired it . . . It is useless to say it, I know, but it rises out of my soul. For you, and for any dear to you, I would do anything. If my career were of that better kind that there was any opportunity or capacity of sacrifice in it, I would embrace any sacrifice for you and for those dear to you. Try to hold me in your mind . . . as ardent and sincere in this one thing . . .[T]hink now and then that there is a man who would give his life, to keep a life you love beside you!' (11,13)

For the first time in his life Carton cares for another human being, an extension of moral sensibility that also extends his capacity for doing good. It is his escape from total self-absorption, from a constantly sentimental view of himself, that enables him to achieve sympathy for and interest in another person. The key word in Carton's speech is "sacrifice"; his willingness to sacrifice his own interests, even his life, in behalf of someone else is our clue to his change of heart and mind. It is now, with him, "others before myself" instead of "myself before others." Of course Carton continues to wear the same mask; he tells Darnay, for example, that he is " 'incapable of all the higher and better flights of men . . . a dissolute dog, who has never done any good and never will.' " But Lucie, who does marry Darnay, at least knows that " 'he is capable of good things, gentle things, even magnanimous things,' " and it is not many years before Carton has a chance to prove to others and to himself that she is right.

With Darnay imprisoned in Paris and awaiting execution as an aristocrat-enemy of the French people, Carton and Mr. Lorry have what is ostensibly a strategy meeting. The meeting, however, turns out to be, for Carton, a more momentous occasion. For it is at this time that he decides how he will fulfill his promise to Lucie: " 'For you, and for any dear to you, I would do anything.' " He tells nothing of his purpose to Mr. Lorry, but his conversation is revealing (III,9): " 'See what a place you fill at seventy-eight. How many people will miss you when you leave it empty. . . . If you could say, with truth. . . "I have secured to myself the love and attachment, the gratitude or respect, of no human creature; I have won myself a tender place in no regard; I have done nothing good or serviceable to be remembered by!" your seventy-eight years would be seventy-eight curses, would they not?'" Carton's love of Lucie and her family as well as his desire to be "missed" and "remembered," to secure the "love," "gratitude," and "respect" of others and to win a "tender place" in their thoughts, lead him to resolve to sacrifice his life in place of Darnay.

Carton now has, says Dickens, "the settled manner of a tired man, who had wandered and struggled and got lost, but who at length struck into his road and saw its end." For Dickens, as for Carton himself, this movement from total self-absorption to sympathetic indentification with humanity has all the overtones and importance of spiritual salvation, and so no less than three times within this chapter (III,9) he has Carton repeat the same words: "I am the resurrection and the life, saith the Lord: he that believeth in me, though he were dead, yet shall he live: and whosoever liveth and believeth in me, shall never die." This anticipates Carton's own death and, presumably, his salvation; it also anticipates, perhaps, the death within him of the last vestiges of egoism. Dickens wishes to make clear that the manner of these deaths, and the very fact that they occur, ensure for Carton the prospect of spiritual grace at last. He has been self-indulgent and selfish, but it is never too late to mend and to grow, and he has grown late but in the right ways. The Biblical cadences of many of the last parts of the novel add support to the idea that Carton's final purgation of selfishness and arrogance is symbolically tantamount for Dickens to religious justification. *A Tale of Two Cities,* with its final emphasis on salvation through sacrifice, is patently one of Dickens' most "Christian" novels. Dickens's interest, however, is not in orthodox religious justification *per se* but rather, as in *Dombey and Son,* in humane behavior.

And so Carton forces Darnay to change places with

him—Darnay to be freed, Carton to be executed in his place. Carton's final act is one of pure and gratuitous unselfishness, a fact emphasized again and again by the language of the novel's last pages.

The girl whom Carton supports just before they are both executed tells him: "'I think you were sent to me by Heaven.'" Carton's death is a Dickensian canonization. The saint here is a secular one, but the ideal of selflessness remains paramount. It is fitting, therefore, that Carton's only earthly reward is the satisfaction he feels in doing something definitive for someone else—something he would have been incapable of doing or feeling had not his love for Lucie melted away his self-absorption. The novel's famous last paragraphs express, melodramatically but eloquently, Carton's state of mind at the very end of his life. He dies with "the peacefullest man's face ever beheld . . . [H]e looked sublime and prophetic." His final thoughts articulate the moral advantages of selflessness and sympathy over selfish indifference: "'It is a far, far better thing that I do, than I have ever done; it is a far, far better rest that I go to, than I have ever known.'" In a letter to Bulwer-Lytton, Dickens not surprisingly described the ending he provided for *A Tale of Two Cities* as constituting in part "an act of divine justice."

Despite many surface differences between *Dombey and Son* and *A Tale of Two Cities*, the moral seems to be essentially the same in both novels: the salvation of man depends upon his cultivation of *feeling*. Sydney Carton, like Mr. Dombey, begins in arrogant indifference and ends in sympathetic and selfless commitment. In both novels the moral development of the protagonist represents Dickens's vision of the only way in which mankind can achieve lasting grace.

III

Great Expectations (1860-61) is perhaps Dickens's most single-minded treatment of the problems of self-absorption and self-knowledge. These problems are particularly emphasized not only by the story the novel tells—that of a boy's growth to manhood—but also by the *way* in which it is told. For the narrative structure of *Great Expectations,* by its very nature, underlines the problems of egoism and moral development. This is because we have before us simultaneously in this novel two points of view other than that of the author himself: that of the young Pip, the protagonist who expresses his feelings and attitudes as he matures; and that of the older and more mature Pip, the narrator who comments from the vantage-point of his maturity upon the development of his younger self. Beyond the older Pip there is of course Dickens himself, who is watching over the shoulders of both. The narrative structure most clearly emphasizes the differences in vision and attitude, in values and perspective, that separate the mature Pip from his younger self—and it dictates that throughout the course of the story, as the young Pip matures, he will move closer and closer to the perspective of his older self. When the protagonist finally catches up with and becomes the narrator—when the distance between the two is dissolved—then the novel must end. From the beginning of the story onward the phenomenon of human moral development is always before us.

Pip, who is raised "by hand" by his sister and his brother-in-law, seems to be a sensitive and satisfied youngster when we first see him (through the eyes of his older self). The central event of the novel's opening pages is his accidental meeting with an escaped convict on the marshes. Terrified that he will be murdered if he does not obey the desperate man, Pip feeds him and brings him a file for his leg-iron. The convict is later caught and transported, and Pip thinks little more about him after that. Instead, a great deal of his youthful thought is devoted to Satis House—home of the eccentric Miss Havisham, who has invited him to come and "play," and to Miss Havisham's ward Estella, with whom Pip begins to fancy he is in love. It is this encounter with apparent wealth that first makes Pip dissatisfied with his life. Estella's calling him "common" changes his life: "I thought . . . how common Estella would consider Joe, a mere blacksmith: how thick his boots, and how course his hands . . . and how Miss Havisham and Estella never sat in a kitchen. . . . That was a memorable day for me, for it made great changes in me" [9]. Pip is immediately contemptuous of what he has never questioned before, and, as his older self says, his attitude helps change the direction of his life. He devotes his time after this to learning how to make himself "uncommon," as though this alone will make him a better person. In his new self-absorption he begins to ignore what is really important—the simple goodness, devotion, and generosity of his friend Joe. He thinks of his way of life instead as a millstone dragging him down from gentility. His dissatisfaction swells, and he begins to feel ashamed of his very home. Everything around him seems "course and common." He is "restless, aspiring, and discontented," and lives in daily fear of being seen by Estella at his blacksmith's work. Even the meals now seem degrading to him; he feels "more ashamed of home than ever." The older Pip has a frequently unsympathetic perspective on his younger self as he tells the story, but even without that help we can see that Pip, as he grows older, is becoming insensitive, ungracious and self-conceited. Instead of listening to more intelligent voices, Pip dreams that Miss Havisham is going to make his fortune some day and enable him to marry Estella. He admits to himself that Estella would probably make him miserable, but his self-indulgent fantasies will not allow him to give up the idea of marrying her.

It is at this stage of Pip's "development" that Mr. Jaggers comes to tell Pip that he has "great expectations." Pip is to be brought up as a gentleman in London, given a liberal allowance, and must wait until his anonymous benefactor identifies himself and makes available the bulk of the property settled upon him. Pip's reaction is immediate: "Miss Havisham was going to make my fortune on a grand scale." He never doubts either that she is his benefactress or that he is worthy of such a change in fortune. He is, thanklessly enough, ready to leave immediately. Everything about the place where he has spent his childhood now seems

ugly and small, including his old room at home—"a mean little room that I should soon be parted from and raised above,
for ever." And yet, we are told, he already feels lonely and is
unable to sleep—an analogue, no doubt, of the subconscious
guilt he must feel when alone with these thankless thoughts.
But except for the "shame" of having consorted with a convict on the marshes years before, Pip's conscious mind seems
to be untroubled by self-reproach. His state of mind at this
point may be gleaned from the following:

> As I passed the church, I felt . . . a sublime compassion
> for the poor creatures who were destined to go there,
> Sunday after Sunday, all their lives through, and to lie
> obscurely at last among the low green moulds. I prom-
> ised myself that I would do something for them one of
> these days, and formed a plan in outline for bestowing
> . . . a gallon of condescension upon everybody in the
> village . . . [All things] seemed, in their dull manner, to
> wear a more respectful air now, and to face round, in
> order that they might stare as long as possible at the
> possessor of such great expectations. (19)

Like Mr. Dombey, Pip sees the world as his own private
audience. Such rampant egoism has a shaky foundation, for it is based on vanity of riches not yet in
hand—nor is the hand of the benefactor known. But Pip continues to think of himself as a prince and to behave like one.
He patronizes everyone, including Joe, whom he says he will
never forget. Joe is not electrified by such generosity; and Pip
is displeased that Joe is "so mightily secure" of him. He
wishes Joe were better educated: "it would have been much
more agreeable if he had been better qualified for a rise in
station." When Pip criticizes Joe's manner to Biddy she
replies that there are many kinds of pride. Pip replies that she
is envious and grudging of his good fortune. And he spends
another sleepless and uncomfortable night.

When Pip goes shopping and informs the tradesmen of
his great expectations, it all becomes "my first decided experience of the stupendous power of money. . . ." Clerks
become obsequious; even the arch-hypocrite Pumblechook,
whom Pip has always despised, seems to him "a sensible

practical good-hearted prime fellow" after a few minutes of crude flattery. When the day of Pip's departure for London arrives, he decides to walk to the coach alone, due mainly to "my sense of the contrast there would be between me and Joe if we went to the coach together." And so he leaves: "the mists had all solemnly risen now, and the world lay spread before me." Pip, like many another character in an English novel, starts out on the road to London to make his way in the world, but unlike many of his counterparts he approaches London neither humble nor destitute. He is instead already a confirmed egoist, a young man too self-absorbed and self-important to realize his true advantages and potentialities. At the end of Chapter 19 the following statement appears: "THIS IS THE END OF THE FIRST STAGE OF PIP'S EXPECTATIONS." This "first stage" represents not only a sudden change of fortune but a stage of character development as well. There are three distinct "stages" in this novel, well-marked both by the action of the novel and by Dickens himself through the use of these capital reminders. The first stage embodies within it the easy corruption of the soul by money or the expectation of it—a selfish egoism that blinds the novel's hero to a great many things, including the new moral direction of his own nature.

In London, Pip moves into Barnard's Inn with Herbert Pocket, Miss Havisham's nephew, and immediately acquires a servant and begins to get himself into debt, conscientiously spending more money than Mr. Jaggers gives him for maintenance. He has gone to London ostensibly to learn, but while he does take lessons from Herbert's father his main avocation seems to be that of dissipation. Such is his idea of a gentleman. He has guilty thoughts from time to time about the home he has left behind, but only from time to time. He finds it easier to repress than to worry, however, and becomes more and more irresponsible—becoming, at the same time, more and more comfortable in his new way of life and in his new insensitivity. These facets of his growing selfishness are thrown into relief by Biddy's announcement, after Pip has been some time in London, that Joe is coming to visit him.

Pip's reaction to this news is enlightening. His feelings are those of "considerable disturbance, some mortification, and a keen sense of incongruity. If I could have kept him away by paying money, I certainly would have paid money . . . As the time approached I should have liked to run away . . ." [27]. His feelings are obvious to Joe, who becomes constrained and awkward in the face of Pip's vaunted new gentility. At the close of their interview Joe tells him that he (Pip) would not find so much fault with him (Joe) if Pip would only think of him as he is in the country and at home. Pip feels ashamed of himself, but the damage is done and Joe leaves.

Shortly thereafter Pip decides to pay his respects at Satis House. It is his first trip back to his home town and he finds the question of where to stay a perplexing one. He obviously does not want to go home, and so creates for himself a number of reasons to justify his staying at a nearby inn. It would really be more convenient: "I should be an inconvenience at Joe's; I was not expected, and my bed would not be ready; I should be too far from Miss Havisham's. . . . All other swindlers upon earth are nothing to the self-swindlers, and with such pretences did I cheat myself" [28]. Thus Pip, the "self-swindler," establishes for himself the pattern of avoiding his old home whenever possible, much to the older Pip's retrospective chagrin. All of these actions are those of a young man totally unresponsive to the feelings of others. The mature narrator is well aware of this.

Pip keeps away from Joe primarily because he knows that Estella is contemptuous of him. As she says: " 'what was fit company for you once would be quite unfit company for you now.' " Pip agrees, and is even more certain that since Miss Havisham has adopted both Estella and himself "it could not fail to be her intention to bring us together." Leaving the town, Pip takes a circuitous route to avoid being seen, and on the way runs into Trabb's boy, an acquaintance of his youth, who insists on shouting after him, in choric fashion, " 'Don't know yah, don't know yah, 'pon my soul, don't know yah!' " Back in London Pip attempts to salve his burning conscience by sending a barrel of oysters and a "penitential codfish" to Joe. He now tells Herbert Pocket that he is hopelessly in love with Estella. When Herbert warns him that this can lead only to misery and that he should try to detach himself, Pip's only answer is that he "can't help it" and that it is "impossible" for him to change. The guiding principle of his life seems to be that self-indulgence must always get the better of reason and common sense, and that any attempt to reverse the equation would be fruitless.

Chapter 34 is devoted primarily to Pip's own summary of the effects of his great expectations upon his character. The point of view is primarily that of the older Pip:

> As I had grown accustomed to my expectations, I had insensibly begun to notice their effect upon myself and those around me. Their influence on my own character I disguised from my recognition as much as possible, but I know very well that it was not all good. I lived in a state of chronic uneasiness respecting my behaviour to Joe. My conscience was not by any means comfortable about Biddy. When I woke up in the night . . . I used to think, with a weariness of my spirits, that I should have been happier and better if I had never seen Miss Havisham's face, and had risen to manhood content to be partners with Joe in the honest old forge . . . My lavish habits led [Herbert's] easy nature into expenses that he could not afford, corrupted the simplicity of his life, and disturbed his peace with anxieties and regrets . . . We spent as much money as we could and got as little for it as people could make up their minds to give us. We were always more or less miserable. . . .

These sentiments, as I have said, are those of the older Pip looking back upon his younger self. The protagonist, implies the narrator, is at this time in his life both insensible to reality and prone to disguise it from his own understanding by imposing upon it the shadow of his own egoism. And yet, to Pip's credit, he is decent enough to be uneasy, even miserable, about the kind of life he is leading. But he does nothing, as yet, to change his ways. As a younger man, Pip was still far from having attained a level of self-knowledge which would have forced him to alter his life—a level which, obviously, the narrator has reached as an older man. *Great Expectations,* as I have said, is the story of how the protagonist of the novel becomes the narrator. At this stage, however, there is obviously still a wide distance between them, for the younger Pip, though he has his moments of guilt and despair, has not as yet seen the totality of his selfishness and folly. The period of self-discovery and bitter repentance is still some little way off.

On his twenty-first birthday Pip visits Mr. Jaggers, expecting to learn something more about his benefactor and to come into a more considerable portion of his property. Mr. Jaggers greets him with a bank-note for five hundred pounds, which will not even pay his debts, and no further information. Shortly thereafter he again visits Satis House and now finally begins to understand, after several of Miss Havisham's eccentric exclamations, that Estella is a pawn of hers designed to wreak her revenge upon men for the treatment she has had from them. Such a state of affairs has been obvious to us for some time, but Pip only sees it now. He also sees that he is to be tormented by Estella for a while, but still he does not doubt that she will ultimately accept him.

When Pip is twenty-three his benefactor makes himself known to him. He is, of course, the old convict from the marshes, Abel Magwitch, who has made and saved a great deal of money while in exile and has come back to England, braving possible execution if caught, to see the "gentleman" he has created. It takes Pip some time to understand the truth of his position, and he begins the conversation with Magwitch haughtily: " 'I cannot wish to renew that chance intercourse with you of long ago. . . . I am glad to believe you have repented and recovered yourself . . . But our ways are different ways . . ." [39]. Gradually the facts are revealed to Pip, whose pride is not proof against this shock to his self-conceit: "All the truth of my position came flashing on me, and its disappointments, dangers, disgraces, consequences of all kinds rushed in in such a multitude that I was borne down by them and had to struggle for every breath I drew" [39]. Pip's initial reaction to Magwitch's revelation does him no justice. It does not occur to him, for example, to feel grateful to the convict, or even to thank him for depriving himself in order to enrich Pip. Instead, in his shallowness, Pip is repelled by the man and heartbroken that his "expectations" have had so humble a source (39): "The abhorrence in which I held the man, the dread I had of him, the repugnance with which I shrank from him could not have been exceeded if he had been some terrible beast . . . I recoiled from his touch as if he had been a snake . . . O that he had never come! That he had left me at the forge—far from contented, yet, by comparison, happy!" Pip, in his callous ingratitude, at least begins to see the moral harm wreaked upon him by his "expectations." Money has made him proud, superficial, and miserable; his financial expectations have generated others—expectations now, as he sees, hopeless. He will never be able to marry Estella. Miss Havisham not only has not intended them for one another—she has had nothing whatsoever to do with his social elevation. He has been living in a dream world of flabby self-indulgence. These truths all come home to him now; "the ship in which I had sailed" goes "to pieces." Most painful of all to Pip is the realization that he has deserted Joe for these ego-fantasies. More present to him now than anything else is a sense of his own "worthless conduct." To complete Pip's despair, Magwitch tells him that he is in England on pain of death if caught and must be carefully hidden. Pip, who of course undertakes to protect Magwitch as fully as possible, nevertheless resolves to take no more of his money.

There is a double irony here. It is certainly ironic that Pip's great expectations, his arrogance and selfishness, have been based on money saved by a criminal, and it is also ironic that Pip's pride, which has grown large on the spoils he is now rejecting, dictates that he must, for reasons of self-respect, take no more of those spoils. Money, arrogance, and ingratitude have been holding sway over his character as we come, so we are told, to the end of another climactic stage of Pip's moral development: "THIS IS THE END OF THE SECOND STAGE OF PIP'S EXPECTATIONS." At the end of the first stage Pip was just starting off for London after having been apprised of his expectations, patronizing everyone around him as he went. Now he has learned the source of his expectations, begins to see how selfishly he has been behaving, and wishes he had never had any expectations at all—thus also slighting the devotion of poor Magwitch, whose uncouthness repels the conventional sense of surface decorum Pip has acquired as a result of Magwitch's own money. The first stage of Pip's ordeal of education in values was dominated by what later writers such as George Eliot and George Meredith might call animal egoism; the second stage, just now ended, is that which they might call rational despair born of a sharpening of moral vision. The third stage, that of self-revelation and increasing selflessness, would seem to lie ahead. And so in fact it does.

The final movement of the novel opens with Pip's seemingly unquenchable dislike for his benefactor still rampant. Magwitch is "disagreeable . . . uncouth, noisy, and greedy." Pip feels "pursued by the creature who had made me," and recoils from him "with a stronger repulsion the more he admired me and the fonder he was of me." That Pip feels repelled by Magwitch is of course much less the convict's fault than it is Pip's own. His knee-jerk reaction to Magwitch is the result of his superficial judgment—a judgment of surfaces—and his sanguine assurance all along that Miss Havisham was making his fortune for him. It is a blow to his ego to discover that Miss Havisham is really Magwitch; in his selfish egoism he rejects Magwitch as he had rejected Joe earlier. It seems that he is most uninterested in those who have demonstrated their love for him most fully. He is interested only in what he does not have—and that, at this moment, is gentility and Estella. He tells Mr. Jaggers that he has always supposed that Miss Havisham was his benefactress, and Mr. Jaggers replies, appropriately, that he is not responsible for that. Pip then tells Herbert that he cannot accept any more money from Magwitch, as if his money is worse than the hard-hearted and perverted Miss Havisham's money would have been—Miss Havisham, who has not a fraction of the feeling for Pip that Magwitch has. Pip is

appropriately miserable, and yet there is still something quite
wrong with his moral perspective. Speaking of Magwitch, he
says to Herbert: " 'Think of him! Look at him! . . . The
dreadful truth is. . . that he is attached to me. . . . Was there
ever such a fate!' " He tells Herbert that he must "break" with
Magwitch; the convict whose money has helped to form Pip's
execrable values is beneath his contempt for the sin of having
dared to be grateful to the boy who fed him on the marshes
years ago.

Pip is now mainly concerned with keeping Magwitch out
of the way of the police and the executioner. As Pip sees the
extent to which the convict is attached to him his heart begins
to soften toward him, and for the first time he approaches an
understanding of the sanctifying value of human attachment
and fellow feeling. He wishes that he had never left Joe's
forge and that Miss Havisham had never had him brought
over to play with Estella and tortured him thereafter with
visions of Estella's unattainable beauty. With these things in
mind he makes another trip down to Satis House, where he
accuses Miss Havisham of leading him on in his suppositions
that she was his benefactress and that she intended Estella for
him. Miss Havisham's reply (" 'You made your own snares.
I never made them.' ") and Estella's (" 'I have tried to warn
you of this. . . . But you would not be warned. . . .' ") are
both entirely correct; Pip's delusions have been based on his
own self-indulgent fantasies. The chapter (44) ends with
Estella's announcement that she is going to marry the boorish
Bentley Drummle, and the thoroughly miserable Pip returns
to London. There he busies himself once again with the
protection of Magwitch, whose loyalty and devotion now
seem to him more valuable: "I little supposed my heart could
ever be as heavy and anxious at parting from him as it was
now . . . I was always full of fears for the rash man who was
in hiding" [46].

Pip is summoned back to Satis House by Miss
Havisham, who, finally beset by guilt for the unhappiness she
has wantonly helped to inject into the life of the blacksmith's
boy, is determined to make some amends. Pip, who has

begun learning lately to think of others before himself, asks her to help him buy Herbert Pocket a partnership in a trading house. She agrees, and asks him if he ever can forgive her. He replies: " 'I can do it now. There have been sore mistakes; and my life has been a blind and thankless one; and I want forgiveness and direction far too much to be bitter with you' " [49]. Pip's egoism has been diluted by his new knowledge of himself, which in turn enables him to sympathize with and understand more fully what is outside of himself. He now acknowledges his earlier blindness and his want of compassion. The ordeal of his education in values, which is the central subject of *Great Expectations,* is nearing its end.

The ordeal, however, is not quite over. Pip is enticed back to his old environs once again by a note whose writer seems to know all about Magwitch's presence in England. He goes out onto the marshes to meet the writer of the note, Orlick, the murderer of Pip's sister, who says he is going to kill Pip for past slights (such as having him fired from Miss Havisham's service). When Pip thinks that he is certainly going to die at the hands of this man his mind quickly runs over "all the consequences of such a death." Magwitch would be captured, believing Pip had deserted him; Herbert would wonder what he had been up to; Joe and Biddy would never know how sorry he was for his past ingratitude. It occurs to Pip that he has done little good in the world and that his own selfishness has blinded him to the things that are most healthy for the soul in this world—friendship, self-sacrifice, and concern for others. As he is about to die (or so he thinks), he writhes in fear not of death itself but of how he will undoubtedly be "misremembered" after his death: "none would ever know what I had suffered, how true I had meant to be, what an agony I had passed through . . . I saw myself despised by unborn generations . . ." [53]. The similarity of Pip's sentiments here to those of Sydney Carton before the performance of his ultimate sacrifice is patently striking. Pip's rescue, like Sydney's, occurs with the onset of these purifying sentiments. For Pip is now saved, both physically and morally; he has finally managed his own spiritual rescue.

His being snatched away from Orlick and death at this point is a kind of physical analogue of what morally and psychologically has already occurred. And so Pip is free to return to London, where plans for Magwitch's escape from England are about to be put into effect.

The attempted getaway fails, and Magwitch is badly wounded in the course of it. Pip's new capacity for empathy is emphasized in these final chapters again and again. He is with his benefactor in the jail-hospital all day and every day:

> For now my repugnance to him had all melted away, and in the hunted wounded shackled creature who held my hand in his, I only saw a man who had meant to be my benefactor, and who had felt affectionately, gratefully, and generously towards me with great constancy through a series of years. I only saw in him a much better man than I had been to Joe. . .'I will never stir from your side,' said I [to him], 'when I am suffered to be near you. Please God, I will be as true to you as you have been to me!' (54)

When Magwitch is brought to trial, Pip, now more affected by gratitude and generosity than by the figure he may cut, stands by the dock and holds the prisoner's hand. When Magwitch is sentenced to death, Pip undertakes a number of appeals in his behalf. But the convict dies in prison before the sentence can be carried out, and Pip goes home alone to undergo the final stage of his ordeal—which takes the form of a serious and protracted illness of unspecified nature, a climactic physical analogue of his psychic revolution. As was the case with Mr. Dombey, this is the final suffering before moral grace, the last tumultuous stage of the advance toward *caritas*.

Joe nurses him back to health and pays his debts, and Pip feels more keenly than ever his ingratitude and past folly. As he begins to recover his old spirits, however, he senses in Joe a shrinking away, as if Joe fears that Pip's old haughtiness and condescension will reassert itself (57): "Had I given Joe no reason to doubt my constancy, and to think that in prosperity I should grow cold to him and cast him off? Had I given Joe's innocent heart no cause to feel instinctively that, as I got stronger, his hold upon me would be weaker, and that he had better loosen it in time and let me go, before I plucked myself away?" The chapter ends as Pip says to Joe: " 'I feel thankful that I have been ill. . . .' " The illness for which Pip is thankful is, of course, more than merely physical. He has suffered to be saved.

The action of the novel's final chapter, with its two famous endings, takes place years later when Pip returns from a residence abroad. Both versions emphasize the moral uses of suffering. In the original ending, wherein Pip and Estella meet and then part again, Pip comes away from their short interview convinced that for Estella "suffering had been stronger than Miss Havisham's teaching, and had given her a heart to understand what my heart used to be." In this version that is the novel's final sentence, and it suggests that for Estella, as for Pip himself, the ordeal of an education in values has resulted in the extinction of hard-heartedness and self-absorption in lieu of more fully developed moral vision. Appropriately enough, it gives final emphasis to the theme of the purgative and thus salutary value of suffering. In the revised ending, in which Pip and Estella meet but, it is suggested, will not part again from one another, the moral uses of suffering are even more strongly emphasized. In this version Estella says to Pip: " 'suffering has been stronger than all other teaching, and has taught me to understand what your heart used to be. I have been bent and broken, but—I hope—into a better shape' " [59]. This sentence describes succinctly the course Dickens has plotted for the salvation of his protagonists. Like Estella, Pip has been bent and broken but has emerged from his ordeal a better and more complete person. His arrogance and indifference to others, like that of Mr. Dombey and Sydney Carton, have been paid for in terms of physical and psychic upheaval. Suffering is again seen as a prerequisite of Grace. And Grace here, as in the other novels, is in turn seen as a concomitant of increased fellow feeling; feeling for others before self is what Dickens's sentient protagonists must achieve in the process of their moral ordeals.

There are fewer sub plots in *Great Expectations* than in most of Dickens's other novels—especially the later ones—and this is primarily because almost everything in the novel gains its importance from how it relates to Pip himself. His development is both the novel's story and its structure; his mind is at the center of almost every chapter. By the end of the novel the protagonist has caught up both in knowledge and in age with the narrator—and there is nowhere further to go. Pip has become himself, and so the novel ends. Like David Copperfield, he has indeed turned out to be the hero of his own life.

GEORGE ELIOT (1819-1880)
National Portrait Gallery, London

Chapter Four

George Eliot

The story of most of George Eliot's novels is that of a character's mental growth, a central movement surrounded by several sub plots concerned with the mental growth (or lack thereof) of more peripheral characters. The moral education of the human being—his movement from egoism to more objective moral vision—is always a radical theme in these novels. George Eliot believed that art has a social, moral mission—that its twin goals should be the destruction of egoism and the creation of sympathy for others. Like Dickens, she also believed that suffering leads to—is even a prerequisite of—increased understanding of and sympathy for one's fellow men. The moral process in her novels is from experience to vision to sympathy—or, to state it another way, from egoism through despair to objectivity. This process usually leads the protagonist from self-absorption through self-examination and thence to self-knowledge and greater understanding both of himself and of those among whom he lives. The painful movement from innocence to experience is, for George Eliot, what is needed to expiate the tragic flaw of egoism so central to the nature of most of her characters, a movement possible only with the dissipation of moral blindness and the growth of feeling. George Eliot's constant goal was to awaken and enlarge the sympathy and the moral perception of her readers by confronting them in her novels with characters who become similarly awakened to the possibilities of moral growth.

Ignorance, both of self and of the world, is for George Eliot the result of faulty moral vision, while understanding and sympathy come from the knowledge of empathic experience. The end of self-absorption is for most of her characters the beginning of true experience and fellow-feeling. Thus it is not surprising that George Eliot's novels include many passages relevant in one way or another to *vision,* to the way people see or avoid seeing. As a character moves toward moral vision his understanding both of the world and of himself increases. George Eliot always hoped that her readers, in the course of reading any particular novel of hers, would undergo this development in conjunction with her characters. She was able to combine a powerful social vision with the expert and sensitive analysis of people's private motives, and thus her novels are usually both chronicles of manners and histories of a soul. Her constant theme is that man must learn to know himself and to live without illusion—else he will never emerge from his prison of egoism.

I

Adam Bede (1859) has as its central subject the mental growth of the title character. There are other egoists in this novel, but their stories are really less important than Adam's, and thus George Eliot gives his name to the book. Arthur Donnithorne, throughout most of the novel, pursues self-indulgence with little reflection; Hetty Sorrel's selfishness grows, finally, into a sort of solipsism (signified in part by her penchant for mirror-gazing); even Dinah Morris gives the impression at times of being more concerned with her own spiritual status than with anybody else's happiness. These themes are all important and they are all emphasized, but primarily as moral analogues to the novel's central focus—Adam Bede's growth to sympathy and vision. Thus it is on his development that I shall concentrate in my discussion of the novel.

Adam's egoism throughout the first two-thirds or so of the novel takes the form primarily of an unsympathetic measuring of others against himself and an intolerance of their weaknesses. He is a hard man, impatient with the failings of his fellow human beings. Virtue and conscientiousness come naturally to him, and throughout much of the novel Adam, basking in the glow of his own goodness, is unable or unwilling to understand the needs and desires of those around him. The novel traces his development from a man with little comprehension of others to a man capable of sympathy and fellow-feeling—once again, a movement from moral blindness to moral vision.

In the opening pages of the novel Adam is introduced to us as a man who "will have his way," an energetic laborer whose doctrine of work he preaches constantly and emphatically at his fellow\workmen: " 'I hate to see a man's arms drop down as if he was shot, before the clock's fairly struck, just as if he'd never a bit o' pride and delight in 's work.' " [1,I]. George Eliot intends us to see here that Adam is right in principle but wrong in spirit, for he is lecturing good men who simply want to leave their work at the end of the day and enjoy diversion. Adam, however, finds pleasure only in work and cannot or will not understand why others do not feel the same way.

Next comes Dinah Morris's preaching on the Green, after which Seth Bede tells Dinah about Adam's infatuation with Hetty Sorrel, a niece of the Poysers. Seth feels that Hetty is not worthy of Adam's love, but here George Eliot's narrative voice interposes and comments to the effect that love, because it is an acknowledgment of a being "greater and better" than one's self, "is hardly distinguishable from religious feeling . . . [O]ur love at its highest flood rushes beyond its object and loses itself in the sense of divine mystery" [1,III]. This is the novelist's first overt expression of her paramount theme, which is the destruction of egoism through the ennobling effects on the self of love for others. The ability to love outside of one's self is by definition a denial of the primacy of self; therefore love, on these grounds alone, is an act of moral exaltation for any individual. For George Eliot, as for Dickens, the ability to feel for others is invested with religious significance. Deep within him Adam does have "this blessed gift of venerating love," but the suggestion seems to be that his vision is tainted by subjectivity to the extent that he is unable to see that the object of his love is unworthy of it. This point is made several times by Seth, a sensible man, and by Adam's mother Lisbeth, who is not particularly sensible but who seems to

have throughout the novel an unusual gift of prophecy
(" 'An' he so wise at bookin' an' figurin', and not to know
no better nor that!' ").

But by far the most damaging weakness in Adam
throughout the novel's early chapters is his hard-hearted
intolerance of the weaknesses of his father, who, as he has
gotten older and more dependent upon his two strong sons,
has started to drink more and to work less. Adam finds his
father's behavior inexcusable and tortures his poor mother
with periodic threats to walk out on the family. Lisbeth tells
him: " 'Thee mun forgie thy feyther—thee munna be so bitter
again' him. He war a good feyther to thee afore he took to th'
drink. He's a clever workman, an' taught thee thy trade,
remember, an's niver gen me a blow nor so much as an ill
word—no, not even in 's drink . . . [T]hee't allays so
hard upo' thy feyther, Adam' " [1, IV]. Adam replies: " 'I
know there's a duty to be done by my father, but it isn't my
duty to encourage him in running headlong to ruin.' " But as he
waits up for his delinquent father, Adam begins to take
Lisbeth's words to heart: "They that are strong ought to bear
the infirmities of those that are weak, and not to please
themselves."

The first stage of Adam's ordeal, of his movement
toward a more sympathetic moral vision, now comes immediately upon him with the sudden accidental drowning of
his father and his resulting feelings of guilt as he reflects upon
his hard attitude toward the old man. It is now too late for
these thoughts, of course, but Adam resolves to be less severe
with others in the future: "Adam's mind rushed back over the
past in a flood of relenting and pity. When death, the great
Reconciler, has come, it is never our tenderness that we repent of, but our severity" [1, IV] . Adam promises to be
more sympathetic, and relieves his feelings by working even
harder. His unbending admiration for serious commitment to
work, however, seems no less abated, and we have the feeling
that while he may be somewhat softened by the death of his
father he is essentially the same inflexible person: " 'the natur
o' things doesn't change, though it seems as if one's own life

was nothing but change. The square o' four is sixteen, and you must lengthen your lever in proportion to your weight, is as true when a man's miserable as when he's happy . . .' " [1,XI]. And yet a few pages further on, just before Adam's father is laid to rest, Adam admits for the first time in the novel that mathematics may not be able to calculate everything. He says to Lisbeth: " 'figures tell us a fine deal, and we couldn't go far without 'em, but they don't tell us about folks' feelings. It's a nicer job to calculate *them*' " [1,XIV]. Adam has begun to recognize the importance of others' feelings even though such feelings are still a mystery to him. Repenting of a severity which now can never be expiated, Adam begins to concern himself with the feelings of others as well as the quality of their work. Still, however, he does not abandon that doctrine of work which is the primary element of his judgment of others. It is precisely this tendency to judge, to find fault, that Adam must (and does) relinquish as the novel progresses. We always feel that Adam is capable of fellow feeling, primarily because he himself is aware, at least to some extent, of the hard inflexibility of his own nature. He tells Arthur Donnithorne: " 'I don't remember ever being see-saw . . . [I]t isn't my way to be see-saw about anything: I think my fault lies th' other way. When I've said a thing, if it's only to myself, it's hard for me to go back' " [1,XVI].

In the famous seventeenth chapter of *Adam Bede,* "In Which the Story Pauses A Little," George Eliot, after enunciating her doctrine of literary realism, reiterates what she feels to be the single most important function of literature: the awakening and the extension of human fellow feeling. She says here: "let us love that . . . beauty . . . which lies in no secret of proportion, but in the secret of deep human sympathy . . . It isn't notions sets people doing the right thing—it's feelings " [2, XVII]. And as if to underline this pronouncement, George Eliot places just after this chapter the funeral of Adam's father and gives in some detail Adam's thoughts upon this sad occasion:

> 'Ah, I was always too hard,' Adam said to himself.
> 'It's a sore fault in me I'm so hot and out o' patience

with people when they do wrong, and my heart gets shut up against 'em, so as I can't bring myself to forgive 'em. I see clear enough there's more pride nor love in my soul, for I could sooner make a thousand strokes with th' hammer for my father than bring myself to say a kind word to him. And there went plenty o' pride and temper to the strokes, as the devil *will* be having his finger in what we call our duties, as well as our sins. Mayhap the best thing I ever did in my life was only doing what was easiest for myself. It's allays been easier for me to work nor to sit still, but the real tough job for me 'ud be to master my own will and temper, and go right against my own pride. It seems to me now, if I was to find father at home to-night, I should behave different; but there's no knowing—perhaps nothing 'ud be a lesson to us if it didn't come too late.' (2,XVIII)

The death of his father has made Adam, for the first time in his life, stop to question his own conduct. He rightly condemns himself for being "too hard" and too proud of himself as a workman and for lacking sympathy for the failings of others. He correctly accuses himself of lacking the generosity of easy forgiveness, of being more proud than loving. It is easier for him to work hard than to be kind, apparently, but at least he recognizes this—and also that there can be as much devilishness in "duty" as in "sin." If working is what comes easiest to him, then he often does what is easy. At least Adam sees, though, that he must master his will, his temper, and his pride, and such a recognition augurs well for the direction of his future moral development. While Adam is not yet in despair, he is edging away from the initial stage of his moral development—self-absorption—and toward that crucial second stage: the misery that is the initial result of suddenly increased clarity of vision. The personal suffering which is a concomitant of moral development is a necessary prerequisite, for George Eliot, of the attainment of fellow feeling. As Adam himself says, " 'perhaps nothing 'ud be a lesson to us if it didn't come too late' "; in this novel he has to repent of hard-heartedness several times until finally he is able to act emphatically *before* it is "too late." Should the reader fail to anticipate these prospective stages of Adam's moral progression, George Eliot underlines them for him:

> Perhaps here lay the secret of the hardness he had ac-
> cused himself of: he had too little fellow-feeling with the
> weakness that errs in spite of foreseen circumstances.
> Without this fellow-feeling, how are we to get enough
> patience and charity towards our stumbling, falling
> companions in the long and changeful journey? And
> there is but one way in which a strong determined soul
> can learn it—by getting his heart-strings bound round
> the weak and erring, so that he must share not only the
> outward consequence of their error, but their inward
> suffering. That is a long and hard lesson, and Adam had
> at present only learned the alphabet of it in his father's
> sudden death . . . . (2, XIX)

Sympathy for others, born of suffering within one's self, is the
"long and hard lesson" Adam must learn. As in Dickens, suffering seems to be a stepladder to Grace, while fellow
feeling, charity and empathy are looked upon as the most
salutary goals for all humanity. The lack of feeling for others,
which has been the source of Adam's egoism, has also been
the most serious flaw in his moral structure. It is this flaw in
Adam, and in her readers too, that George Eliot is dedicated
both to exposing and expunging.

The next several chapters deal with Adam's growing love
for Hetty and his total unawareness of her infatuation both
with Arthur and her own beauty. Lisbeth again warns Adam
against Hetty's shallowness, only to be told by her son that he
will do as he likes. When he is with Hetty, Adam mistakes her
day dreaming (about being a great lady as Arthur's wife) for
love of himself. Adam, George Eliot reminds us during one of
his visits to the Hall Farm, "must suffer one day," and his increasing confidence in Hetty's attachment to himself is
leading him further in that direction.

At the end of Book 2, Adam visits his old friend and
tutor Bartle Massey, the crotchety but kind-hearted anti-
feminist. When Adam expresses some scruples about increasing his income (and thereby his ability to support his
mother) by managing the woods belonging to Arthur's par-
simonious grandfather, old Squire Donnithorne, Bartle

chastises him for his inflexible pride: " 'You must learn to deal with odd and even in life, as well as in figures . . . [Y] ou're over-hasty and proud, and apt to set your teeth against folks that don't square to your notions' " [2, XXI] . Once again it is suggested that Adam's doctrine of work ("figures"), his temperament and his pride, have gotten in the way of his humanity. Nevertheless he does accept the position of manager of the Donnithorne woods.

Adam continues to be preoccupied with his thoughts of Hetty. He sees that she too is preoccupied about something, but takes it once again to be a symptom of her love for him. Adam's self-absorption prevents his seeing the true state of Hetty's emotions; he has, as George Eliot tells us, "woven for himself an ingenious web of probabilities—the surest screen a wise man can place between himself and the truth." The egoist imposes outward upon things the shadows of his own perception. A major barrier to Adam's vision, however, is soon removed. He sees Arthur and Hetty kissing each other in the wood and, in his mortification and anger, picks a fight with Arthur and knocks him down. He is immediately thereafter "sickened at the vanity of his own rage" and apologizes to the guilty Arthur: " 'perhaps I judged you too harsh—I'm apt to be harsh . . . We're not all put together alike, and we may misjudge one another' " [4, XXVIII] . Adam for the first time demonstrates concretely the softening effect his father's death has had on him. His admission articulates both his own quickness to condemn and his understanding of the inevitable differences among different people, differences which must always be taken into account in human interrelationships. The irony here, however, is that his misjudgment this time takes the form of an acceptance as the truth of Arthur's false version of the relationship that exists between Hetty and himself. Though Adam swallows the story, he remains unable to forgive Arthur for interposing himself between Hetty and his own love for her: " 'I know forgiveness is a man's duty, but, to my thinking, that can only mean as you're to give up all thoughts o' taking revenge: it can never mean as you're t' have your old feelings back again. . .' His exasperation. . .deafened him to any plea for the mis-called friend who had wrought this misery. Adam . . . was bitterly jealous . . ." [4, XXIX]. Adam's hardness is still an element of his character; despite his desire to be magnanimous, revenge remains an uppermost thought.

As time goes by Adam feels more and more confident of Hetty's love for him. He proposes to her and is shyly accepted. Thus his shock, disappointment and rage are the more violent when, shortly before they are to be married, Hetty runs away from the Hall Farm. Adam, who goes in search of her, recognizes both his own imperceptiveness ("He had been foolishly sanguine and confident") and his increased desire for vengeance against "that man [Arthur] who had selfishly played with her heart—had perhaps even deliberately lured her away." His desire for vengeancc will be much the greater, of course, when he learns of Hetty's pregnancy. Adam is unable to find Hetty and returns home defeated and despairing. For the first time in his life he acknowledges the suddenly overwhelming desire within him to lean on others, both for moral support and for solace. He turns for help first to Seth ("the strong man, accustomed to suppress the signs of sorrow, had felt his heart swell like a child's at this first approach of sympathy. He fell on Seth's neck and sobbed"), then to Mr. Irwine, the Rector ("' it's the right thing. I can't stand alone in this way any longer'"), and finally to Bartle Massey [5, XXXVIII-XXXIX].

Mr. Irwine has just learned of Hetty's apprehension on the charge of child-murder, and when Adam comes to confide in him the Rector feels bound to tell him all he knows. The effect of this news upon Adam is electric:

'Is *he* to go free, while they lay all the punishment on her . . . so weak and young . . . I can't bear it . . . . O God, it's too hard to lay upon me—it's hard to think she's wicked . . . I'll make him go and look at her in her misery—he shall look at her till he can't forget it—it shall follow him night and day—as long as he lives it shall follow him—he shan't escape wi' lies this time—I'll fetch him, I'll drag him myself.' (5, XXXIX)

Adam's immediate reaction to the news of Hetty's tragedy is, even now, that of murderous hatred for Arthur rather than that of sympathy for Hetty. Even though the desire for revenge is what is emphasized in this passage, however, it is clear that the second stage of Adam's moral development (despair and increased moral vision) is not far off (" 'I can't bear it . . . . O God, it's too hard to lay upon me' ").

The scene now moves to Stoniton, the place of Hetty's imminent trial. Adam takes a room there accompanied by Bartle Massey; Mr. Irwine and Martin Poyser also are at hand, waiting to testify in Hetty's behalf. Arthur, however, has not as yet appeared, and Adam's wrath against him grows. He is still too much the judge (" 'I hold him the guiltiest before God' ") and too little the pardoner, and this is what causes Mr. Irwine to fear for Arthur's life should he return at this juncture. In his conversations with Adam, Mr. Irwine stresses the need for "fellow-feeling," for sympathy, tolerance, and understanding, and from this point onward the novel studies the effects of Adam's misery upon his bruised moral perspective. His spiritual crisis, as it deepens and widens, is reflected for example in his physical appearance: "His face has got thinner [and] he has the sunken eyes, the neglected beard of a man just risen from a sick-bed. His heavy black hair hangs over his forehead, and there is no active impulse . . . which inclines him to push it off, that he may be more awake to what is around him" [5, XLI]. This is once again the physical analogue of a psychological ordeal. In the same chapter Adam tells Mr. Irwine that all he wants is " 'justice. I want him to feel what she feels . . . [H]e shall feel it . . . if there's a just God . . . [H]e knows nothing about it—he suffers nothing.' "

Adam's lack of charity finally exasperates Mr. Irwine, and his answer to Adam's complaint is a crucial moment in the novel:

> 'he *will* suffer, long and bitterly. He has a heart and a conscience . . . . Why do you crave vengeance in this way? No amount of torture that you could inflict on *him* would benefit *her* . . . [Y]ou have no right to say

> that the guilt of her crime lies with him, and that he
> ought to bear the punishment. It is not for us men to ap-
> portion the shares of moral guilt and retribution . . .
> The evil consequences that may lie folded in a single act
> of selfish indulgence, is a thought so awful that it ought
> surely to awaken some feeling less presumptuous than a
> rash desire to punish . . . .' (5, XLI)

Adam here is being rebuked for precisely the same failings he
has carried with him since we first met him: lack of sympathy
for others and the self-righteous implulse to judge their actions.

In judging so readily, Adam's presumptuous attitude is
no less an example of "selfish indulgence" than Arthur's
moments with Hetty; both stand condemned of egoism.
Self-indulgence is again identified as the antipode of fellow
feeling. Mr. Irwine's final speech to Adam is another crucial
choric statement : " 'Men's lives are as thoroughly blended
with each other as the air they breathe . . . . [S]o does every
sin cause suffering to others besides those who commit it
. . .[A]s long as you indulge [your present feelings], as long
as you do not see that to fix your mind on Arthur's punishment is revenge, and not justice, you are in danger of being
led on to . . . some great wrong' " [5, XLI]. The most important reason for sympathy and understanding, says George
Eliot (again and again), is the fact that all men's lives are in-
extricably interrelated. One cannot be hard and selfish
without poisoning in some way a number of other lives.

Egoism, as we know, leads inevitably to despair. It is
into despair that Adam now plunges, and more deeply than
ever before. This, as we also know, is a stage of moral
development which is a necessary prerequisite for the attainment of ultimate sympathy and more objective vision. The
climax of Adam's suffering, his moral revelation, now occurs.

> Energetic natures, strong for all strenuous deeds, will
> often rush away from a hopeless sufferer as if they were
> hard-hearted. It is the overmastering sense of pain that
> drives them . . . Deep, unspeakable suffering may well
> be called a baptism, a regeneration, the initiation into a
> new state . . . Adam [looked] back on all the previous

years as if they had been a dim sleepy existence, and he had only now awaked to full consciousness. It seemed to him as if he had always before thought it a light thing that men should suffer; as if all that he had himself endured and called sorrow before, was only a moment's stroke that had never left a bruise. Doubtless a great anguish may do the work of years, and we may come out from that baptism of fire with a soul full of awe and new pity.

'O God,' Adam groaned. . .'and men have suffered like this before. . .and poor helpless young things have suffered like her. . . .I'll stand by her—I'll own her—for all she's been deceitful. They oughtn't to cast her off. . . .We hand folks over to God's mercy, and show none ourselves. I used to be hard sometimes: I'll never be hard again!' (5, XLII)

This passage marks the height of Adam's despair and his movement toward the third and final stage of his moral development (that is, sympathetic vision). It also reveals a good deal about George Eliot's conception of the nature of this psychic process. Suffering, for George Eliot as for Dickens, must precede "the initiation into a new state"—that is, a state of increased fellow feeling. For George Eliot, as for Dickens, such a conversion has specifically religious overtones. Suffering, for her, is "a baptism, a regeneration"; it is, in other words, a source of life itself, or at least a source of meaningful, conscious, sentient life. Adam now has, for the first time, a "full consciousness." Heretofore he had not thought much about the suffering of others—had accepted it as simply an inevitable concomitant of existence. But "a great anguish may do the work of years," and so Adam's own suffering has taught him how to be sympathetic to, how to pity, that of others. George Eliot characterizes this phenomenon as a "baptism of fire" out of which the soul emerges "full of new awe and new pity." This last phrase inevitably calls to mind Aristotle's account of the effects a witnessed tragedy has on its audience. Adam's experience of suffering is by no means vicarious; but it is cathartic, purging as it does the last remnants of his intolerance and inflexibility in judging others—thus his new understanding, finally, of the virtue of mercy: " 'I used to be hard sometimes: I'll never be hard again.' " Herewith Adam starts on the final part of his journey toward moral vision and fellow feeling. In doing so he is once again reinforced by Bartle Massey, who tells him that " 'it's a great thing in a man's life to be able to stand by a neighbour, and uphold him in . . . trouble.' " And so Adam goes to the trial and attempts to support Hetty in *her* ordeal. Like Pip at Magwitch's trial, compassion finally overpowers fastidiousness in him. She is judged guilty of the crime of child-murder and taken back to the prison to await her execution several days hence. Adam finally says to Dinah: " 'Tell her, I forgive her.' "

Now comes a time of suspense during which Adam and the others await the fatal hour, hoping for a last-minute pardon for Hetty. Before Adam starts off to visit her in her cell, Bartle Massey tries once again to console him: " 'There may good come out of this that we don't see.' " Adam hotly denies this, but the very next scene (5, XLVI) proves Bartle right—for in it Adam has the opportunity to bring to fruition his new fellow feeling. Hetty asks Adam for forgiveness; Adam says he does forgive her, and as he does so he feels "a sense of relief from what was becoming unbearable" and begins to weep. Adam's catharsis here represents the end of the second stage of his moral development—the last moment of despair before more sympathetic vision becomes an unreflecting habit. George Eliot emphasizes the importance in Adam's development of the capacity to "forgive" by repeating the word several times more during this scene. Hetty tells Adam to tell Arthur that she forgives him, which she does in order that God may forgive her. She has been coached in this by Dinah, but she too seems to feel the necessity of forgiving. Then, as the last few minutes approach, Arthur shows up with that infamous pardon, and Hetty is eventually transported rather than executed.

With Hetty's exit from the scene and Arthur's return, Adam reassesses his attitude toward the latter and discovers that he no longer wishes to be revenged upon the young squire. Walking through the environs where he had fought with

Arthur, Adam now sees the wood as "the boundary mark of his youth—the sign, to him, of the time when some of his earliest, strongest feelings had left him." At this point he meets Arthur, who is also walking remorsefully through the wood. The impulse to inflict pain upon Arthur is no longer a part of Adam, particularly when he sees in Arthur's face unmistakable signs of the kind of suffering he has known so well himself: "Adam knew what suffering was—he could not lay a cruel finger on a bruised man. He felt no impulse that he needed to resist. . . ." Adam tells Arthur: " 'If I can help to mend anything, I will. Anger 'ull mend nothing, I know. We've had enough o' that.' " But when Arthur starts talking about making amends to the Poysers for what has happened, Adam begins to feel "his old severity returning": " 'The time's past for that, sir. A man should make sacrifices to keep clear of doing a wrong; sacrifices won't undo it when it's done . . . I don't see how the thing's to be made any other than hard. There's a sort o' damage. . .that can't be made up for' " [5,XLVII]. Adam has learned that "sacrifice" is desirable *before* the fact and not after it, but he is indignant with Arthur. Arthur reminds Adam that the future is more important than the satisfaction of one's momentary indignation. Despite the recent death of his grandfather and his coming into the Donnithorne estates, Arthur has resolved to make the sacrifice of going away for a number of years, hoping that by doing so he may prevent the Poysers and Adam himself from moving away and thus disrupting the community. Arthur concludes his plea against "unreasonable conduct" with these words (5,XLVIII): " 'Perhaps you've never done anything you've had bitterly to repent of in your life, Adam; if you had, you would be more generous. You would know then that it's worse for me than for you . . . Shan't I carry the thought of her about with me as much as you will? And don't you think you would suffer more if you'd been in fault?' " Adam, who is of course no stranger to such suffering, is deeply moved by what Arthur says and resolves to help keep the community together in Arthur's absence. His response to Arthur is another crucial moment in the process of his movement toward moral vision:

> 'It's true what you say, sir: I'm hard—it's in my
> nature. I was too hard with my father, for doing wrong.
> I've been a bit hard t' everybody but *her.* I felt as if
> nobody pitied her enough—her suffering cut into me so;
> and when I thought the folks at the Farm were too hard
> with her, I said I'd never be hard to anybody myself
> again. But feeling overmuch about her has perhaps
> made me unfair to you. I've known what it is in my life
> to repent and feel it's too late: I felt I'd been too harsh to
> my father when he was gone from me—I feel it now,
> when I think of him. I've no right to be hard towards
> them as have done wrong and repent . . . I'll stay, sir:
> I'll do the best I can. It's all I've got to think of now—to
> do my work well, and make the world a bit better place
> for them as can enjoy it.' (5,XLVIII)

At the end of this speech Adam shakes hands with Arthur,
"feeling that sorrow was more bearable now hatred was
gone."

Adam's statement indicates that he has reached the final
stage of his psychic development, that of fellow-feeling and
objective moral vision. He has recognized and repented of the
"hardness" in his nature before; now he also sees that the
mission of man upon this earth is not to judge others but to
"make the world a bit better place for them" through feeling
and sympathetic understanding. This is the conversion
George Eliot wishes for her readers as well as her characters.
Adam's is a moral baptism, the waters of which we are meant
to take upon ourselves in our everyday relations with our
neighbors. For George Eliot, as for Dickens, it is of
paramount importance that people "feel enough," as Adam
puts it; without feeling, life is devoid of human fulfillment
and spiritual meaning.

Book 6 of *Adam Bede* is concerned chiefly with getting
Adam and Dinah together at last as a kind of final
apotheosis. What is constantly emphasized in the novel's
final pages is Adam's ever-growing sympathy for others and
the moral importance, for him and for others, of this new-
found fellow feeling. Adam still talks occasionally about the

necessity of doing one's work well, but he now says such things with a different emphasis: " 'A good solid bit o' work lasts: if it's only laying a floor down, somebody's the better for it being done well, besides the man as does it' " [6, L]. The "somebody" was missing from Adam's exhortation to his fellow workmen in the novel's opening chapter.

George Eliot now pauses to expatiate once again upon the moral process she has been at such pains to describe and define throughout the course of *Adam Bede:*

> in the last years or so, Adam had been getting more and more indulgent toward Seth. It was part of that growing tenderness which came from the sorrow at work within him.
>
> For Adam . . . had not outlived his sorrow—had not felt it slip from him as a temporary burthen, and leave him the same man again. Do any of us? God forbid. It would be a poor result of all our anguish and our wrestling, if we won nothing but our old selves at the end of it—if we could return to the same blind loves, the same self-confident blame, the same light thoughts of human suffering, the same frivolous gossip over blighted human lives. . . . Let us rather be thankful that our sorrow lives in us as an indestructible force, only changing its form, as forces do, and passing from pain into sympathy—the one poor word which includes all our best insight and our best love . . . . [T]his transformation of pain into sympathy had [not] completely taken place in Adam yet. . . . He did not know that the power of loving was all the while gaining new force within him; that the new sensibilities bought by deep experience were so many new fibres by which it was . . . necessary to him, that his nature should intertwine with another. Yet he was aware that common affection and friendship were more precious to him than they used to be. . . . (6, L)

In this passage George Eliot speaks explicitly about the transformation of pain into sympathy and of sympathy into love, of "sorrow" as a prerequisite of "tenderness." Adam's growing tenderness results from the sorrow at work within him. Personal suffering, for George Eliot as for Dickens, is the most effective destroyer of blindness, unimpaired self-confidence, callousness toward others, and frivolity in human relations. It never leaves us shallowly the same. "All our best insight and our best love" are included in that sympathy for others which grows out of suffering. Thus with Adam's growing fellow feeling comes the power to love once again. His "new sensibilities bought by deep experience" incline him toward that kind of selfless love which is the most complete denial of egoism—and he falls in love with Dinah. The increased importance for him of affection and friendship and his new interest in and sympathy for his neighbors are concomitants of his capacity to love a woman once again. Like Amelia in *Vanity Fair,* Adam discovers the need to "intertwine" his life inexorably with somebody else's: self-sufficiency is a dead end. Love for others—the ultimate exorcism of egoism—is the chief result of his moral education. Adam's ordeal is therefore also his moral salvation. He can now love Dinah. He needs only to discover her love for him—in which he is helped considerably by the keen instincts of his mother.

Lisbeth has detected Dinah's attraction to Adam and announces her discovery one Sunday morning. The announcement speeds Adam's recognition of his own regenerated capacity to love:

> Again and again his vision was interrupted by wonder at the strength of his own feeling, at the strength and sweetness of this new love—almost like the wonder a man feels at the added power he finds in himself for an art which he had laid aside for a space. How is it that the poets have said so many fine things about our first love, so few about our later love? . . . The boy's flute-like voice has its own spring charm; but the man should yield a richer, deeper music. (6, LI)

That "richer, deeper music" is the deeper *feeling* which is the result of experience, disappointment, and suffering.

Adam expresses his new feeling to Dinah when he proposes to her: " 'it's the same with love and happiness as with sorrow—the more we know of it the better we can feel what other people's lives are or might be, and so we shall only

be more tender to 'em, and wishful to help 'em. The more
knowledge a man has, the better he'll do 's work; and feeling's
a sort o' knowledge' " [6, LII]. "Feeling," which is
"knowledge," makes one more sympathetic to and understanding of "other people's lives"; such feeling can only be
born of experience, of suffering. Adam muses upon this
theme once again after his proposal to Dinah has met with an
equivocal negative on the ground that marriage would interfere with her missionary work: " 'I should never ha' come
to know that [Dinah's] love 'ud be the greatest o' blessings to
me, if what I counted a blessing hadn't been wrenched and
torn away from me, and left me with a greater and a better
comfort' " [6, LIII]. As Bartle Massey once said, " 'There
may good come out of [suffering] that we don't see' "—and
here is George Eliot's most explicit expression of that good.
The movement from self-absorption to self-knowledge carries
with it a sorrow that gives the sensibility both an emotional
and a moral expansion.

> [T] he fuller life which a sad experience has brought us is
> worth our own personal share of pain; surely it is not
> possible to feel otherwise, any more than it would be
> possible for a man with cataract to regret the painful
> process by which his dim blurred sight of men as trees
> walking had been exchanged for clear outline and ef-
> fulgent day. The growth of higher feeling within us is
> like the growth of faculty, bringing with it a sense of
> added strength: we can no more wish to return to a
> narrower sympathy, than a painter or a musician can
> wish to return to his cruder manner, or a philosopher to
> his less complete formula . . . [Thus Adam's] love for
> Dinah was better and more precious to him; for it was
> the outgrowth of that fuller life which had come to him
> from his acquaintance with deep sorrow. (6, LIV)

Suffering, for George Eliot, is purgative; it brings "higher
feeling" and "added strength." The movement from
"narrower sympathy" to a "fuller life" comes, she says here,
from "acquaintance with deep sorrow," which also brings
with it a transformation of "blurred" vision into "clear outline
and effulgent day." The spiritual expansion resulting from

suffering deflates self and pride and replaces them with increased fellow feeling and sharpened moral vision.

Dinah, like Adam, finally realizes that there can be as much of the devil in duty as in sin, and accepts Adam. They are married by Mr. Irwine, who reflects appropriately upon the "better harvest from that painful seed-time" he had witnessed not long before. And the novel's Epilogue, which gives us a brief picture of Adam and Dinah seven years after their marriage, concludes on a note equally appropriate to all that has gone before. " 'Come in, Adam, and rest,' " says Dinah; " 'it has been a hard day for thee.' "

II

Middlemarch (1871-72) abounds with egoists. Lydgate's egoism, his "spots of commonness," resides in his numerous prejudices, many of which are a result of the pride he feels in his birth, his immaculate gentility, and his intellectual gifts and energies. Rosamond is completely self-absorbed, a total solipsist incapable of thinking of anyone or anything beyond her own immediate wants. Fred Vincy's egoism lies in the self-indulgence of an unreflecting carelessness. Bulstrode's egoism is inseparable from his ponderous self-righteousness and self-conceit. Casaubon's incapacity to feel for others and his monomaniac pursuit of his own illusory goals are symptoms of his heartless egoism.

George Eliot's articulation in this novel of her theme of the horrors of solipsism, however, resides primarily in the person of Dorothea Brooke. Dorothea is the novel's central character, and her psychological development interests the author more than anything else in *Middlemarch*. The moral development (or lack thereof) of the other characters in the novel is of great importance, of course, for one of the novel's paramount themes is the interconnectedness of all existences. As a matter of convenience I shall focus on Dorothea. But in each of the various stories that *Middlemarch* tells, the movement toward or away from moral vision is again one of George Eliot's constant concerns. Moral growth or stagnation is the theme in each case. Dorothea's story is simply the most important among others—and perhaps the most interesting.

Dorothea's egoism is not as easily identifiable as is that of the other major characters in the novel. But while it is much more subtle, it is no less radical than theirs; and it is fundamental to the story of her moral growth. Dorothea's egoism lies primarily in self-indulgence born of a combination of blind idealism, lack of intellectual discrimination and common sense, and stubborn and misplaced self-confidence. Egoism is no less a flaw which suffering has to mend just because it happens to take the form of a vision of duty. As in *Adam Bede,* there can be as much of the devil in duty as in sin. Like Adam, Dorothea is fundamentally a good person. Her self-indulgent pride, however, is a result not of hard-heartedness but of a sentimental, idealistic, and obstinate failure to *see,* to assess both herself and others correctly. She lacks both self-knowledge and worldly wisdom but feels, like Isabel Archer, that she has both. Self-confidence and a resulting self-indulgence are the cornerstones of both her egoism and the near-tragedy of her life. The novel traces her development from this state of self-delusion to one, finally, of self-knowledge, and by the end of the novel Dorothea's blind self-indulgence has been replaced by objective moral vision and common sense born of a fuller knowledge of herself and the world she lives in.

Dorothea is introduced in the opening pages of the novel as a young woman with less common sense than her younger sister Celia. Her lack of judgment is attributed to a "love of extremes" and an "insistence on regulating life according to notions" both eccentric and inflexible: "Her mind was theoretic, and yearned by its nature after some lofty conception of the world . . . [S]he was enamoured of intensity and greatness, and rash in embracing whatever seemed to her to have those aspects . . ." [1, 1]. Here, in language similar indeed to that James was to use a few years later in describing the mind of Isabel Archer, George Eliot illuminates the basic elements of Dorothea's moral shallowness. To be both "theoretic" and "rash" is quite clearly to be on dangerous ground. Dorothea dreams of marrying a man like Hooker or Milton, the major advantage of such a marriage being, apparently, that one's husband could be "a sort of father, and could teach you Hebrew." Her idealism is not unlike that of Don Quixote, with whom she is explicitly compared in Chapter 2. In a world devoid both of meaning and of God—and in which, therefore, a modern Saint Theresa is an impossibility—Dorothea dreams of martyrdom, of the delight of self-sacrifice, and thinks of herself as being above worldly phenomena—such as physical love, for example. It is no accident that her nickname is that of an extinct animal ("Dodo"). When she first meets Mr. Casaubon she thinks he resembles Locke and dreams of the self-mortification (Celia calls it simply "giving up") available in marriage to such a man. Casaubon, of course, is a pathetically empty man, cold and humorless, whose "scholarship" is vacuous. But Dorothea dreams of "spiritual communion" with him; and George Eliot defines her particular form of blindness at this point as a penchant for making "large inferences" based on small (or non-existent) facts and having at her command therefore, like Elizabeth Bennet, a too "liberal allowance of conclusions."

For Dorothea, Casaubon becomes magnified into "a living Bossuet," a "modern Augustine who united the glories of doctor and saint." The narrator of *Middlemarch,* never shy, says that Dorothea's "interpretations are illimitable . . . and coloured by a diffused thimbleful of matter in the shape of knowledge." Her "notions about marriage took their colour entirely from an exalted enthusiasm about the ends of life, an enthusiasm which was lit chiefly by its own fire . . ." [1, 3]. Dorothea's ideas are self-reflexive; they feed on themselves. Marriage to Casaubon seems to her to provide an ample opportunity for the self-sacrifice and blind attachment her ardent nature craves. Her self-blinding vision of duty obscures for her both Casaubon's real nature and her own, which is not really suited to the kind of existence she thinks she wants. Her worship of Casaubon becomes an extreme form of self-

indulgence, perversely and stubbornly reinforced by the un-
enthusiastic assessment of her infatuation offered by relatives
and friends. Marriage to Casaubon, she thinks, will enlarge
her mind and thus make her a freer woman; "It would be like
marrying Pascal." Such a marriage would enable her to "see
how it was possible to lead a grand life here—now—in
England." Dorothea fails to see that such a life is *not* possible
here—now—in England, that even were such a life possible it
would not be possible as Casaubon's wife, and that in any
case such a life, remote from physical reality, would not
satisfy her. What she really needs as an object of devotion is a
genuine husband and a family; she is temperamentally unsuited, as she will discover, to become the servant of a narrow
and passionless man. Her physical short-sightedness, a symbol of her psychological condition, leads her to think of
marriage with Casaubon as an event which could open up to
her "the treasures of past ages" and provide her with
"understanding, sympathy, and guidance"—precisely the
things her marriage to Casaubon will make it impossible for
her to have. In all of this she is, as the narrator says, both
"wilful" and "blind"; and George Eliot emphasizes this
assessment in the epigraph for Chapter 4: "Our deeds are
fetters that we forge ourselves."

As Dorothea's betrothal to Casaubon edges closer and
closer to becoming a reality, Celia and her uncle become
more energetic in their warnings. But Casaubon's outrageously frigid letter of proposal merely confirms
Dorothea's belief in his superiority. She thinks that "a fuller
life was opening before her"; but what has really happened,
Geoge Eliot is quick to tell us, is that "the radiance of her
transfigured girlhood fell on the first object that came within
its level." Dorothea is grateful to Casaubon for "loving" her,
but he has never said that he does—and indeed he does not.
This "Protestant Pope" merely sees Dorothea as a potentially
valuable amanuensis, a helpmate in his arid labors. Were
Dorothea possessed of the slightest modicum of self-
knowledge one might say that the situation was not entirely
unlike that of St. John Rivers and Jane Eyre. When, to the

astonishment of all, the engagement is finally announced, Chettam calls Casaubon a "mummy" and Mrs. Cadwallader labels him a "bladder for dried peas." And they are right. Mr. Casaubon, who thinks that the poets have "exaggerated the force of masculine passion" and feels none himself, is hardly likely to become more passionate. Dorothea, meanwhile, does not inflame him further by telling him that she expects to perform for him the combined duties of Milton's daughters. Dorothea's "alleged cleverness," says the author at this point, is really a rampant naivety; she is unable to see "the emptiness of other people's pretensions" because she has so many of her own.

The marriage is doomed from the beginning, even as the bride and groom prepare to depart on their honeymoon to Rome (where the groom plans to spend most of his time in the Vatican Museum). Each partner in the marriage has gravely misjudged the other. For Dorothea, as we have seen, Casaubon is "the mere occasion which has set alight the fine inflammable material of her youthful illusions." But Casaubon too is "the centre of his own world," and he imagines that he has married a woman with no ideas other than the central one of serving him. He does not understand that such a life is not enough for Dorothea—indeed, how should he, when Dorothea herself does not understand this? Each of them has constructed a mental image of the other, a metaphor which expresses and contains only that which each sees or wants to see in the other. George Eliot does not say that this is the case, but her intimation of it is unmistakable: "we all of us, grave or light, get our thoughts entangled in metaphors, and act fatally on the strength of them" [1, 10]. Dorothea is yearning for a life "filled with action at once rational and ardent," and she is the only person among those who know her husband who believes that marriage to him can provide her with such a life. When Lady Chettam remarks to Mrs. Cadwallader that Dorothea is "headstrong," the rector's wife replies that Dorothea will hate her husband before they have been married a year.

That prediction, as it turns out, is a conservative one.

For when we next see Dorothea, in Rome six weeks after her marriage, her disillusionment has already begun. Though she has not as yet fully discerned that her blind self-indulgence could well turn out to be an instrument of destruction for her marriage, she has begun to see that she may have misjudged both her husband and herself. He has not as yet opened to her a fuller life; and she is temperamentally unsuited to such a narrow one. Dorothea, who has "turned all her small allowance of knowledge into principles," is now "in tumultuous preoccupation with her personal lot." She has been experiencing the ruins of Rome epistemologically, beginning to find in them a tangible analogue of the erosion of her own enthusiasms and expectations. Like Isabel Archer, Dorothea examines her disappointment in some detail during an extended retrospective meditation. George Eliot says:

> [W]e begin by knowing little and believing much, and we sometimes end by inverting the quantities. Still . . . Mr. Casaubon . . . had not actively assisted in creating any illusions about himself. . . . [I]n the weeks since her marriage, Dorothea had not distinctly observed, but felt with a stifling depression, that the large vistas and wide fresh air which she had dreamed of finding in her husband's mind were replaced by anterooms and winding passages which seemed to lead nowhither . . . Having once embarked on your marital voyage, it is impossible not to be aware that you make no way and that the sea is not within sight—that, in fact, you are exploring an enclosed basin. . . .[H]er husband . . . had begun to affect her with a sort of mental shiver: he had perhaps the best intention of acquitting himself worthily, but only of acquitting himself. (2,20)

It is necessary to Dorothea that she feel that her devotedness is worthy of its object, and now, for the first time, she is beginning to wonder if it is. Her loving reverence has been jarred by a wider acquaintance with her husband. Dorothea began by "knowing little and believing much"—believing, that is, what she wanted to believe in order to satisfy her own egoistic needs; and she is in the process now of "inverting the quantities"—that is, more and more she is believing little and knowing much. The fact that Casaubon "had not actively assisted in creating any illusions about himself" underlines the importance of Dorothea's own sentimental view of him before their marriage. Her blindness is responsible for her disillusionment; Casaubon himself is the same man, only now seen by her more fully. Dorothea's perception, and not the object of that perception, is what is most materially changed; it was more or less the same with Elizabeth in her relations with Darcy in *Pride and Prejudice*. During their courtship Casaubon was not acting in any way; Dorothea simply read him incorrectly. He is shallower, more egotistical, than she had thought, and in discovering this Dorothea begins to understand more fully both her own shallowness of judgment and her own real emotional needs. Her discovery that the "large vistas" she had wanted and expected to find as a result of her marriage "lead nowhither" but to "an enclosed basin" due to Casaubon's arid narrow-mindedness marks the onset of her disillusionment and thus also the beginning of her "education."

There follows almost immediately a passage which details the specific reasons Dorothea has for that "mental shiver" of hers in the presence of her husband:

> There is hardly any contact more depressing to a young ardent creature than that of a mind in which years full of knowledge seem to have issued in a blank absence of interest or sympathy . . . [S]he was gradually ceasing to expect with her former delightful confidence that she should see any wide opening where she followed him . . . These [things] might have remained longer unfelt by Dorothea if she had been encouraged to pour forth her . . . . feeling—if he would have held her hands between his and listened with the delight of tenderness and understanding to all the little histories which made up her experience, and would have given her the same sort of intimacy in return . . . or if she could have fed her affection with those childlike caresses which are the bent of every sweet woman, who has begun by showering kisses on the hard pate of her bald doll, creating a happy soul within that woodenness from the wealth of her own love. . . . Mr Casaubon . . . [would only

pronounce] her, with his unfailing propriety, to be of a most affectionate and truly feminine nature, indicating at the same time by politely reaching a chair for her that he regarded these manifestations as rather crude and startling. . . . She was humiliated to find herself a mere victim of feeling . . . She was as blind to his inward troubles as he to hers . . .[It all seemed to her] like a catastrophe, changing all prospects . . .[T]he . . . years to come [were] not so clear to her as [they] had been. (2, 20)

The imagery here denotes constriction, narrowing, shrinking. As Dorothea's understanding of her husband and herself widens she begins to see how effectively she has imprisoned herself through her own egoism and that of her husband. As her sense of Casaubon's lack of feeling becomes more pronounced she begins to understand that her mistake was overabundance of feeling; she is a "victim" of it. George Eliot means us to see that what has led Dorothea astray is her tendency to indulge her ardent and untutored feelings, which more often than not are misplaced as a result of a metaphysical vision of duty which blinds her to hard reality. George Eliot argues in all of her novels for sympathy for one's neighbors, feeling for one's fellows: yet here she also demonstrates the dangers of an excess of misplaced feeling. Feeling, when it annihilates common sense and reason, tends to sentimentalize, to distort, objects of vision into things we would like them to be. We fail to see things clearly due to sub-jectification. This was Emma Woodhouse's deficiency, and it is Dorothea's as well in a different context. In the case of both, too often, subject determines object and gives it color; objective vision disappears. The self-indulgence born of self-absorption is capable of distorting the epistemological balance of everything outside of us. Dorothea's sense of "duty," the passage tells us, has "blinded" her to her husband's real nature, just as his own self-absorption has blinded Casaubon to Dorothea's desires and needs. The last part of the passage suggests, however, that Dorothea's mode of vision is undergoing some rearrangement. The future is not so clear to her as it once was, which means that she is beginning to see it differently. Her new vision parallels the beginning of her discovery of her own nature and her real needs as a woman and a wife.

The first formal visit to Dorothea of Will Ladislaw helps shake her out of her "self-absorbed discontent," though after Will leaves Dorothea is surprised at her own quick readiness to confide in him. She is amazed to discover also that her view of her marriage seems unlike that of everyone else around her. She sees that she "must have made some original romance for herself in this marriage," and her husband's particular crustiness re-enforces her suspicion that for her "some dear expectation" has died that day. The day has indeed been a tumultuous one for Dorothea; George Eliot sums it up tersely:

> We are all of us born in moral stupidity, taking the world as an udder to feed our supreme selves. Dorothea had early begun to emerge from that stupidity, but yet it had been easier to her to imagine how she would devote herself to Mr Casaubon, and become wise and strong in his strength and wisdom, than to conceive with that distinctiveness which is no longer reflection but feeling—an idea wrought back to the directness of sense, like the solidity of objects—that he had an equivalent centre of self, whence lights and shadows must always fall with a certain difference. (2,21)

The paramount image here is an emblem of egoism, recalling as it does the old idea of the world as a great breast at which only fools suck. "Moral stupidity" is putting one's self before the world, feeding from it instead of feeding it. Dorothea's self-conceit consists in just this—that she has been thinking of her husband as a great man who will make her a great woman. Such "feeding" has obliterated for her his true nature, which requires to be fed without hope of gain or advancement to the feeder. She must give all, for he has nothing to give. Dorothea, who has hoped to become wise as his wife, is beginning to discover that the great breast contains, in Mrs. Cadwallader's words, only "dried peas," and that a life of abject giving, getting nothing in return, will not suit her after all. Thus she is beginning to "emerge" from "moral stupidity"; she is slowly returning "to the directness of sense." Mr. Casaubon, she discovers, has an ego; and this discovery is a prerequisite to the discovery of her own.

Despite Dorothea's slowly growing self-awareness her immense naivety is still insisted upon by the author again and again. As a child, says George Eliot, Dorothea had "believed in the gratitude of wasps"; as a woman her paramount desire is to "make life beautiful" for "everybody." During his second visit to Dorothea, Will calls it all a "fanaticism of sympathy. . . .It is of no use to try and take care of all the world. . . . .Would you turn all the youth of the world into a tragic chorus, wailing and moralising over misery? I suspect that you have some false belief in the virtues of misery, and want to make your life a martyrdom' " [2, 22]. Will speaks, of course, with the author's approval; misery is indeed no virtue, and Dorothea's fanaticism does seem to preclude any possibility of genuine happiness. And martyrdom is beyond both her reach and her desire, if she only knew it. Dorothea's reply to him is ingenuously perfect: " 'I cannot help believing in glorious things in a blind sort of way.' " There is nothing wrong, for George Eliot, with believing in goodness, glory and virtue so long as one has one's eyes open and is not "blind" to the objective here-and-now. Dorothea's failure so far has resulted from her inability to combine idealism with common sense and lucid judgment.

When we next see Dorothea it is just after her return to Lowick from Rome. We encounter her as she meditates even more candidly upon the disillusionment marriage has brought with it. This moment is a pivotal one as far as Dorothea's moral education is concerned; I must quote from the novel at some length:

> The very furniture in the room seemed to have shrunk since she saw it before. . . . The bright fire of dry oak-boughs burning on logs seemed an incongruous renewal of life and glow—like the figure of Dorothea herself. . . . .The duties of her married life, contemplated as so great beforehand, seemed to be shrinking with the furniture and the white vapour-walled landscape. The clear heights where she expected to walk in full communion

had become difficult to see even in her imagination. . . .
When would the days begin of that active wifely devotion which was to strengthen her husband's life and exalt
her own? Never perhaps. . . .[She still hoped that] duty
would present itself in some new form of inspiration and
give a new meaning to wifely love.

Meanwhile . . . there was the stifling oppression of
that gentlewoman's world . . . .Marriage had not even
filled her leisure with the ruminant joy of unchecked
tenderness. Her blooming full-pulsed youth stood there
in a moral imprisonment which made itself one with the
chill, colourless, narrowed landscape, with the shrunken
furniture, the never-read books, and the ghostly stag in a
pale fantastic world. . . . All existence seemed to beat
with a lower pulse than her own, and her religious faith
was a solitary cry, the struggle out of a nightmare in
which every object was withering and shrinking away
from her. Each remembered thing in the room was dis-
enchanted . . . till her wandering gaze came to the
group of miniatures, and meaning: it was the miniature
of Mr Casaubon's aunt Julia, who had made the unfortunate marriage—of Will Ladislaw's grandmother . . .
What breadths of experience Dorothea seemed to have
passed over since she first looked at this miniature! She
felt a new companionship with it. . . . Here was a
woman who had known some difficulty about marriage.
Nay, the colours deepened, the lips and chin seemed to
get larger, the hair and eyes seemed to be sending out
light, the face was masculine, and beamed on her with
that full gaze which tells her on whom it falls that she is
too interesting for the slightest movement of her eyelid
to pass unnoticed and uninterpreted. The vivid presentation came like a pleasant glow to Dorothea: she
felt herself smiling . . . . (3, 28)

In this remarkable passage Dorothea experiences her surroundings epistemologically; topography becomes a
metaphor for her state of mind. Dorothea sees Lowick in
terms of her own shrunken expectations and disillusionment.
She no longer has any misconceptions as to the "duties of her
married life"; the "clear heights where she expected to walk
in full communion" have become shrouded by disappointment. They are difficult to see now, even in her imagination;
that is, imagination is being subdued by reason, a consumma-

tion always devoutly to be wished for for George Eliot—for subjectivity is always self-blinding. The substitution of a sort of metaphysical dimness where before there was brightness (that is, more confidence in the powers of perception), a phenomenon of revised vision which is insisted upon again and again by the language of this passage, epitomizes also a rearrangement of Dorothea's own bright but unenlightened hopes. She still hopes that some form of "duty" and "inspiration" may possibly come her way, but in the meantime all she feels is "oppression" and uselessness. She has not even found any "tenderness" in her marriage. George Eliot says very directly indeed that Dorothea's "imprisonment" is a "moral" one, and that she feels her life becoming as "chill," "colourless," and "narrowed" as the "landscape" she ponders from the window of her room at Lowick. Dorothea's "moral imprisonment," however, is mostly her own doing, for her former "ideas and hopes" were based primarily on stubborn self-confidence, misjudgment, misplaced idealism, and inexperience. The "withering" and "shrinking" of Dorothea's "disenchantment" abates, however, as she gazes at the group of miniatures and, as George Eliot is careful to tell us, "meaning." Dorothea now identifies herself with her husband's aunt Julia, who also made an "unfortunate marriage." She begins to feel that she has "passed over" great "breadths of experience" since she last looked at the miniature, and indeed she has. She has both recognized the inadequacy of her marriage to Casaubon and, as the final sentences of the passage quoted make clear, she has begun to feel the attraction Will Ladislaw has for her. She had seen a great deal of Will while in Rome. Her recognition of her preference for his company is not as yet, perhaps, a totally conscious one, but it is clearly present within her. At the end of the passage, when Aunt Julia commences to look, to Dorothea, like Will, it is clear that Dorothea has at least begun to accept the idea that she has been wrong. She had assessed both her husband and her own nature incorrectly. The kind of man who would in all probability make her happy is not a dry and middle-aged modern Locke or Pascal but rather a young man both more ardent and less serious than her present husband. She is beginning to discover, in other words, that she is a woman who needs a man; this "vivid presentation" comes to Dorothea "like a pleasant glow."

(The withering oppression Dorothea feels in her narrowed and shrunken world, which the language of the passage insists upon again and again, is something we will encounter more than once in the course of this study—in *Daniel Deronda,* for example, and even more so in *The Portrait of A Lady.* The theme of "moral imprisonment" is as important for James as it is for George Eliot, and indeed it is probable that James, who read George Eliot avidly, had in mind such a passage as the one just quoted here, as well as several in *Daniel Deronda,* when he sat down to ponder the story of *The Portrait of A Lady* and the psyche of its famous heroine. James's comments about George Eliot and his own novel, made in his preface to *The Portrait of A Lady,* in essays on George Eliot's novels, and elsewhere, tend to substantiate these hypotheses.)

As time passes Dorothea begins to find that she has less and less patience with her husband at a time when he, a man with a heart condition which is apparently now being aggravated by an increasingly unsatisfactory home life, needs it most. Casaubon, disillusioned in his young wife, treats her less affectionately than politely and often becomes vexed with her upon slight provocation. "Dorothea thought she could have been patient with John Milton, but she had never imagined him behaving . . . stupidly undiscerning and odiously unjust" [3, 29]. She finds some pleasure in correspondence with Will, in which he continually chides her for her "fanatical sympathy."

Some time later, when Will visits Lowick, Dorothea tells him that it has always seemed to her that she ought to use her life " 'to help some one who did great works, so that his burthen might be lighter,' " but she says this less emphatically than nostalgically; and in fact, says George Eliot, Dorothea is "no longer struggling against the perception of facts, but adjusting herself to their clearest perception. . . ." Dorothea's vision, as her moral education advances, becomes less subjective and less obstinately selective. And as she becomes increasingly aware of her husband's failures and of her own misconceptions, her attitude toward Casaubon becomes more and more governed by pity and loyalty and less and less by self-satisfying visions of her own martyrdom. The slowly sharpening focus of Dorothea's perception, emphasized by George Eliot again and again, is a concomitant of her new objectivity.

As Dorothea gets to know Will better, her husband becomes increasingly jealous of his cousin and begins to fancy Ladislaw plotting with Dorothea against him. Dorothea, who is incapable of imagining such emotions in the man she has married, goes confidently on from one trumped-up interest to the next, never wholly suspecting the depth of emotion beside her: "her blindness to whatever did not lie in her own pure purpose carried her safely by the side of precipices where vision would have been perilous with fear" [4, 37]. The egoist, no less an egoist for "pure purpose," sees only what concerns himself and is unable, because of the shallowness of his perception, to see into the hearts of others. It is, once again, a deficiency of *vision*—both physical and spiritual. George Eliot puts it, succinctly, another way: "Will not a tiny speck very close to our vision blot out the glory of the world, and leave only a margin by which we see the blot? I know no speck so troublesome as self"[4,42]. When "self" gets in the way of "vision," we fail to "see" the "world" and instead see only self. This is a further development of a principle George Eliot articulates earlier in the famous "pier-glass" passage (3,27), in which she says that for each of us the "candle of egoism" will reflect upon the surfaces of things in such a way as to ensure that we will see those surfaces only as our egoism makes them appear to us. Dorothea may be "pure" in spirit, but she has been spiritually blind; her egoism is in large measure the result in her of an imbalance of the epistemological elements of perception. Her "tendency to immoderate attachment," as Casaubon calls it, is the result of an imagination that cannot imagine beyond itself.

Casaubon's symptoms become more alarming. When Lydgate tells him that his death could come at any time, he rejects Dorothea's passionate sympathy and locks himself in his study, writing instructions for her use after his death. Such behavior calls up for Dorothea an image of "all the paths of her young hope which she should never find again . . . Was it her fault that she had believed in him . . . ?" The answer is—yes. It is her fault, for her husband, as we have been told, had never actively assisted in the creation of any illusions about himself; Dorothea created these for herself. But her disillusionment is a necessary part of her education in the art of moral vision, and she is learning that, like any other human being, she cannot exist solely by being useful and dutiful; she too needs love and mutual affection. She is not, in fact, temperamentally suited for the type of martyrdom she had yearned for. Even her vision of martyrdom was faulty, for instead of "fellowship in high knowledge" she has had to settle for "questionable riddle-guessing." Her existence is a tomb that locks her up from life—which, in the form of Will Ladislaw, seems to be receding into the distance.

When Casaubon asks her to promise him something without first knowing what it is, she assumes he wishes her to commit herself to finishing the endless and valueless scholarly tasks at which he has been laboring. In terror she pictures to herself "shattered mummies," "crushed ruins," "weariness and impatience," and working "as in a treadmill fruitlessly"—and she hesitates. Casaubon, who wants her to promise not to marry Will Ladislaw after his death, is deeply hurt by her hesitation. Dorothea, however, ultimately decides that "she must bind herself to a fellowship from which she shrank." Having seen how much she has idealized her marriage, Dorothea is prepared, at last, to blame herself and yield to her husband's wishes, whatever they might be. By this time, however, Casaubon is dead, and his testamentary codicil relating to Dorothea and Will becomes known to all.

Dorothea's response to the news that her husband's will forbids her to marry Ladislaw upon pain of disinheritance moves her further along the path of self-knowledge; she had

been groping her way slowly before, but now her moral
education is quickly accelerated: "her life was taking on a
new form. . . . Everything was changing its aspect: her
husband's conduct, her own duteous feeling towards him,
every struggle between them—and yet more, her whole relation to Will Ladislaw. Her world was in a state of convulsive
change. . . . [She now felt] a violent shock of repulsion from
her departed husband . . ." [5, 50]. The "stirring of new
organs," together with the explicit suggestion of a romantic
attachment to Will, stimulates further mental reorganization
on Dorothea's part. Her discovery of "hidden alienation"
and "suspicion" in her late marriage begins to subjugate her
past "pity" for Casaubon and puts in its place "only the
retrospect of painful subjection to a husband whose thoughts
had been lower than she had believed, whose exorbitant
claims for himself had . . . blinded [him]." Seeing that she
had misjudged Casaubon, Dorothea's faith in her own
powers of perception begins to waver even more violently. As
it does so she sees more and more to like in Will, who is
capable of entering "into everyone's feelings, and [who]
could take the pressure of their thought instead of urging his
own with iron resistance." The act of entering into the
thoughts of others instead of constantly urging one's own is
an act of which Dorothea heretofore has been largely incapable. It is an important element of her widening moral vision that, as her admiration for Will increases, she begins to
think of others more than of herself.

Sometime later, when Will confesses to Dorothea his
love for her, she finally begins to realize how important the
genuine love of a man is to her. Her reaction to his declaration is one of unmitigated (but unexpressed) joy. Indeed, "It
was all one flash to Dorothea"; she needs this relationship to
give her life meaning and interest, and she finally understands
this. How much she needs Will she has still to discover;
however, the small amount of the rest of the novel that concerns Dorothea is the dénouement of her story. While
Lydgate and Bulstrode face great crises in these final sections,
Dorothea's battle is almost over. She and Will have yet, of

course, to agree on marriage, but Dorothea's spiritual ordeal has for the most part been resolved by the forces of reason. She realizes that martyrdom and sainthood, the apparent concomitants of "duty," are empty for her, and that she, like most others, needs human and not metaphysical love.

Dorothea's friends, meanwhile, watch her closely in case she should "fall under some new illusion," and they think that perhaps she has fallen under one when she undertakes a spirited defense of Lydgate, who has been accused of impropriety in his association with the unfortunate Bulstrode. Despite her quixotism, Dorothea happens to be right this time. She feels a peculiar kinship with the idealistic and egotistical Lydgate and tells him how easy it is for her to sympathize with one " 'who had meant to lead a higher life than the common, and to find out better ways.' " When Lydgate tells her that he is particularly concerned for his wife, who married him " 'without knowing what she was going into,' " Dorothea, "with keen memory of her own life," is drawn even closer to him in sympathy. She herself knows well how destructive can be the "invisible barriers" between husband and wife. Lydgate, on his part, wonders about her life: " 'Casaubon must have raised some heroic hallucination in her. I wonder if she could have any other sort of passion for a man . . . [H]er love might help a man more than her money' " [8,76]. Dorothea's "heroic hallucination," however, has been exploded, and she has become capable of another sort of passion for a man. That this is indeed the case becomes patently manifest even to Dorothea herself.

Dorothea, who has gone to see Rosamond Lydgate in order to explain and justify to her Lydgate's conduct (which he is unable to do himself), finds her and Will Ladislaw in what she considers a compromising tableau. She leaves quickly, goes about her business as usual, and then collapses when she gets home under the weight of bitter disappointment. In doubting Will's love for her she discovers at last her own passionate love for him:

the waves of suffering shook her too thoroughly to leave any power of thought. She could only cry in loud

whispers . . . after her lost belief which she had planted
and kept alive from a very little seed since the days in
Rome—after her lost joy of clinging with silent love and
faith to one who, misprized by others, was worthy in her
thought—after her sweet dim perspective of hope . . . .
[W]ith a full consciousness which had never awakened
before, she stretched out her arms towards him and
cried with bitter cries that their nearness was a parting
vision: she discovered her passion to herself in the un-
shrinking utterance of despair . . . [S]he had waked to a
new condition: she felt as if her soul had been liberated
from its terrible conflict. . . . (8, 80)

Dorothea's long-standing "silent love" for Will is finally
acknowledged to herself. It is love—not duty, devotion or
sacrifice—that she needs. Her "consciousness" is "full" now
because she has discovered her own nature, her own needs; it
had "never awakened before." In "discovering" her
"passion," Dorothea has literally discovered herself. Thus
she awakes "to a new condition," to a new feeling of
"liberation." For her too suffering has been productive; for
the fruit of her grief, as George Eliot goes on to make clear, is
rational thought and self-understanding.

It only remains, then, for Dorothea to make her
confession to Will himself, and it is settled; Casaubon's
suspicion, based perhaps on a clearer understanding of
Dorothea's nature than anyone, including Dorothea herself,
had thought possible, is justified. When Celia reminds
Dorothea that if she marries Will she will have to give up her
philanthropic plans for the improvement of mankind,
Dorothea replies simply that she has "never carried out any
plan yet.'"

In the Finale to *Middlemarch,* George Eliot delves briefly into Dorothea's future life and summarizes its meaning:

No life would have been possible to Dorothea which
was not filled with emotion, and she had now a life [as a
mother] filled with a beneficent activity which she had
not the doubtful pains of discovering and marking out
for herself . . . Many who knew her, thought it a pity
that so substantive and rare a creature should have been

absorbed into the life of another, and be only known in
a certain circle as a wife and mother. But no one stated
exactly what else there was in her power she ought
rather to have done. . . . Certainly the determining acts
of her life were not ideally beautiful. They were the mixed
result of young and noble impulse struggling amidst the
conditions of an imperfect social state, in which great
feelings will often take the aspect of error, and great faith
the aspect of illusion.

The final sentences (which could as well describe what
happens—more tragically—to Isabel Archer in *The Portrait
of A Lady*) deserve the most careful attention. Dorothea cannot be a Saint Theresa "here—now—in England" because
there is no room, no function, for sainthood in a society not
grounded on faith in any extra-societal foundation. In such a
society any individual is most completely fulfilled by doing
those things only which he or she is most humanly capable of
doing. When one yearns for religious justification in a world
without a Providence the result is "error" and "illusion."
"For there is no creature," concludes the Finale, "whose inward being is so strong that it is not greatly determined by
what lies outside it." Finding out what lies outside of her is
Dorothea's most important and significant accomplishment.
In doing so she also finds the life most suited to her—one
whose direction she need not keep on trying to "discover"
and "mark out for herself." As a wife and mother, Dorothea,
like Amelia Sedley, has satisfied her yearnings for devotion
and love. She has also done her "duty"; there is really
nothing else "she ought rather to have done." Like Lydgate,
Bulstrode, Casaubon, Fred, Rosamond and the other egoists
in this novel, Dorothea's self-absorption blinds her for some
time to her life's real duty—that is, being "absorbed into the
life of another." More fully than any of them, however, she
realizes her mistake, recognizes her own needs, and thus is
able to immerse herself in "beneficent activity" in behalf of
others—an apotheosis George Eliot, no feminist, argues and
hopes for. Like Dickens and Trollope, she sees salvation in
fellow feeling. Dorothea's story, only one of four in
Middlemarch, is probably the most illustrative of this general

theme and thus expresses in the telling of it—which both begins and ends the novel—George Eliot's most important lessons.

III

The egoism of Gwendolen Harleth in George Eliot's *Daniel Deronda* (1876) is patently less subtle than that of either Adam Bede or Dorothea Brooke. Because it is more deeply rooted, more radical, than theirs, Gwendolen's ultimate self-discovery and regeneration is also more convulsive and more dramatic.

Gwendolen's egoism is undoubtedly of a more orthodox variety than that of any protagonist we have encountered thus far in this study. She is selfish, willful, conceited, and arrogant, putting herself always at the center of all concerns and pursuing only those paths calculated to insure self-gratification and the satisfaction of personal ambition. Her egoism, more conventional and obvious than that of George Eliot's earlier protagonists, is perhaps more similar to that of a Paul Dombey. Like her predecessors in George Eliot's earlier novels, however, Gwendolen's ordeal of knowledge also is marked by definitive stages of moral development— specifically in its movement from self-absorption through despair to fellow feeling and more objective perception.

As is so often the case, Gwendolen is not the only egoist in George Eliot's novel. Grandcourt, who resembles Casaubon in some ways, is notable primarily for his possessiveness, selfishness, and self-content. His desire not only to possess but to dominate, to own, marks him throughout the novel as a figure of evil—one not unlike the most radical egoists of Henry James, as we shall see. Once again I shall concentrate in my discussion of *Daniel Deronda* upon the development and growth of a single character, in this case that of Gwendolen Harleth—ignoring, to the extent that it is possible to do so, the disastrous half of the novel that deals with Daniel Deronda and the Jewish question.

Perhaps no other character in English fiction has her thoughts and sentiments so minutely discussed and analyzed as does Gwendolen Harleth. In the development of Gwendolen's story George Eliot is at her very best. Gwendolen's mind itself is at the center of and provides the setting for some of the novel's most effective passages. The novel's major interest is that of Gwendolen's moral expansion, a psychological movement James, for example, both studied in detail and transferred to the realm of his own fictional world.

The novel's first section, which introduces us to Gwendolen *in medias res* (that is, *after* the action of the last half of Book 1 and most of Book 2), is entitled "The Spoiled Child." We come to it from a reading of George Eliot's general epigraph for *Daniel Deronda,* the first line of which is "Let thy chief terror be of thine own soul." Gwendolen has gone to Leubronn to escape the attentions of Grandcourt, who has offered her marriage despite the existence of his several children by a now-discarded mistress whom Gwendolen had met shortly before her flight abroad. As far as Gwendolen's ambitions in marriage are concerned, the wealthy, gentlemanly and respectable Grandcourt is satisfactory; but Gwendolen has promised his former mistress, Mrs. Glasher, that she will not marry Grandcourt and thus deprive Mrs. Glasher's children of their inheritance. When we first meet Gwendolen she is gambling recklessly at Leubronn; George Eliot describes her as having a "dynamic" form of beauty marred somewhat by an "evil genius" radiating "unrest rather than . . . undisturbed charm" and drawing the attention of others "coercively" rather than "consentingly." It is a purposefully ominous introduction. The novel's opening chapter goes on to embellish the initial unflattering impression we have of Gwendolen. She looks around the room "with a survey too markedly cold and neutral not to have in it a little of that nature which we call art concealing"; "she had visions of being followed by a *cortège* who would worship her as a goddess of luck"; her bad luck at the gambling tables merely makes her defiant and blind to "any end beyond the satisfaction of enraged existence," an attitude George Eliot labels "the puerile stupidity of a dominant impulse." Gwendolen's moral stupidity lies chiefly in her indulgence of her own feelings, which tend to be selfish and unenlightened, and in her pride. The sin of pride is reflected in the opinion of onlookers that, with her hair arranged in coils and in her green and silver habit, Gwendolen "has got herself up as a sort of serpent." George Eliot says: "In Gwendolen's habits of mind it had been taken for granted that she knew she was admirable and that she herself was admired." The first chapter ends with Gwendolen's assertion that she is always "bored"; she seems to feel that the world exists primarily in order to amuse her and that it is not doing a very satisfactory job. (We already know what George Eliot thinks of the "udder" theory, of which Gwendolen seems to be a partisan.) Gwendolen blames her bad gambling luck on Daniel Deronda, with whom she is as yet unacquainted but who has been watching her gamble with obvious disapproval. Thus our introduction to Gwendolen Harleth.

In Chapter 2 Gwendolen receives a letter from her mother announcing that the family's slender means have evaporated completely due to the failure of some investments. Gwendolen's disappointment, characteristically, is for herself rather than for her mother and her four younger "superfluous" sisters: "The implicit confidence that her destiny must be one of luxurious ease . . . had been . . . fed . . . by her youthful blood and that sense of superior claims which made a large part of her consciousness." Gwendolen's sense of her own superior claims is so strong within her that she feels no sorrow for the plight of her mother: "if Gwendolen had been at this moment disposed to feel pity, she would have bestowed it on herself—for was she not naturally and rightfully the chief object of her mamma's anxiety too?" Gwendolen, however, feels not pity but anger. Why should this happen to *her?* She resolves to sell a necklace in order to provide herself with one last stake at the gambling tables. She believes in her own luck:

> It is possible to have a strong self-love without any self-satisfaction, rather with a self-discontent which is the

> more intense because one's own little core of egoistic
> sensibility is a supreme care; but Gwendolen knew
> nothing of such inward strife. She had a *naive* delight in
> her fortunate self, which any but the harshest saintliness
> will have some indulgence for in a girl who had every
> day seen a pleasant reflection of that self in her friends'
> flattery as well as in the looking-glass. (1, 2)

Gwendolen's overmastering "delight" in herself, then, is her
most distinguishing characteristic—one which is the logical
result of an undisciplined and unenlightened bringing-up.
Gwendolen's egoism, her "self-love," is in large part a result
of naivety, of a faulty education, of precisely this absence of
"inward strife"; and it is to be one of Deronda's roles in the
novel to provide her, through his moral vision, with a
spiritual jolt which will lead her to "inward strife" and thence
to a more objective perspective upon herself and the rest of
the world. George Eliot's tone here is demonstrably less sympathetic than it is likely to be in passages dealing with her
other erring heroes and heroines; but then Gwendolen is
more blatantly in need of moral correction than any of them.
George Eliot, however, becomes more sympathetic to Gwendolen the more she moves, later on, toward moral vision. For
George Eliot was never wholly without the fellow feeling she
was constantly prescribing for her readers.

Gwendolen receives a package containing the necklace
she has just pawned—obviously from Deronda—and that
same day, obeying her mother's request, sets off on the return
trip to England, where she immediately chafes under the new
austerity conditions imposed by necessity upon the family
home at Offendene. As always, her concern is mainly for
herself; she has for years had a sense "that so exceptional a
person as herself could hardly remain in ordinary circumstances or in a social position less than advantageous" [1,
3]. While Gwendolen's mother worries about money, Gwendolen sits in front of her mirror likening herself to Saint
Cecilia. She resolutely refuses to give music lessons to her
younger sisters. When both her mother and her uncle, the
Rector of Pennicote, circuitously suggest to Gwendolen that
marriage would provide an avenue of escape from the vexa-

tion she feels at home, she makes it clear that she will marry only when doing so will bring her "social promotion" and still enable her to "do what she liked": "She meant to do what was pleasant to herself in a striking manner; or rather, whatever she could do so as to strike others with admiration . . ."[1,4]. Gwendolen is another for whom the rest of the world is considered an interested audience. Everything she does is the result of self-indulgence and pride; always she plays "the princess in exile," her "inborn energy of egoistic desire" unchecked by her mother or anyone else. "Egoism" and "egoistic" are terms George Eliot applies specifically to Gwendolen often throughout this novel; her view of Gwendolen in these early pages is neatly summarized in the epigraph for Chapter 5, a brief passage quoted from *Much Ado About Nothing:* "Her wit/Values itself so highly, that to her/All matter else seems weak."

The novel now goes back to the time of the family's first arrival at Offendene—the period preceding Gwendolen's flight abroad and the sudden reversal of the family's fortunes. Gwendolen's "egoistic ambitions" are occupying her mind. She dreams of becoming a great actress. She encourages a middle-aged clergyman of the neighborhood to fall in love with her and then laughs at him. She knows nothing, says George Eliot, about "human relations," and blames the unhappiness of her current life upon "the pettiness of circumstances" beyond her control. She has no "inward strife." Having little to amuse her, she encourages her cousin Rex Gascoigne to fall in love with her, doing, as always, exactly "what pleases" her: "Gwendolen was perfectly aware that her cousin was in love with her; but she had no idea that the matter was of any consequence, having never had the slightest visitation of painful love herself" [1, 7]. Gwendolen's inability to love, to put herself second to any other human being, defines the nature of her egoistic self-absorption and explains why, as George Eliot puts it, she is "apt to think rather of those who saw her than of those whom she could not see." What is out of her sight is literally out of her mind—thus her "moral stupidity." When she is told that

Rex has had a fall from a horse she is unable to summon up even the mildest sympathy for him; and when Rex, packed off back to school by his father, asks Gwendolen if she will miss him, she replies: " 'Of course. Every one is of consequence in this dreary country . . .' The perception that poor Rex wanted to be tender made her curl up and harden like a sea-anemone at the touch of a finger" [1, 7]. "The life of passion," says George Eliot, "had begun negatively in her." Gwendolen tells her mother that night that she shall " 'never love anybody. I can't love people. I hate them.' " She is at least marginally aware of her own emptiness.

After Rex's departure things are duller than ever for Gwendolen and she begins to think of marriage as an "escape" from "being expected to please everybody" but herself. Why should she not marry? She is, as she tells her mother, " 'charming . . . I am contented with myself.' " It is suggested that one explanation for Gwendolen's new interest in marriage is the rumor that Henleigh Mallinger Grand-court, wealthy sportsman and heir presumptive to the nearby Mallinger estates and a baronetcy, will be present at the neighborhood's annual Archery Meeting. Gwendolen, needless to say, sets out to dazzle him—for "pre-eminence is sweet to those who love it, even under mediocre cir-cumstances." For her it is a matter of pride; she must be first with the county's first man—in order to reject him when the time comes. Cherishing her own independence, she has "not considered that the desire to conquer is itself a sort of subjec-tion," and looks forward to meeting Grandcourt as a test of her powers.

When they finally do meet, Gwendolen, to her surprise, discovers that this man of calm, cold, and distinguished manners is agreeable to her. Like Mr. Dombey in pursuit of Edith Granger, Gwendolen seeks what she believes to be a kindred spirit of arrogance. She exerts herself to gain Grand-court's "homage"; she will not be satisfied until he declares his love—which she is sure he must do. She assumes all along that her understanding of the male character is complete, never realizing how totally ignorant she remains of "human

relations." She feels that she needs no "help in drawing conclusions" about others. Gwendolen's blindness is emphasized
again and again by her assertion to herself that, should she
agree to marry Grandcourt (certainly a "social promotion"
for her), "she would most probably be able to manage him
thoroughly" and to continue "doing as she liked." Marriage
to Grandcourt, should she reach for it, would be for her, she
becomes convinced, "the gate into a larger freedom." Grandcourt, meanwhile, hints at his love for her. But for this consummate egoist, love translates into a desire to possess an ex-
quisite ornament and to bend an obviously refractory nature
to his own will—to "master" a "spirit," as George Eliot puts
it. Gwendolen, of course, is as totally ignorant of his true
nature as she is of human nature in general.

It is at this stage of affairs that Grandcourt's lackey Mr.
Lush, who fears that a marriage between Gwendolen and
Grandcourt would dilute his own influence with his
employer, arranges for Gwendolen to meet Mrs. Glasher.
The shock of Mrs. Glasher's revelations causes a revulsion of
feeling in Gwendolen; and, having promised Mrs. Glasher
that she will not marry Grandcourt, she sets off abruptly for
Leubronn, where we found her at the opening of the novel.
Late events have convinced her that "There is nothing worth
caring for."

We next see Gwendolen at the time of her return to
Offendene from Europe after the collapse of the family fortunes—that is to say, the novel now returns to the present.
Her "self-delight" has "faded before the sense of futility" inherent in the collapse of the family's fortunes and her
previous disillusionment in Grandcourt. For once she begins
to feel a little sorry for someone else—in this case her mother.
Her sympathy, however, does not last long. When her mother
tells her that they are to move into a small cottage nearby,
Gwendolen's haughty spirit reasserts itself: " 'I will not submit to it, ' " she says. " 'Everything has gone against me. People have come near me only to blight me.' " Once again
Gwendolen sees the "pettiness of circumstances" as
directed against herself. She is horrified when her mother

suggests that she take a position as a governess in order to help out the family. She announces that her "life is [her] own affair," but soon begins to realize that perhaps after all she will have to consider seriously going to work. While her pride remains for the most part undiluted, it finally dawns upon her that she may not be so special a ward of Fate after all: "for the first time the conditions of this world seemed to her like a hurrying crowd in which she had got astray, no more cared for and protected than a myriad of other girls . . ." [3, 21]. But she continues to think of her troubles as those which "might well enter into the biography of celebrities and remarkable persons. And if she had heard her immediate acquaintances cross-examined as to whether they thought her remarkable, the first who said 'No' would have surprised her" [3, 21]. Gwendolen's self-conceit remains substantial.

Gwendolen has always thought of herself as a talented singer and actress and decides to consult her friend Herr Klesmer—a composer, pianist, and teacher of music—on the subject of a career for herself on the stage. Her drawing-room performances have usually been unfettered by criticism, and in the present crisis Gwendolen feels "clever enough for anything . . . 'I *am* beautiful.' " Klesmer, an honest man and a dedicated artist, advises her to abandon the idea. Gwendolen, who thinks she knows what such a career would entail ("betrayed by her habitual consciousness of having valuable information to bestow," as George Eliot puts it), is numbed by Klesmer's contention that only " 'arduous, unceasing work' " will prepare her for a career on the stage. Klesmer tells her that she has no conception of what true excellence is. Gwendolen, shocked by this assertion of her ignorance, had always believed "that to present herself in public on the stage must produce an effect such as she had been used to feel certain of in private life." She ascribes Klesmer's judgment not to her own inadequacies but to "fallible" and "biassed" sentiment on his part. Some later reflection, however, shakes her self-confidence at least to the point where she fears that her talent might not be sufficiently recognized. The "layers of egoistic disappointment and irritation" within her cannot obfuscate the necessity of abandoning the project, and Gwendolen now makes an attempt to face her situation more realistically:

> For the first time since her consciousness began, she was having a vision of herself on the common level, and had lost the innate sense that there were reasons why she should not be slighted, elbowed, jostled—treated like a passenger with a third-class ticket. . . . Every word that Klesmer had said seemed to have been branded into her memory, as most words are which bring with them a new set of impressions and make an epoch for us. (3, 23)

Gwendolen's self-confidence, for the first time in her life, begins to waver. The "new set of impressions" which are making an "epoch" for her suggests that perhaps she is not at the center of the universe after all. Her unreflecting egoism here receives one of its first serious jolts.

Soon, however, Gwendolen falls back into some of the old cadences. She complains again that the family ought not to have to live in a cottage and that she herself ought not to have to be a governess: " 'It seems to me a very extraordinary world if people in our position must sink in this way all at once.' " George Eliot comments here that "it was never [Gwendolen's] aspiration to express herself virtuously so much as cleverly. . . . No religious view of trouble helped her: her troubles had in her opinion all been caused by other people's disagreeable or wicked conduct . . ." [3, 24]. Gwendolen's perspective on the world is patently devoid of both objectivity and sympathy. Her solipsistic existence dictates the view that when pleasure or satisfaction is denied her it is because "others" have slighted her. George Eliot specifically criticizes Gwendolen's contemptuous attitude toward labouring for one's happiness and fulfillment—here in connection with her disinclination to become a governess: "the fact which wrought upon her was her invariable observation that for a lady to become a governess—to 'take a situation'—was to descend in life and to be treated at best with a compassionate patronage. And poor Gwendolen had never dissociated happiness from personal pre-eminence and *éclat"* [3, 24]. Gwendolen's equation of "happiness" with "personal pre-eminence" is both the symptom and the definition of her blind self-absorption. George Eliot goes on to say here, however, that Gwendolen is not so much unlike many others as to suggest that we should "cast her out of our compassion." And indeed, ultimately there is no reason to do so; it is the progress of Gwendolen's realization, through growing moral awareness, that happiness and *éclat* are not symbiotic after all that defines the nature of her education in values.

As the prospect of becoming a governess draws nearer, Gwendolen's resentment of the world's treatment of her deepens. For her, the universe has been reduced "to an unjust infliction of pain"; George Eliot asks us to "imagine one who had been made to believe in his own divinity finding all homage withdrawn." At this critical juncture Grandcourt turns up again and asks permission to call. Gwendolen is sure that he plans to propose marriage to her formally and finds herself now wishing that she had never heard of Mrs. Glasher and her children. She decides to permit him to call, resolving to reject him despite a very present "vision of what Grandcourt might do" for her family and herself should she marry him after all.

On the day Grandcourt is to come, Gwendolen has decided—or so she thinks—to refuse him. But as the time draws nearer she begins to equivocate, indulging in a series of rationalizations and false premises which George Eliot labels the result of a "constructive imagination":

> She had given a sort of promise [to Mrs. Glasher]. But would another woman who married Grandcourt be in fact the decisive obstacle to her wishes, or be doing her and her [children] any real injury? Might it not be just as well, nay better, that Grandcourt should marry? For what could not a woman do when she was married, if she knew how to assert herself? Here all was constructive imagination. Gwendolen had about as accurate a conception of marriage—that is to say, of the mutual influences, demands, duties of man and woman in the

state of matrimony—as she had of magnetic currents
and the law of storms. (3, 27)

The phrase "constructive imagination" is repeated, for
George Eliot wishes us to see how self-deluded Gwendolen's
solipsistic ignorance of the world has made her. Gwendolen
will no more be able to "manage" the masterful Grandcourt
than the man in the moon. And there is no way her marriage
to Grandcourt could benefit Mrs. Glasher, since in any case
Grandcourt will do just as he likes about her and her children.
A child born to Gwendolen and Grandcourt, however, could
quite obviously damage the claims of Mrs. Glasher's
children. The blindness born of the distortions of excessive
subjectivity most clearly characterizes Gwendolen's reasoning here. She admits to herself quite candidly that she does
not love Grandcourt, but the prospect of being able to "exercise her power" over him, one way or the other, is exciting to
her: "she had the white reins in her hands again." As he is
about to arrive she considers how easy it would be for her to
make "all things easy for 'poor mama' " —nonetheless she
is still (she thinks) resolved to refuse him.

Grandcourt comes, he proposes, and Gwendolen is
transfixed: "ah, piteous equality in the need to
dominate!—she was overcome like the thirsty one who is
drawn towards the seeming water in the desert, overcome by
the suffused sense that here in this man's homage to her lay
the rescue from helpless subjection to an oppressive lot" [3,
27]. Gwendolen does not love him, but she loves his
"homage" and the prospect of the power of domination. Her
egoism, her love of pre-eminence, is too much for her, and so
of course she accepts Grandcourt. Her decision is in large
measure the result of her usual penchant for instant self-
indulgence: "her vision was filled by her own release from the
[prospect of being a governess], and her mother's release
from Sawyer's Cottage." She is of course ignorant of the fact
that Grandcourt knows the full details of her late domestic
crises and is aware as well that she has met Mrs. Glasher.
Gwendolen thinks he does not know about her meeting with
the lady, and would be mortified (and is later) if she thought

that he knew of the meeting and thus that she is willing to marry him in spite of this view into his past. In sum, Gwendolen is not aware of many of the factors that will determine the nature and the direction of her marriage; and in any case she knows as much about the state of marriage as about "magnetic currents and the law of storms." (This is the first of several metaphors from science in this novel which emphasize the pre-determined and unchanging balance of influences regulating the relationship between individuals in constantly close proximity.) Gwendolen does not, after all, know Grandcourt himself very well; she does not know of *his* egoism, *his* need for the subjection of others to *his* power. Like Dorothea, Gwendolen does not take into account the equivalent center of self of her prospective husband. When Grandcourt promises her that she shall have whatever she likes he is not thinking of her freedom. Gwendolen, meanwhile, dreams of "command and luxury," believing that " 'everything is to be as I like!' "

Gwendolen's subsequent mental post-mortem takes place in a chapter whose epigraph quotes La Rochefoucauld: "Il est plus aisé de connoître l'homme en général que de connoître un homme en particulier." Gwendolen has become uneasy about the moral direction of her own conduct:

> It was new to her that a question of right or wrong in her conduct should rouse her terror; she had known no compunction that atoning caresses and presents could not lay to rest. But here had come a moment when something like a new consciousness was awakened . . . The brilliant position she had longed for, the imagined freedom she would create for herself in marriage, the deliverance from the dull insignificance of her girlhood—all were immediately before her; and yet they had come to her hunger like food with the taint of sacrilege upon it, which she must snatch with terror. (4, 28)

Gwendolen's ordeal of moral education has by no means reached its climax—she is not as yet plunged in despair; and yet here, for the first time, even in her "blindness," Gwendolen's previous lack of "compunction" about her own

behavior begins to give way before the advent of "a new consciousness" of moral responsibility for her own actions. At
last she is experiencing "inward strife." She realizes that she
has consented to the marriage out of purely selfish motives.
Now, before her marriage, she begins to question the intelligence of her decision—realizing that of course she is "not
going to marry for her mama's sake." Nor is she going to
marry for love. Her assessment of Grandcourt is ominous
both in its lack of warmth and in its lack of understanding:
" 'he is very proud. But so am I. We shall match each other
. . . He really is not disgusting.' " Gwendolen is not nearly so
strong or masterful a person as Grandcourt, and her failure
to realize this in advance will spell misery for her later on. She
understands Grandcourt no better than she understands
anyone else; a lifetime of self-absorption has almost annihilated objective perception.

Gwendolen's greatest failure is of course her total ignorance—because of her inability to interest herself in and
thus understand others—of the kind of relationship she is
likely to have with Grandcourt after they are married.
George Eliot insists on making this clear to the reader
wherever she can:

> She was thinking of him, whatever he might be, as a man
> over whom she was going to have indefinite power; and
> her loving him having never been a question with her,
> any agreeableness he had was so much gain. Poor
> Gwendolen had no awe of unmanageable forces in the
> state of matrimony, but regarded it as altogether a
> matter of management, in which she would know how
> to act . . . Grandcourt himself was not jealous of
> anything unless it threatened his mastery—which he did
> not think himself likely to lose. (4, 28)

Gwendolen does have enough intelligence to question from
time to time her picture of her life as Grandcourt's wife.
Sometimes, in conversation with him, it seems to her "as if
she had consented to mount a chariot where another held the
reins"; but Gwendolen's egoism is still her most potent
motivating force: it is "not in her nature to leap out in the

eyes of the world." She remains ignorant of the "un-manageable forces" which will determine her future as a wife.

Meanwhile, as she sees more of the Mallingers and Deronda, Gwendolen finds herself becoming increasingly desirous of the latter's good opinion of her. She is not aware, perhaps, of the source of this desire; George Eliot suggests that

> We make the goodness of others a reason for exorbitant demands on them. This sort of effect was penetrating Gwendolen. . . . [T]here had been changes going on within her since that time at Leubronn [when Deronda saw her gambling and returned her necklace]: the struggle of mind attending a conscious error had wakened something like a new soul, which had better, but also worse, possibilities than her former poise of crude self-confidence: among the forces she had come to dread was something within her that troubled satisfaction. (4, 29)

Gwendolen's "new soul," George Eliot seems to be suggesting, is a newly developing conscience, a psychic growth feeding on her increasing dependence on Deronda's expanding moral authority over her. Deronda, for his part, has not actively assisted in encouraging her in this since the incident at Leubronn. But Gwendolen, who feels that she has never met anyone like him before, simply begins to feel more and more that he will always know what is right. As it turns out, of course, Deronda ultimately becomes the chief agent of her moral regeneration—and so in this, at least, she has chosen wisely. Indeed, her intuitive response to his moral authority may well be seen as a sign of latent or undeveloped moral sensibility in her—which is ultimately one source, within herself, of her moral regeneration. The "changes" mentioned here also signal, finally, the growth in Gwendolen of real feeling for another person—not just the desire to please, but genuine attachment and dependence. Gwendolen, her self-satisfaction "troubled" and newly "conscious" of "error" now that her mind, no longer merely dormant, is at last capable of "struggle," is edging slowly toward a modicum of fellow feeling.

Gwendolen's perception, however, has not as yet become significantly more acute. It does not occur to her, for example, that Grandcourt might know why she is marrying him and yet consent to marry her anyway in order to satisfy his own overwhelming urge to possess, and to control what he possesses. She marries him in bad faith, and his knowledge of this, while it in no way excuses his later cruelty, at least goes part of the way toward explaining it. For the rest of the explanation an understanding of Grandcourt's nature is necessary, and this Gwendolen lacks. The only thing that can disturb his cold self-satisfaction, George Eliot makes it clear to us, is "a sense of imperfect mastery."

The chapter in which Gwendolen marries Grandcourt has this as its epigraph: "A wild dedication of yourself/ To unpath'd waters, undream'd shores." A little choric prattle, in which it is made explicitly clear that almost everyone except Gwendolen is aware of Grandcourt's true nature, introduces us once more to the heroine herself, whom we now see savoring her triumph and only a little upset as a result of Deronda's close observation of her and her own miserable thoughts. At this critical juncture George Eliot gives us a large slice of Gwendolen's mental tumult, making it quite plain that Gwendolen's "education" is only in its incipient stages:

> Whatever uneasiness a growing conscience had created, was disregarded as an ailment might have been, amidst the gratification of that ambitious vanity and desire for luxury within her which it would take a great deal of slow poisoning to kill. This morning she could not have said truly that she repented her acceptance of Grandcourt or that any fears in hazy perspective could hinder the glowing effects of the immediate scene in which she was the central object . . . [Gwendolen experienced] a sort of exulting defiance as she felt herself standing at the game of life with many eyes upon her, daring everything to win much—or if to lose, still with *éclat* and a sense of importance . . . [S]he thought that she was entering on a fuller power of managing circumstance—with all the official strength of marriage, which some women made so poor a use of. That in-

toxication of youthful egoism out of which she had been shaken by trouble, humiliation, and a new sense of culpability, had returned upon her under the newly-fed strength of the old fumes. She did not in the least present the ideal of the tearful, tremulous bride. Poor Gwendolen, whom some had judged much too forward and instructed in the world's ways!—with her erect head and elastic footsteps she was walking amid illusions. . . . (4, 31)

Gwendolen's slowly "growing conscience" is not sufficiently developed as yet to annihilate the "gratification" she feels in the satisfaction of her "ambitious vanity and desire for luxury." The "slow poisoning" of these feelings is of course just a little way off. But, as usual, Gwendolen is living for the dizzying self-indulgence of the moment—in this case being the "central object" of the "immediate scene." Like Michael Henchard in *The Mayor of Casterbridge,* she does not have the habit of reflection. While she begins to sense soon afterwards that a cord of some sort has been flung over her neck, her primary emotion is that of "exulting defiance" and the sweetness of having "many eyes upon her." For her, "*éclat* and a sense of importance" are rewards sufficiently gratifying to shroud most of her doubts in momentary indifference. She thinks, anyway, that marriage will give her a "fuller power of managing circumstance." For George Eliot, Gwendolen's regression to the "intoxication of youthful egoism" is both pitiful and tragic—for it leads her once again to walk "amid illusions." The shattering of these illusions will bring to Gwendolen ultimately both the suffering of unhappiness and the providential opportunity to attain moral vision. As in all great tragedy, pain will be productive; suffering must precede salvation.

As she bids her mother good-bye, Gwendolen tells her plainly that she does not love Grandcourt, and so goes off with him with an "infusion of dread" gnawing at her triumphant happiness. At Ryelands she receives Mrs. Glasher's diamonds and that disconcerting note from the lady herself, and thus begins her married life in a state of guilt and terror.

We next see Gwendolen some weeks later on a visit she
and her husband pay to the Mallingers. Deronda thinks she is
unhappy, but she tells him only that she is bored. He says that
"'what we call the dulness of things is a disease in ourselves.'"
Gwendolen replies: "'Ah, I see! The fault I find in the
world is my own fault.'" Deronda does not contradict her; it
is an idea he will impress upon her again and again, a theme
that becomes his favorite weapon against her self-absorption.
Deronda finds in her "a dreary lack of the ideas that might
help her . . . She was clearly an ill-educated, worldly girl" with
"a native love of homage, and belief in her own power." He
feels sorry for her, considers her worth saving, and decides
not to discourage her obviously growing dependence upon
his own opinions and views. Gwendolen, for her part, has
begun to consider Deronda "a part of her conscience."

And now, once again, George Eliot moves us firmly
back into Gwendolen's mind, and we see clearly that at last
the ordeal of her education in values has begun in earnest.
She has discovered that she has misjudged both her own
powers and Grandcourt's. We see her, as a wife, magnifying
"the satisfactions of her pride, on which she nourished her
strength." And we also see her finally plunged into that state
of despair which for George Eliot represents both a necessary
purging of past blindness and a cleansing of perception re-
quisite for future moral progress. Here are the climactic
moments of Gwendolen's self-discovery:

> Poor Gwendolen was conscious of an uneasy,
> transforming process—all the old nature shaken to its
> depths, its hopes spoiled, its pleasures perturbed, but
> still showing wholeness and strength in the will to
> reassert itself . . . [She] no longer felt inclined to kiss her
> fortunate image in the glass; she looked at it with
> wonder that she could be so miserable. One belief which
> had accompanied her through her unmarried life as a
> self-cajoling superstition, encouraged by the subordina-
> tion of every one about her—the belief in her own power
> of dominating—was utterly gone. Already, in seven
> short weeks, which seemed half her life, her husband
> had gained a mastery which she could no more resist

than she could have resisted the benumbing effect from the touch of a torpedo [crampfish]. Gwendolen's will had seemed imperious in its small girlish sway; but it was the will of a creature with a large discourse of imaginative fears: a shadow would have been enough to relax its hold . . . [A]ll her easy arrangement of her future power over her husband to make him do better than he might be inclined to do, were now as futile as the burnt-out lights which set off a child's pageant. [She now had a] sense of being blameworthy . . . [a] gnawing trouble in her consciousness. . . . [S]he was frightened at Grandcourt. The poor thing had passed from her girlish sauciness of superiority . . . into an amazed perception of her former ignorance . . .[and] of her present ignorance as to what their[married]life . . . might turn into . . . [She had seen Grandcourt] in the light of a creature such as she could understand and manage: but marriage had nullified all such interchange, and Grandcourt had become a blank uncertainty to her in everything but this, that he would do just what he willed, and that she had neither devices at her command to determine his will, nor any rational means of escaping it . . . . (5, 35)

The language of this passage insists on the "transforming process" going on in Gwendolen's mind—"all the old nature shaken to its depths." The old egoistic supports are no longer either available to Gwendolen or sufficient for her peace of mind. Her overwhelming sense is that of misery born of self-blame, which has become a "gnawing trouble in her con-sciousness." No longer can she avoid *thinking,* "inward strife." The self-will she had thought of as strong was so only among the weaker members of her own family and in her own imaginings of the future. Her "belief in her own power of dominating," a confidence in self based largely on imagina-tion, is now gone, and she is left only with remorse. Like Dorothea, Gwendolen has discovered that marriage has bestowed on her less freedom than she had before—not more. It has been foreordained that Grandcourt will master her—she can no more resist his influence than she can resist the "benumbing effect" of an eel. And so she has passed from unreflecting egoism to "an amazed perception of her former ignorance"—a phenomenon which quite patently links her with protagonists we have previously encountered as well as with those we shall soon meet (Gwendolen's feeling of stupefied helplessness in dealing with her husband is most notably similar to the plight of Isabel Archer in *The Portrait of A Lady*). The language here, as a matter of fact, is startlingly similar to that of the scene in *Pride and Prejudice* in which Elizabeth Bennet finally reaches *her* self-recognition. Gwendolen, then, has begun to pass from a state of total self-absorption and moral blindness to one of self-questioning and misery. As the novel continues to tell her story we will see her edge closer to that objective moral vision, that sympathy for others, which is so important to George Eliot and so dominant a preoccupation in all of her novels.

George Eliot moves from this important scene to a closer examination of the relationship between Gwendolen and Deronda, a relationship destined to become central to the completion of Gwendolen's moral conversion. The word "conversion," as a matter of fact, appears quite pointedly in George Eliot's summation of the foundations of Deronda's attraction for Gwendolen:

> It is one of the secrets in the change of mental poise which has been fitly named conversion, that to many among us neither heaven nor earth has any revelation till some personality touches theirs with a peculiar influence, subduing them into receptiveness . . . [Deronda's influence upon Gwendolen] had entered into the current of that self-suspicion and self-blame which awakens a new consciousness . . . [Gwendolen's] feelings had turned this man, only a few years older than herself, into a priest. . . . (5, 35)

Gwendolen's "change of mental poise" is awaking in her "a new consciousness" of herself and of others, making her, little by little, desire to be a better person (she wishes, for example, to make Deronda aware that she wants " 'to be something better if I could' "). That George Eliot uses the word "conversion" to describe what is going on in Gwendolen and defines Deronda's role in Gwendolen's life as that of a "priest" underscores the religious overtones she attaches to the kind of moral growth she is depicting in Gwendolen's story. (Gwendolen, we may also recall, did not "repent" of what she was doing on her wedding day.) Religiosity, for George Eliot, resides in the expansion of one's vision of the world and concomitant increase in feeling for his fellow beings. In *Adam Bede,* as we have seen, she labels this process a "baptism of fire"; for her, as for Dickens, it always has the overtones of salvation.

Deronda continues to expound such themes and other ones for Gwendolen's benefit: " 'those who would be comparatively uninteresting beforehand may become worthier of sympathy when they do something that awakens in them a keen remorse. Lives are enlarged in different ways. I daresay some would never get their eyes opened if it were not for a violent shock from the consequences of their own actions' " [5, 36]. Gwendolen's sensibilities are slowly being "enlarged" as a result of her past folly and her ultimate recognition of it; she is becoming "worthier of sympathy." Happily, her reaction to Deronda's speeches is to submit "her mind to rebuke"; she feels that she is "wrong and miserable." Sometimes she asks him what she should do to improve her life. Deronda's answer is also George Eliot's: " 'Look on other lives besides your own. See what their troubles are, and how they are borne. Try to care for what is best in thought and action—something that is good apart from the accidents of your own lot' " [5,36]. Deronda's advice to Gwendolen is not wholly different from that tendered Adam Bede. Sympathy for others and the renunciation of one's own selfish desires are insisted on as a spiritual cure for both protagonists. Expansion of one's moral sensibilities is the prescribed antidote for egoism.

The conversations between Gwendolen and Deronda continue. He tells her that she is "selfish and ignorant"; she feels "remorse for having injured others." She says she has been punished for her folly, but knows no way of escaping the misery of her present life (Grandcourt's name, of course, is never mentioned). Deronda suggests to Gwendolen that she order her life " 'so as to make any possible amends, and keep away from doing any sort of injury again.' " When Gwendolen complains bitterly that she is powerless to change her life, Deronda replies by stating one of George Eliot's most characteristic views: " 'That is the bitterest of all—to wear the yoke of our own wrongdoing . . . [But one] who has committed irremediable errors may be scourged by that consciousness into a higher course than is common . . . Feeling what it is to have spoiled one life may well make us long to save other lives from being spoiled' " [5, 36]. Folly and its inevitable aftermath of suffering and misery are the best guides, for George Eliot, to "a higher course"; pain may often lead one to moral regeneration. This was also a central lesson of *Adam Bede*.

Gwendolen is moved by Deronda's vehemence but feels that there is not much hope for herself: " 'I am selfish. I have never thought much of any one's feelings. . . .' " Gwendolen, at least, has come to a more rational view of her own failings. Deronda answers her on this occasion with these words:

'some real knowledge[of life]would give you an interest in the world beyond the small drama of personal desires. . . . The refuge you are needing from personal trouble is the higher, the religious life, which holds an enthusiasm for something more than our own appetites and vanities . . . [F]or us who have to struggle for our wisdom, the higher life must be a region in which the affections are clad with knowledge . . . Take the present suffering as a painful letting in of light. . . . I don't think you could have escaped the painful process in some form or other . . . Keep your dread fixed on the idea of increasing that remorse which is so bitter to you . . . Try to take hold of your sensibility, and use it as if it were a faculty, like vision.' (5, 36)

Deronda has defined accurately Gwendolen's past existence as a "small drama of personal desires"; its smallness has been due to a dearth of ideas and sympathies. He prescribes for her the "religious life," which for George Eliot, as well as for Deronda himself, means a life of affections, a life of selflessness, feeling, and knowledge. Gwendolen's "present suffering" is an instrument of spiritual salvation—that "painful letting in of light" which constitutes the "painful process" of moral education. Meditation is an effective means of increasing one's "remorse," which in turn will enlarge one's sympathies. "Sensibility" and "vision" are, must be, interdependent; the growth of feeling for others enables one to exorcise the blindness of self-absorption and to cultivate in its place self-knowledge, objectivity, and a sense of proportion.

In her newly found objectivity, Gwendolen admits to herself how foolish she had been ever to suppose that she could "manage" Grandcourt. Grandcourt, meanwhile, is both jealous and resentful of her new intimacy with Deronda and decides that he must humiliate her into total passivity. To do this, he determines to play a trump he has been holding for some time—he chooses to let Gwendolen know that he has been aware all along that when Gwendolen married him she was conversant with the story and the consequences of his previous alliance with Mrs. Glasher. Gwendolen has been dreading the discovery of this knowledge for some time, feeling that if he knows that she has always known he will more than ever be inclined to treat her high-handedly. To perform this final humiliation of his wife, Grandcourt, like Mr. Dombey, decides to use a hated ambassador—in this case Mr. Lush. "Want of sympathy condemns us to a corresponding stupidity," George Eliot tells us, and Grandcourt, in the moral stupidity of his cold-hearted egoism, does not see that his wife is attempting to alter the spiritual texture of her existence. He remains as blind to her real nature as she had been to his earlier in their relationship. He remains essentially the same, in other words, while his wife's sensibilities are slowly expanding.

To remove Gwendolen from Deronda's proximity, Grandcourt determines to take her yachting on the Mediterranean—and so it is on Grandcourt's yacht off the Italian coast that we next encounter Gwendolen. She is as miserably unhappy as ever, of course, but has become objective enough to understand that she is largely to blame for her

catastrophic marriage: "she [had] meant to rule and have her
own way . . . [But] she was not one of the narrow-brained.
. . . She had a root of conscience in her, and the process of
purgatory had begun for her on the green earth: she knew
that she had been wrong" [7, 54]. Gwendolen's "purgatory"
is that state of despair which follows the torture of self-
conceit and precedes the final grace of selflessness. More and
more, as the novel nears its conclusion, Gwendolen finds
herself capable of facing squarely her past folly while considering the most efficacious means of avoiding further moral
lapses: "The vision of her past wrong-doing, and what it had
brought on her, came with a pale ghostly illumination over
every imagined deed that was a rash effort at freedom, such
as she had made in her marriage . . . [Deronda's] power over
her had begun in the raising of a self-discontent which could
be satisfied only by genuine change" [7, 54]. Gwendolen has
moved from selfish indifference to the feelings of others
through "self-discontent" to almost total dependence upon
the sensibilities of a fellow human being. She has acquired the
capacity at least to begin to understand and appreciate the
symbiosis of fruitful human relationships; once again this
new capacity is evoked by George Eliot in terms of "vision."
Gwendolen's new understanding, in its turn, makes her begin
to hate her husband passionately, for Grandcourt is a perfect
specimen of inert respectability devoid of any capacity for
human sympathy.

Deronda, who has been visiting his mother in Genoa,
meets the Grandcourts accidentally after they have put into
the port for minor repairs on the yacht. Grandcourt, immediately suspicious of Deronda's presence and disinclined
to leave his wife alone for a minute, insists that she go out
sailing with him while they are waiting for the repairs to be
completed. It is then that the accident occurs which almost
destroys Gwendolen's sanity but which ultimately gives her,
like Dorothea Brooke, another chance to grope toward happiness and fulfillment. Grandcourt, in the course of putting
his sailboat about, is knocked into the water by the boom.
Gwendolen moves mechanically to toss him a rope, freezes

into immobility, and Grandcourt goes under. She dives in after him, but it is never clear whether she does this in a last-minute attempt to save him or to end her own life. She is rescued by fishermen and brought back to her hotel, "a wild amazed consciousness in her eyes, as if she had waked up in a world where some judgment was impending" [7, 55].

Deronda, of course, attends her immediately. She is hysterical, confusing her murderous hatred for her late husband with the act of murder itself. She calls herself a guilty woman, a murderess, and hopes incoherently that the present catastrophe might help to "scourge [her] into something better." In her panic of guilt, she confesses at some length to Deronda:

> 'I used to think I could never be wicked. I thought of wicked people as if they were a long way off me. Since then I have been wicked. I have felt wicked. And everything has been a punishment to me—all the things I used to wish for. . . . I ought not to have married. That was the beginning of it. I wronged some one else. I broke my promise. I meant to get pleasure for myself, and it all turned to misery.' (7, 56)

This is a moment of catharsis for Gwendolen. After it she slowly begins to regain her rationality, a more placid and profound rationality based on the tragedy of her past egoism—tragic now in that the high price of her "pleasure," as she sees, has turned that pleasure into "misery." For Deronda, Gwendolen's self-discovery explicitly has the importance and sanctity of salvation, as the language of his thoughts makes clear:

> her remorse was the precious sign of a recoverable nature; it was the culmination of that self-disapproval which had been the awakening of a new life within her; it marked her off from those whose only regret is failure in securing their evil wish. Deronda could not utter one word to diminish that sacred aversion to her worst self—that thorn-pressure which must come with the crowning of the sorrowful Better, suffering because of the Worse. (7, 56)

The "worst self" undergoes the "thorn-pressure" of suffering and sorrow in order to be reborn into the "better self"; "self-disapproval" is a prerequisite to "the awakening of a new life." Gwendolen's awakening, both literally and figuratively, prefigures her conversion to moral vision, and thus her salvation; the Christian terminology used here makes this patent.

Deronda continues to play priest to Gwendolen's penitent. She still fears that she is too "wicked" to become "worthy," and continues to dwell on her past mistakes. Referring to " 'the self-abhorrence that stings us into better striving,' " Deronda tells her: " 'I believe that you may become worthier than you have ever yet been—worthy to lead a life that may be a blessing. No evil dooms us hopelessly except the evil we love, and desire to continue in, and make no effort to escape from. You *have* made efforts—you will go on making them' " [7, 57]. Man, in George Eliot's system of modified determinism, must ultimately be partly responsible for his own actions because his character determines in some measure what those actions are. His character is his fate; his fate, whatever it may be, is partly determined by himself. Deeds may have unalterable consequences, but a man can determine his deeds as easily as he can let his deeds determine what he himself is. He is capable, then, of exercising his will or amending his conduct; and if he will attempt to improve or elevate those elements of his character that are destructive and selfish, he may very well succeed. Thus it is possible for some, such as Adam Bede and Gwendolen Harleth, to undergo those stages of moral progression I have been attempting to identify and define here. For others, such as Rosamond Vincy and Henleigh Grandcourt, such conversion is not possible because of the unchangeability of their characters and the determining nature of their deeds upon themselves.

George Eliot introduces the final Book of the novel with a statement about the gradualness and yet the revolutionary nature of Gwendolen's moral conversion:

> If the swiftest thinking has about the pace of a greyhound, the slowest must be supposed to move, like the limpet, by an apparent sticking, which after a good

while is discerned to be a slight progression. Such
differences are manifest in the variable intensity which
we call human experience, from the revolutionary rush
to change which makes a new inner and outer life, to
that quiet recurrence of the familiar, which has no other
epochs than those of hunger and the heavens.

Something of this contrast was seen in the year's experience which had turned the brilliant, self-confident
Gwendolen Harleth of the Archery Meeting into the
crushed penitent impelled to confess her unworthiness
where it would have been her happiness to be held
worthy. . . . (8, 58)

"Experience" is a "progression" toward "a new inner and
outer life" for Gwendolen; it is the process by which inor-
dinate self-confidence may turn into penitence.

We now see Gwendolen back at home, miserable but
more tender to everyone than she has ever been before. Her
mind is becoming more placid and her existence at
Offendene, while not exciting, is a relief to her:

All that brief experience of a quiet home which had once
seemed a dulness to be fled from, now came back to her
as a restful escape, a station where she found the breath
of morning and the unreproaching voice of birds, after
following a lure through a long Satanic masquerade,
which she had entered with an intoxicated belief in its
disguises, and had seen the end of in shrieking fear lest
she herself had become one of the evil spirits who were
dropping their human mummery and hissing around her
with serpent tongues. (8, 64)

Things have not materially changed. It is just that Gwendolen, emerging from "a long Satanic masquerade,"
perceives them differently now. Once again the Biblical
language of this passage insists that Gwendolen's moral
growth may be compared with religious salvation. That such
salvation is generated by human rather than supernatural
agencies is emphasized as George Eliot expands her
statement: "It is hard to say how much we could forgive
ourselves if we were secure from judgment by an other whose
opinion is the breathing-medium of all our joy . . ." [8, 64].
Like Dickens, George Eliot believes that the redemption of

humanity may be found in the feelings of individuals for one another.

Deronda now arrives at Offendene at Gwendolen's request, and she launches immediately into the question of her husband's bequests. Shrinking from the house and the money Grandcourt has left her, she tells Deronda: " 'I think I could bear to be poor, if you think I ought . . . I want to be good—not like what I have been . . .' " [8, 65]. Deronda praises her sentiment: " 'You shrink from taking what was his. You want to keep yourself pure from profiting by his death. Your feeling even urges you to some self-punishment—some scourging of the self that disobeyed your better will—the will that struggled against temptation' " [8, 65]. Again, this is the language of the Bible. But when Gwendolen suggests taking from Grandcourt's estate an income sufficient only for her mother to live on, Deronda demurs. He tells her that the " 'future beneficence' " of her life " 'will be best furthered' " by hiding from the world the pain of her conscience, and that she ought to consider an income from Grandcourt's estate as a positive means to do good in the world:

> 'What makes life dreary is the want of motive; but once beginning to act with . . . penitential, loving purpose . . . there will be unexpected satisfactions—there will be newly-opening needs—continually coming to carry you on from day to day. You will find your life growing like a plant. . . . This sorrow, which has cut down to the root, has come to you while you are so young—try to think of it, not as a spoiling of your life, but as a preparation for it . . . [Y]ou have been saved from the worst evils that might have come from your marriage, which you feel was wrong. You have had a vision of injurious, selfish action—a vision of possible degradation. . . . And it has come to you in your spring-time. Think of it as a preparation. You can, you will, be among the best of women, such as make others glad that they were born.' (8, 65)

Gwendolen's life is viewed here as having undergone organic growth, growth that has been a "preparation" for life rather than an advance toward death. The providential direction of her life will enable her to be sympathetic and empathic, "among the best of women." Egoism, selfishness, and their attendant despair have been the necessary prerequisites of a "loving purpose." Like Adam Bede, Gwendolen may henceforth attempt to make life better for others.

Deronda's lecture has a galvanizing effect upon Gwendolen:

> The words were like the touch of a miraculous hand to Gwendolen. Mingled emotions streamed through her frame with a strength that seemed the beginning of a new existence, having some new powers or other which stirred in her vaguely. So pregnant is the divine hope of moral recovery with the energy that fulfils it. So potent in us is the infused action of another soul, before which we bow in complete love. . . . It is only by remembering the searching anguish which had changed the aspect of the world for her that we can understand her behaviour to Deronda—the unreflecting openness, nay, the importunate pleading, with which she expressed her dependence on him. . . She identified him with the struggling regenerative process in her. . .Mighty Love had laid his hand upon her . . . . (8, 65)

Gwendolen's final elevation to the status of moral Election is seen here as the concomitant of a new self-consciousness and, more importantly, of an ability to *love*. The act of love is in itself a denial of egoism, a declaration of the ability to put others before one's self. This passage defines Gwendolen's movement from *cupiditas* to *caritas*. The moral anguish which is a concomitant of *cupiditas* has led her to "the divine hope of moral recovery" and "a new existence"; this is the effect of her "baptism," of the continuing "struggling regenerative process in her." Gwendolen's new view of the world has for George Eliot all the importance of the "miraculous."

In Chapter 69, George Eliot summarizes the state of mind to which Gwendolen's moral education has led her, and its epigraph aptly quotes from *The Prelude,* itself a work whose subject is the growth of a mind: "The human nature unto which I felt/That I belonged, and reverenced with love,/Was not a punctual presence, but a spirit/Diffused through time and space . . . . " George Eliot then goes on, in her usual way, to draw some general conclusions from the specific story she has been recounting:

> [Gwendolen] was experiencing some of that peaceful melancholy which comes from the renunciation of demands for self, and from taking the ordinary good of existence . . . as a gift above expectation . . . There is a way of looking at our life daily as an escape, and taking the quiet return of morn and evening—still more the star-like out-growing of some pure fellow-feeling, some generous impulse breaking our inward darkness—as a salvation that reconciles us to hardship. Those who have a self-knowledge prompting such self-accusation as Hamlet's, can understand this habitual feeling of rescue. And it was felt by Gwendolen as she lived through and through again the terrible history of her temptations, from their first form of illusory self-pleasing when she struggled away from the hold of conscience, to their latest form of an urgent hatred dragging her towards its satisfaction, while she prayed and cried for the help of that conscience which she had once forsaken. She was now dwelling on every word of Deronda's that pointed to her past deliverance from the worst evil in herself and the worst infliction of it on others, and on every word that carried a force to resist self-despair. (8, 69)

In this passage George Eliot explicitly identifies the moral process she has arranged for her heroine to undergo. Gwendolen began in a state of "illusory self-pleasing," moved from this state to one of "self-despair," and has now come under the new influence of a growth of "conscience." Her "renunciation of demands for self" leads to "fellow-feeling," "generous impulse," and a new humility, a moral advance seen by George Eliot as the only kind of "salvation" achievable in this world—one inevitably based, as George Eliot also makes clear, on "self-knowledge." Gwendolen's ordeal of self-discovery is now nearly over. She is moving from "inward darkness" into "daylight," from "temptation" toward "deliverance."

Deronda now returns for his final interview with Gwendolen before departing for the East with Mirah. His announcement of his plans represents Gwendolen's final reversal—for she has fallen in love with him: "she was . . . feeling the pressure of a vast mysterious movement . . . [She was] being dislodged from her supremacy in her own world, and getting a sense that her horizon was but a dipping onward of an existence with which her own was revolving" [8, 69]. To see oneself at the periphery of existence instead of at the center of it is perhaps that state of mind most nearly approaching the antithesis of egoism. Gwendolen's vision is no longer clouded by pride and self-interest; no longer does she see the rest of the world as her private audience. Her final words to Deronda denote her new humility: " 'I have been a cruel woman . . . [but it will be] better with me . . . for having known you . . . You have been very good to me. I have deserved nothing . . . What good have I been? Only harm' " [8, 69]. After Deronda leaves, Gwendolen tearfully promises her mother: " 'I shall live, I shall be better.' " And on Deronda's wedding day he receives a letter from Gwendolen which says in part: " 'I have remembered your words—that I may live to be one of the best of women, who make others glad that they were born . . . It is better—it shall be better with me because I have known you' " [8, 70]. Gwendolen, who loves Deronda, has been able by an act of will to conquer any jealousy or resentment she may feel—something that would have been impossible for her when we first met her. By becoming able to relate to others, she has saved herself.

Daniel Deronda is the history of two souls, Daniel's and Gwendolen's. I have ignored Daniel's story, which occupies the other half of the novel, because it does not specifically fit the general pattern I am concerned with in these pages. Deronda discovers, both literally and figuratively, his true identity, and hypothesizes from his discovery a new kind of existence for himself; but his self-discovery is not preceded by self-conceit or lack of sympathy. His major failings in the early sections of the novel are indolence, excessive self-reliance, and occasional arrogance. These are symptoms of self-indulgence, perhaps, but Deronda is never so much an egoist as the other protagonists we have met thus far. He is basically a compassionate, generous, and selfless man, and indeed it is exactly this that his long story tells us. Gwendolen's story, on the other hand, is the story of her own expanding psyche, of her acquisition of the moral and spiritual virtues which are embodied in Deronda virtually from the beginning of the novel.

GEORGE MEREDITH (1828-1909)
National Portrait Gallery, London

Chapter Five

George Meredith

Meredith's method in most of his novels is to analyze the psychological texture of the characters he has created and in this way to explain their behavior. Meredith believed in evolution, and his view of character development in his novels is, not surprisingly, patently evolutionary. Thus as the course of his psychological analysis advances, his characters are often changed through a kind of organic growth. This also helps explain the metaphors from physical nature he frequently employs in dealing with the development of his protagonists. Like George Eliot before him and Henry James after him, Meredith believed that only by involving himself with other people in society does a person learn what he is. This process of learning in turn explains the evolution of personal change in his novels and suggests that he too is deeply concerned with the "education" of his protagonists. *The Ordeal of Richard Feverel* (1859) is an account of the education of a Meredithian protagonist; *The Egoist* (1879), to a lesser extent, is another.

Like George Eliot once again, Meredith believed that the novel should not merely entertain but also teach people about themselves. This is another reason why the theme of education—of both protagonists and readers—is a radical one in Meredith's novels. The character learns from his own mistakes and the reader in turn learns from the character's education. This, of course, is also the method of George Eliot; as her protagonists move toward moral vision, her readers are being educated to the necessity of human fellowship. In George Eliot's novels, as we have seen, the educational process is from egoism to despair to fellow feeling. In Meredith's novels it is often from animal egoism to rationality to unselfish love—or from blood to brain to spirit, to use Meredith's own terms. He believed that all sentient beings capable of moral growth undergo this organic process.

195

One of Meredith's most constant themes is what he calls the "comedy of egoism," which arises, he believes, out of man's failure to perceive his place in the human hierarchy and his vision of himself at the center of the world. As Meredith's own *An Essay on Comedy* (1877) and the Prelude to *The Egoist* make clear, the irrational man must be ridiculed, not tolerated. In these important statements Meredith speaks of the value of laughter and the need for the perception of folly and "Olympian" mockery instead of sympathetic identification. What Meredith calls the "Comic Spirit" provides moral progress by deflating egoism and establishing in its place a sense of proportion. In *The Egoist,* and to a lesser extent in the earlier *Ordeal of Richard Feverel,* the ironic attitude of the Comic Spirit is maintained throughout. The main sin of most of Meredith's major characters in both novels is egoism; in fact the theme of egoism and the need to conquer it, along with the theme of the loveless marriage, is typical of many of Meredith's poems and novels (*Modern Love* and *Beauchamp's Career* are other examples). These twin themes are also fundamental, of course, to *Middlemarch* and *Daniel Deronda.* Meredith was preoccupied, almost obsessed, with the phenomenon of egoism.

One form egoism frequently takes in his novels is the unreasonable desire of some people to *possess* others entirely. Among the many egoists in *The Ordeal of Richard Feverel,* for example, Sir Austin, like Mr. Dombey, is prominent for his desire to possess completely the heart and soul of his son. Richard's "ordeal" is his moral education, an education that advances him painfully and even tragically from a state of innocence to a state of exhausted experience. Among the egoists in *The Egoist,* Sir Willoughby Patterne is prominent for his desire to possess his fiancée completely, body and mind. His egoism is both a cause and a reflection of his inability to understand and appreciate the thoughts and desires of others, and this failing, as might be expected, leads directly to his downfall. His egoism makes his overthrow inevitable.

Both of these novels abound with egoists. In *The Ordeal of Richard Feverel,* however, the particular pattern I have been attempting to elucidate in these pages is present, while in *The Egoist,* despite its alluring title, it is not. In my discussion of *The Ordeal of Richard Feverel,* as in the discussions of novels previously examined in this study, I shall be concerned primarily with the particular pattern which best illustrates the didactic thrust of the whole. Thus the focus of my discussion of *Feverel* will be on the career of Richard himself, even though many others in the novel, including Adrian, Berry, Mountfalcon, and Sandoe, are also egoists. Egoism in them is a natural outgrowth of sensualism. Sir Austin's mountainous egoism resides in a combination of several factors—his self-confidence, his egregious sentimentality, his specious scientism, and his selfish desire to play Providence to his son. For Sir Austin, however—as for St. John Rivers before him and Sir Willoughby Patterne after him—there is no self-discovery; the moral process I have been attempting to define in these novels is for him incomplete. Lady Blandish's letter to Austin Wentworth at the end of *Feverel* (XLVI) makes this abundantly clear:

> 'There was his son lying all but dead, and the man was still unconvinced of the folly he had been guilty of . . . [He still] deceived himself in the belief that he was acting righteously. . . . [H]e could not even then see his error . . . His mad self-deceit would not leave him . . . I [am not] *quite sure* that he is an altered man even now the blow has struck him . . . If he can look on [Lucy] and not see his *sin,* I almost fear God will never enlighten him.'

Richard, however, must bear the brunt of his father's folly, and the story of the novel is that of his difficult growth to maturity.

Before examining *The Ordeal of Richard Feverel* in more detail, however, I should like to add a few words more about *The Egoist,* which at least on the surface might seem a novel admirably fit for larger concern here. But in fact it is not. Sir Willoughby Patterne, like Sir Austin Feverel, is a consummate egoist who learns practically nothing from the defeats he encounters as a result of his moral blindness. At the end of the novel, while perhaps not as sure of himself as he is at the beginning, Sir Willoughby still falls far short of meaningful self-discovery:

> The mysteries of his own bosom were bare to him, but he could comprehend them only in their immediate relation to the world outside . . . The discovery he made was that in the gratification of the egoistic instinct we may so beset ourselves as to deal a slaughtering wound upon Self to whatsoever quarter we turn. Willoughby's interpretation of his discovery was directed by pity; he had no other strong emotion left in him. He pitied himself, and he reached the conclusion that he suffered because he was active; he could not be quiescent. Had it not been for his devotion to his house and name, never would he have stood twice the victim of womankind. Had he been selfish, he would have been the happiest of men! (XLVII)

This is as close as Willoughby ever gets to understanding self. For Meredith, who detested self-pity as the worst form of sentimentality, Willoughby has learned very little from his various humiliations. The baronet sees his disappointment as being a result of the world's vengeful cruelties rather than of his own moral and emotional limitations. He does not even recognize his own selfishness. Willoughby *feels* the "wound upon Self" but does not *understand* it or its origins, and this is why Meredith has to articulate what has happened for him and for us. We should not confuse self-pity with self-knowledge. Willoughby is sadder but very little wiser. He merely hurts. He is still desirous both of the possession of others and their good opinion, and little else matters to him. If he must appear humbled to the world to achieve these ends, then he will appear humbled. He is concerned only with the "immediate relation" of his feelings "to the world outside." He is still essentially the same man, forcing Laetitia Dale to marry him in order to rescue what is left of his dignity while helping to facilitate Clara Middleton's betrothal to Vernon Whitford both in order to appear magnanimous before the world and to salve his jealousy and wounded pride by disappointing his friend de Craye, who is also in love with Clara. At the very end of *The Egoist* Sir Willoughby still thinks of himself as a generous victim. His very minimal development, which consists mostly of an increased awareness of and desire to avoid pain, does not illustrate Meredith's central lesson of the destruction of selfishness through selfless love.

While Sir Willoughby is an egoist who remains for the most part self-deceived, the novel's other major character, Clara Middleton, undergoes self-discovery without ever having been genuinely an egoist. While it is possible to argue, as some have, that Clara's romanticism, asceticism, and willfulness are forms of self-indulgence, it would nevertheless be unfair and inaccurate to say that her major impulse is that of selfishness or self-interest. On the contrary, her nature is empathic, discerning, and open. Her major failing throughout the novel's first two hundred pages is a lack of self-knowledge, and we should not confuse mere ignorance of self with egoism. The two are compatible but not symbiotic. It is Clara's inexperience that leads her to mistake Willoughby's true nature and to believe for a time that she could be happy as his wife. As she gets to know him better, however, she discovers that he repels her, and in understanding what it is about him that repels her she also begins to understand more fully her own nature and its needs: to be free, to remain in marriage individual and unyoked, to retain at all times an "inner life" apart from anyone else. Like Jane Eyre, Clara cannot exist without these; and like St. John Rivers, the possessive Willoughby cannot comprehend or tolerate these needs in intimates. When Clara finally understands her own needs she also perceives that her nature demands an entirely different sort of husband: "Her cry for freedom was a cry to be free to love. She discovered it, half-shuddering: to love—oh, no, no shape of man, nor improbable nature either—but to love unselfishness and helpfulness and planted strength in something" [XXI]. Such unselfish, unpossessive love is impossible between herself and Willoughby. But Clara is able to find the kind of unfettering love she needs in Vernon Whitford, who must in his turn overcome the self-indulgence of his ascetic detachment in order to make the relationship a whole one.

While Clara discovers the nature of her own nature, however, neither her naivety about self nor her self-regard is ever so radical as to justify condemning her as a true egoist; were we in any doubt about this, there is the omnipresent example of Sir Willoughby to make it more patently clear. Surely it is unnecessary to prove what the novel's title and story declare openly: that Sir Willoughby is an egoist. However, as I have said, his moral development is virtually nil, and therefore any possibility of self-discovery is impeded. Like the pattern of Sir Willoughby's moral development, such as it is, Clara's too essentially fails to fit our pattern of egoism and self-discovery. She is really not, as some readers of this novel have suggested, much like Isabel Archer in *The Portrait of A Lady*. Isabel's self-indulgence, as we shall see, is more like Dorothea Brooke's than it is like Clara's. For Isabel and Dorothea, blind self-ignorance and what Henry James calls "a certain nobleness of imagination" lead to tragic error and a final dissipation of stubborn and untutored self-conceit. Clara's early naivety leads her quickly to reflection, self-discovery, and the avoidance of tragic error. She is inexperienced but not so self-absorbed as to lose totally the faculty of objective perception.

There are other egoists in *The Egoist,* of course: the ladies of the county and Colonel de Craye are notable primarily for the self-indulgence of an idle aimlessness; and Dr. Middleton's selfishness takes the form of total absorption in the pursuit of his own comfort and ease. But whereas most of the others (except Vernon) are unable to overcome the pull of selfish concerns, Clara's experiences enable her to mature psychically and emotionally. Her "education," which is not a terribly radical one, consists of her acceptance of Willoughby's proposal of marriage, her attempts to free herself from her commitment, and her final escape from him. Like Richard Feverel's education, Clara's is an ordeal through experience. Unlike Richard, however, she is never totally self-absorbed and morally blind. And unlike Richard, Willoughby undergoes no significant moral expansion. This is why *The Ordeal of Richard Feverel* will be discussed in some detail in the following pages while *The Egoist* will not.

(One might well ask at this point why then, in my discussion of *Jane Eyre,* I dwelt at such length on the moral failures of St. John Rivers; for like Sir Willoughby, St. John is an egoist who undergoes no tangible expansion of sensibility. But St. John's importance in *Jane Eyre* is tied largely to the contrast insisted upon by Charlotte Brontë between his essential nature and that of Rochester; the novel is structured on the antipodal sensibilities of its two male protagonists. The meaning of the novel, as I argued in Chapter 2, is built on this contrast between a man who discovers himself and a man who does not, while a heroine attempts to choose between them. In *The Egoist,* however, there is no such pattern. The egoists remain egoists, and those who do achieve substantial moral growth were never very far removed from it at the beginning of the novel. Unlike *Jane Eyre, The Egoist* is structured less on antagonistic but thematically complementary psyches than on a simple contrast between egoists who learn nothing and non-egoists who learn more. Thus the organic-evolutionary formula of human development one finds so often in Meredith's novels is for the most part missing in *The Egoist;* it is very much present, however, in *The Ordeal of Richard Feveral.*)

Meredith believed that the novel must affirm human freedom in the face of scientific determinism. But his protagonists usually must survive some sort of moral and spiritual imprisonment or incarceration before they can appreciate and learn to retain their hard-won freedom. In this Meredith is not unlike the authors we have already encountered in this study. In *The Egoist* Clara Middleton, though she feels for a time trapped by a combination of Willoughby's persistence, her father's indifference, and her own inexperience, is never totally a prisoner of her own naivety. She may feel, like Dorothea Brooke, trapped in the house she is living in and surrounded by scenes which seem to reflect in their bleakness her own state of mind—but, unlike Dorothea (and Isabel Archer as well), she is quickly able, as a result of her own perceptiveness before the fact, to disentangle herself. Sir Willoughby, on the other hand, never really escapes from the prison of his own moral blindness. While there is both egoism and self-discovery in *The Egoist,* in sum, they are for the most part separate, unconnected, lacking symbiosis and logical development one from the other. It is as if Meredith, twenty years after *The Ordeal of Richard Feverel,* is despairing of egoistic man's failure to discover himself through any form of self-education or moral experience. In *Feverel,* however—though the human ordeal is brutally, searingly destructive and exhausting—it is at least complete. In it we encounter once again the story of a protagonist's moral education—his progression from a state of virtually total self-blindness to one of objective vision and self-knowledge.

II

Richard Feverel's ordeal is embodied in his attempt to survive and surmount the specious scientific and philosophical prejudices of his father's educational "System," which obfuscates the nature of the world, and to love another human object. Sir Austin Feverel is a monomaniac whose paramount desire in life is to play successfully the role of Providence to his son—to possess him body and soul and thereby to shield him from the corruption and terrors he associates with the world outside of Raynham Abbey. To do this Sir Austin places his entire faith in the scientific control of human nature, which is the bulwark of his educational System for his son; instinct and unpredictability are alien to him and to it. The result of Richard's pernicious upbringing is the subject of the novel. Sir Austin's System works so long as Richard is young and malleable; as an adolescent he is idealistic, honest, and intrepid. He is also, of course, incredibly innocent, generally a poor judge of others. The combination of heroic idealism and personal naivety ultimately spells disaster both to the System and to Richard himself. Richard acknowledges and tolerates the System until he is old enough to fall in love. Love marks the end of the System, for science has no place in its view of things for the spontaneity of instinct. When Sir Austin orders his son to burn the innocent and unaddressed love poetry he has been writing, the System begins to crumble (XII). And when Richard falls in love with Lucy Desborough, the System refuses to accept her because she is not its own choice; it fails to understand that she is a perfect wife for Richard and that it is itself substantially responsible for Richard's excellent choice. The consequences of this blindness initiate the ordeal of Richard Feverel.

As a boy and as an adolescent, Richard promises much. But the prouder he grows the less he sees and thus the more misplaced is his advancing self-confidence. As with most of the protagonists we have already encountered, his egoism blinds him to the true nature of things, and the ultimate discovery of his folly plunges him into misery and despair. At the end of the novel his tragic knowledge of himself and of others is sadly complete.

Richard's two most paramount traits as an adolescent are pride, instilled into him by his father, and innocence, an inevitable result of his father's educational System. Sir Austin is frequently warned about the dangers of blindfolding his son to the full nature of the world outside of Raynham Abbey, but he pays no attention. Adrian Harley, Richard's cousin and tutor, sees the danger quite clearly: " 'combustibles are only the more dangerous for compression. This boy will be ravenous for Earth when he is let loose . . . . ' " One of the results of the enforced circumscribing of Richard's world is the increased importance, in his own eyes, of himself in it. At the age of fifteen, made to feel like royalty, he naturally behaves royally:

> Perhaps the boy with a Destiny was growing up a trifle too conscious of it. His generosity to his occasional companions was princely, but was exercised something too much in the manner of a prince; and notwithstanding his contempt for baseness, he would overlook that more easily than an offence to his pride, which demanded an utter servility when it had once been rendered susceptible . . . There was no middle course for Richard's comrades between high friendship or absolute

slavery . . . [L]ike every insulated mortal, he attributed
. . . deficiency [in] others to the fact of his possessing
a superior nature. (XII)

Richard's pride encompasses the feeling that it is natural that
others should love him. His young cousin Clare Forey
worships him, but "Love of that kind Richard took for
tribute." He is indifferent to her. Meanwhile, as he grows
older, his separation from the female sex breeds in him both a
dangerous sentimentality and an undiscriminating idealism.
In his dreams "he loved them all."

At the age of eighteen Richard meets and falls in love
with Lucy Desborough, the niece of a prosperous farmer of
the neighborhood. The innocent and high-minded Lucy is admirably suited to Richard. The System, which has not picked
her out itself, chooses to brand her as inferior, and Sir Austin
embarks on a tour of London to inspect young ladies who
might be worthy of his son. Sir Austin feels that such a match
may be made scientifically rather than naturally; his friend
Lord Heddon gives him some good advice along the way, advice which of course he chooses to ignore:

> '[A lad is] all the better for a little racketing when he's
> green—feels his bone and muscle—learns to know the
> world. He'll never be a man if he hasn't played at the old
> game one time in his life, and the earlier the better . . .
> [D]epend upon it, when he does break out he'll go to the
> devil . . . . [I]t's a dangerous experiment, that of bring-
> ing up flesh and blood in harness . . . Early excesses the
> frame will recover from: late ones break the con-
> stitution.' (XVIII)

Lord Heddon's statement is particularly prophetic, but Sir
Austin pays no attention. Meanwhile, if he only had sense
enough to see it, his System is producing its greatest
result—perfect love between two perfectly matched personalities. Father and son, Meredith tells us, were both
"looking out for the same thing; only one employed science,
the other instinct, and which hit upon the right it was for time
to decide." The System does not "know its rightful hour of
exaltation."

Sir Austin, recognizing that "pride and sensitiveness were his chief foes" in his battle to win Richard back from Lucy, resorts first to sermonizing: " '[Women] are our ordeal. Love of any human object is the soul's ordeal; and so they are ours, loving them, or not' " [XXII]. Sir Austin, whose own wife ran off with his best friend shortly after Richard's birth, judges the world in the context of his own experience. A victim of his own System, he knows little of human nature despite his pretensions. Richard, whose ordeal is to be more severe than his father's, is also to learn far more of the world's ways than his father has ever learned, and his tragedy will be correspondingly the more incapacitating. He remains at this juncture deaf to Sir Austin's shallow wisdom and pretends to submit to his father's regimen, all the time longing for Lucy. Sir Austin, meanwhile, in his zeal to discover a perfect wife for Richard, becomes more interested in the System than its object: "he lost the tenderness he should have had for his experiment—the living, burning youth at his elbow."

Sir Austin now makes his greatest mistake: he resorts to duplicity. When Richard is nineteen and Sir Austin has decided that his love for Lucy has died, he sends him off to London with Richard's invalid uncle Hippias, ostensibly for Richard to see the great city in all its aspects but actually to get him away from the neighborhood while Lucy visits her uncle. While there she is scheduled to marry her cousin, but Richard discovers the plot and intercepts her on the way. He extracts a promise of marriage from her and houses her with Mrs. Berry, a wise old lady who later turns out to have been Richard's first nurse, fired for having inadvertently seen Sir Austin one night in a state of tears at the bedside of his motherless son. Adrian, meanwhile, attempts in his characteristic fashion to warn Richard about his own innocence: " 'Mystery is the great danger to youth, my son! Mystery is woman's redoubtable weapon, O Richard of the Ordeal!' " But the chivalric Richard, whose inexperience and failure to recognize it are equally damaging, continues to judge all women by Lucy, and to idealize: " 'Oh what noble creatures women are!' '' The marriage plans are settled upon, Sir Austin in ignorance the while. Richard's step is characterized by Meredith as being equivalent in importance in his life to the crossing of the Rubicon in Caesar's; and the comparison leads Meredith on to a statement about the moral dangers inevitable for a nature both unsophisticated and self-confident. What Richard is most lacking—and also, in his pride, most unaware of lacking—is experience:

> Only when they stand on the opposite banks do heroes see what a leap they have taken . . . There they have dreamed; here they must act. There lie youth and irresolution; here manhood and purpose . . . Be your Rubicon big or small, clear or foul, it is the same: you shall not return . . . 'The danger of a little knowledge of things is disputable; *but beware the little knowledge of one's self!'* Richard Feverel was now crossing the River of his Ordeal . . . [w]ithout a suspicion of folly in his acts, or fear of results . . . . (XXX)

Richard's ignorance, both of the world and of himself, is ironically alluded to here in a quotation from *The Pilgrim's Scrip*. He does not realize that he is as yet too young to marry—dreams and gullibility and irresolution are still a part of his youthful inexperience. The moral dangers of the world remain unknown to him and thus he is inordinately susceptible to them. He does not know what they are, nor how to react to them. It is an act of folly for Richard to marry and set up in the world at this stage of his moral development, even though he is undeniably marrying the right woman. In plunging ahead in the pride of his innocence, Richard is also guaranteeing that Lucy will undergo an ordeal as harsh as or harsher than his own. The evil catalyst is "the little knowledge of one's self."

The reaction of Raynham to the news of Richard's marriage and escape with his wife to the Isle of Wight is ironically characteristic. Adrian, who is the first of the family to discover the truth, ascribes Richard's actions to a System of education " 'that does not reckon on the powerful action of curiosity on the juvenile intelligence.' '' Sir Austin's reaction is typical: " 'it is useless to base any system on a human being.' " He blames the human being instead of the System which has attempted to make his son its creature: "Richard was no longer the Richard of his creation—his pride and his joy—but simply a human being with the rest. The bright star had sunk among the mass" [XXXIV]. Now that Richard no longer belongs to him body and soul, Sir Austin shuts him out of his heart. Meredith comments on Sir Austin's error: "If, instead of saying, Base no system on a human being, he had said, Never experimentalize with one, he would have been nearer the truth of his own case" [XXXIV]. Sir Austin is clearly at fault for believing that human nature can be scientifically controlled, and then for being unable to see that the results of the science he has been practicing upon his son should not be laid at the door of the experimental object itself. He decides to do nothing. His cold pronouncement of doom upon his son—" 'Consequences are the natural offspring of acts' "—sounds like a humorless parody of the author of *Adam Bede* (which appeared in the same year). Wisdom, or its appearance, is to Sir Austin more than the love of his son, even when the wisdom is specious and the love precious.

When we next see Richard, during his honeymoon on the Isle of Wight, his sentimentality has swelled appreciably. Imprisoned by his father during all of his previous years, he is now infatuated with all women. Meredith uses the image of Briareus—the hundred-armed Titan—to characterize Richard's moral irresolution. "Vague, shapeless ambition ha[s] replaced love"; Richard has decided that his mission in life is to save fallen women from the consequences of their folly. His romantic knight-errantry obliterates the real world: "Images of airy towers hung around. His fancy performed miraculous feats." The real world is obscured by the mists of self-indulgence.

Wanting reconciliation with his distant father, Richard now decides to go to London for the purpose. Lucy, advised by Adrian to stay behind in order to enhance the prospects of reconciliation, pleads cowardice to Richard, and he goes off to the city. Sir Austin is not so easily placated, however, and stays away. Finding himself with little to do and rationalizing a continued separation from Lucy as the best way to conciliate his father, Richard begins to discover the pleasures of London, and in doing so resolves to put into execution his plan for the regeneration of the fallen women of the city. The results, naturally, are catastrophic. Richard knows nothing about women and very little in general about human nature. In his youthful idealism and zeal he fancies himself an expert on the subject of the human heart. He rushes headlong into a series of self-gratifying escapades in blissful violation of the dictum that, in the language of the novel, one can never cross back over the Rubicon and return to the irresponsibility of youth. Richard, however, is neither mature nor wise. He is deluded by his innocence, his self-confidence, and his rampant sentimentality. As Mrs. Doria Forey says, " 'He is forever in some mad excess of his fancy . . . .' " Lord Heddon is proved a prophet.

Meanwhile, Richard "dallies" with Lucy's love and forgets both about her and his father. As he discovers more and more plainly how attractive he is to women and what power he may exercise over them, his regard both for them and for himself grows. Staying in London becomes a form of self-gratification rather than self-denial. Instead of separating himself from Lucy for the good of their marriage, he is engaged headlong in destroying it. Sir Austin, in his retreat, is apprised of Richard's folly and the dangers inherent in his flirtations, and does nothing. By coming to London and reconciling himself to his son he might still be able to save him; but he does not move. He considers this a test for Richard, part of his ordeal—the ordeal of the Feverels. He remains blind to the fact that the System has groomed Richard for precisely the form of vanity he is now in fact engaged in—and that he himself is now helping to perpetuate his son's ordeal.

Richard pursues "the regeneration of the streets of London, and the profession of moral-scavenger . . . . " He is "flattered" by "the idea that he [is] seeing the world, and [feels]wiser . . . ." All of his friends and relatives perceive his moral stupidity, and yet he insists on his own righteousness. He even undertakes to "save" his own mother from the man she has been living with for the past twenty years. Everyone tells him to go home to his wife, but he is deaf to all in his blind self-assurance. The climax of his moral collapse is his affair with the beautiful Bella, wife of his friend Lord Mountfalcon. Mountfalcon, vacationing on the Isle of Wight, has fallen in love with Lucy and pays his wife, from whom he is separated, to keep Richard away from Lucy as best she can. Bella is simply a prostitute, but Richard sees in her the ideal of fallen womanhood and resolves to save the sex by saving her. Everyone around Richard knows Bella and knows what she is, but Richard perseveres in his delusion. When he is warned about being duped by the unscrupulous Bella, he responds with lectures "on erring women, speaking of them as if he had known them and studied them for years. Clever, beautiful, but betrayed by love, it was the first duty of all true men to cherish and redeem them" [XXXVII] . All women are to be rescued from transgression; Richard begins with Bella. His romantic vanity continues to blind him to reality. The more Richard is urged to return to his wife, the more he argues that he is staying away from her for the sake of their marriage. He thinks Lucy is afraid of meeting Sir Austin; he does not realize that her strength of will keeps her away. She still believes Richard's sole object in town is reconciliation with his father. Mrs. Berry's assessment of the situation, to which no one but Lady Blandish pays any attention, is by far the most sensible: " 'Let that sweet young couple come together, and be wholesome in spite of [Sir Austin] , I say, and then give him time to come round, just like a woman; and round he'll come, and give 'em his blessin' . . .' " [XXXIX].

As Richard gets himself more and more entangled in Bella's nets, his view of his marriage becomes increasingly irrational and jaundiced (XXXIX): "He began to think that the life lying behind him was the life of a fool. What had he done in it? He had burnt a rick and got married . . . Great heavens! how ignoble a flash from the light of his aspirations made his marriage appear!" And so Richard, who thinks Bella "the cleverest woman he had ever met," plunges back into the dangerous waters of the Rubicon. He insists that he is "saving" Bella, doing her good rather than being harmed by her, and snorts at Lady Blandish's assertion that he is deluded. The System has rendered him helpless in the face of human nature. He reacts to everything sentimentally and subjectively (XXXIX): "Her sin was there, but in dreaming to save, he was soft to her sin—drowned it in deep mournfulness . . . Was ever a hero in this fashion won?" Unlike another Richard recalled by the language here, Shakespeare's Richard III, Richard Feverel is everybody's victim.

Richard is finally and unequivocally unfaithful to his wife. Lucy is pregnant, but Richard does not know this. Even Lord Mountfalcon and his parasite Brayder consider Richard a "brute" and his conduct "infamous." Sir Austin, increasingly alarmed at the reports of his son's behavior, at last consents to an audience with him, but their meeting is cold and uneventful. Even the supreme egoist himself can see the nature of his son's folly. He tells Richard that he is ready to receive him and his wife at Raynham, but Richard does not reply. When Richard and Lucy almost meet in London (Mrs. Berry has brought her back to her house), Richard hides and pretends not to know her. He asks Sir Austin to receive Lucy at Raynham without him. Sir Austin says he will receive her when Richard returns with her. Richard demurs. His self-indulgence begins to be tinged with guilt and misery, but he is still blindly sentimental: he will not return to Lucy because, he says, he is no longer worthy of her. At least he is beginning to see the ruinous infamy of his behavior (XLI): " 'Ask me what it is to have taken one of God's precious angels and chained her to misery! Ask me what it is to have plunged a sword into her heart, and to stand over her and see such a creature bleeding! Do I regret that? Why, yes, I do!' " Though somewhat repentant, Richard still sounds like the posturing penitent; sentimentality forces him to play a role. He says, after avoiding Lucy on the street, that " 'God spared her' "; Sir Austin begins to think, ironically enough, that perhaps he was " 'wrong in allowing him so much liberty during his probation.' "

Richard's self-discovery, however, now begins in earnest. Clare Forey, who has married a wealthy middle-aged man at her mother's insistence, commits suicide. She has always been in love with Richard, as everyone except Richard himself seems to have known. He has always treated her with tolerance and condescension. On the occasion of their last meeting, at Clare's wedding, Richard had suggested to her that death would be preferable to such a marriage and had walked off in a cloud of self-righteousness. Clare can bear his indifference but not his contempt; miserable in her marriage, she kills herself, leaving an explicit diary for Richard and her mother to read. Richard reads that he has helped to destroy the happiness of still another woman. He decides that he is " 'not worthy to touch [Lucy's] hand' " and that he will go abroad to "cleanse" himself. His sentimentality is still there, but now more substantially tempered by genuine self-doubt and unhappiness. Lucy, meanwhile, gives birth to a son and is taken by Austin Wentworth to Raynham Abbey, where she is immediately accepted and cherished by Sir Austin. Richard remains abroad.

Chapter XLIII, in which, finally, "Nature Speaks," contains the novel's pivotal scene, the moment of Richard's discovery of the meaning and the value of unselfish love of another human object. Austin Wentworth tracks him down in Germany in the train of yet another woman, this one middle-aged, and informs him that he has a son. Richard is astonished, first by the news and then, increasingly, by his own ridiculous behavior now seen in temperate retrospect. He finds he "can blame nothing but his own baseness." He begins to feel "infinitely vile"; yet, in his despair, he cannot abandon a final attempt at self-justification: "Had he not been nursed to believe he was born for great things? . . . And to feel base and yet born for better is enough to make one grasp at anything cloudy." Meredith quickly deflates this final sentimentalizing: "Briareus of the hundred unoccupied hands may turn to a monstrous donkey with his hind legs aloft, or

twenty thousand jabbering apes." As if to emphasize his
doctrine that nature and natural instinct are always superior
to unbending mechanical science, Meredith makes Richard
undergo the most convulsive part of his moral conversion in a
forest during a walk:

> Where are the dreams of the hero when he learns that he
> has a child? Nature is taking him to her bosom . . . And
> though he knew it not, he was beginning to strike the
> key-notes of Nature. But he did know of a singular har-
> mony that suddenly burst over his whole being . . .
> Something of a religious joy—a strange sacred
> pleasure—was in him . . . [H]e remembered himself;
> and now he was possessed by a proportionate anguish
> . . . [H]e had no longer his fantasies to fall upon. He
> was utterly bare to his sin . . . Then came stern efforts
> to command his misery . . . . [H]is spirit rose . . . .
> (XLIII)

The "religious joy" and "sacred pleasure" Richard feels are
the harbingers of a baptism of love. As in George Eliot's and
Dickens's novels, "anguish" leads from the "misery" attendant upon the follies of egoism ("fantasies") to self-
awareness and genuine feeling—which are in turn viewed by
the novelist as concomitants of spiritual salvation. "He
remembered himself," and in doing so Richard feels a new
and "singular harmony" within him. "Bare to his sin," he
walks on through the German forest. A storm comes up, appropriately enough, and Richard, like Lear, is content to be
buffeted. Finding a leveret in the woods, Richard is transfixed by his sudden feeling of charity and reverence for all
living things:

> [H]is strength went out of him and he shuddered. What
> was it? He asked not. He was in other hands. Vivid as
> lightning the Spirit of Life illumined him. He felt in his
> heart the cry of his child, his darling's touch. With shut
> eyes he saw them both. They drew him from the depths;
> they led him a blind and tottering man. And as they led
> him he had a sense of purification so sweet he shuddered
> again and again. (XLIII)

The "Spirit of Life" which "illumines" Richard represents a "purification" which leaves in its wake the ruins of a sentimental egoism, the seed of more objective vision, and a renewed ability to love. For Meredith, as for our preceding writers, the growth of feeling for others has all the sanctity of religious fulfillment. Understanding his own folly and suffering for it have regenerated Richard into a being capable of unselfish love. And yet Richard's ordeal is not yet over; he must suffer more for his past folly.

The news of Richard's imminent return reaches Raynham. Sir Austin, who has remained blind to the follies of his own nature, has at least begun to question the virtues of the System. He sees that he was wrong to think that " 'anything save blind fortuity would [have brought Richard] such a mate as he should have.' " He admits that "instinct" has "beaten science," but he still thinks of the pernicious System as something detached from his person, as if, because he has discovered some defects in it, it is to blame for what has happened rather than himself. His blind self-conceit remains unshaken. He believes himself false to his System but not to his son.

Meanwhile Richard, on his way home, has gotten himself into one final sentimental entanglement. A letter from Bella reaches him in which she reveals Mountfalcon's plot against Lucy and himself. Without calculating the effects of such an action upon Lucy and the others at Raynham, Richard deliberately insults Mountfalcon and challenges him to a duel. He then returns to Raynham, where "the fulness of his anguish and the madness of the thing he had done" comes upon him when he sees at first hand the "hard earthly misery" he has caused to those he loves. One of the things the System denied him was experience of the world, and this at least he has now sadly had: "His father's studious mind felt itself years behind him, he was so completely altered." His reunion with Lucy is tender but brief. He thinks of "the sweet wonders of life she had made real to him" and wishes he might retract his challenge to Mountfalcon in the interests of "divine happiness." But, tragically enough, "pride said it was impossible," and Richard, admitting to Lucy that he has been a " 'wretched vain fool,' " leaves her again.

Two days later, with Lucy on the verge of madness, comes the news from France of Richard's duel with Mountfalcon, in which Richard has been wounded. The Raynham contingent arrives to nurse him, and Lady Blandish's letter recounts the novel's final events. Egoism and sentimentality are seen to be capable at last of turning comedy into tragedy, life into death. Sir Austin, fearing possible effects upon his grandson, prevents Lucy from seeing Richard during his convalescence and commands her to control herself for the sake of her child. Collapsing under the enormous strain she has been under, Lucy contracts brain fever and dies within a few days. What Lady Blandish terms his " 'mad self-deceit' " never leaves Sir Austin, as we have seen earlier; she includes in her letter to Austin Wentworth the hope that Richard's son may be " 'saved' " from his grandfather. She feels that Sir Austin remains unaltered; and " 'what he has done cannot be undone . . . If he can look on her and not see his *sin,* I almost fear God will never enlighten him.' " Sir Austin informs Richard, who is recovering, of his wife's death: " 'He listened, and smiled. I never saw a smile so sweet and so sad. He said he had seen her die, as if he had passed through his suffering a long time ago . . . Richard will never be what he promised' " [XLVI]. We see him, at the end, lying silent in his bed, striving to image his dead wife's picture upon his brain. He has finally understood the world and himself; he is no longer proud and self-indulgent. Physically, at least, he has survived his ordeal. But emotionally Richard is dead, a victim of the completeness of his moral education.

THOMAS HARDY (1840-1928)
National Portrait Gallery, London

Chapter Six

Thomas Hardy

When we first meet Bathsheba Everdene, the heroine of Hardy's *Far from the Madding Crowd* (1874), she is admiring her reflection in a mirror. The scene both introduces us to and epitomizes the novel's paramount moral precept: the vanity of personal vanity. *Far from the Madding Crowd* addresses itself basically to the question of how to live as painlessly as possible and answers that question by tracing Bathsheba's development from a state of moral solipsism and narrow vision to one of moral expansion and wider sympathy.

In the novel's early pages Bathsheba's thoughts, not unlike those of Hetty Sorrel, are of herself and of the effects she is likely to have upon men. Her vanity is prodigious:

> a small looking-glass was disclosed, in which she proceeded to survey herself attentively. She parted her lips . . . She blushed at herself, and seeing her reflection blush, blushed the more . . . There was no necessity whatever for her looking in the glass. She did not adjust her hat, or pat her hair, or press a dimple into shape, or do one thing to signify that any such intention had been her motive in taking up the glass. She simply observed herself as a fair product of Nature in the feminine kind, her thoughts seeming to glide into far-off though likely dramas in which men would play a part—vistas of possible triumphs--the smiles being of a phase suggesting that hearts were imagined as lost and won. (I)

The losing and winning of hearts is for Bathsheba, like Gwendolen Harleth, a subject of light interest rather than thoughtful concern at this untutored stage of her existence. Such intellectual superficiality is a concomitant of the importance the surface of her own person has for her. Were there any reason to doubt Bathsheba's shallow self-conceit, such doubt would be quickly dispelled by the choric voice of farmer

217

Gabriel Oak, who has been observing her during her unconscious performance. " 'Vanity,' " says Oak, and steps
back into the woods. But the judgment seems to echo resound-
ingly. There is that in Bathsheba's manner, the narrator tells
us, which implies that "the desirability of her existence could
not be questioned. . . ." In this too Bathsheba is not unlike
Gwendolen Harleth. (*Daniel Deronda* appeared just two years
after *Far from the Madding Crowd*, which was widely popular
and was undoubtedly read by George Eliot, who was herself
thought by many people to be the author of this anonymous
success.)

Given her lack of deep thought, it seems logical that
Bathsheba should also be deficient in feeling. She is, in fact, a
flirt. Oak, who is enamored of her despite his quick discern-
ment of her unreflecting egoism, attempts to get to know her
better. She teases him: " 'Now find out my name.' " Oak's
precipitate proposal of marriage elicits an answer patently
demonstrating the depth of her personal vanity, her egoism:

> 'a marriage would be very nice in one sense. People
> would talk about me and think I had won my battle, and
> I should feel triumphant, and all that. But a husband . . .
> [W]hat I mean is that I shouldn't mind being a bride at a
> wedding, if I could be one without a husband. But since
> a woman can't show off in that way by herself, I shan't
> marry—at least yet!' (IV)

Bathsheba loves to "show off," to be at the center of things,
observed and admired by an audience of others. Like Gwendolen's, her major interest is in self-gratification, in the
"triumph" of marriage rather than its responsibilities. And so
she rejects Oak. She is honest, at least, about the importance
of herself to herself. But her inability to empathize beyond
the barrier of self betokens future disappointment and
remorse.

Not long after Oak's suit has been rejected Bathsheba's
prosperous uncle dies, and she inherits his large farm and
leaves the neighborhood of Oak's farm and impecunious
obscurity for Weatherbury. Shortly thereafter, too, Oak loses
his sheep herd and his farm through a gratuitous Hardyesque

accident and decides to look for work in the vicinity of
Weatherbury. He is hired as a shepherd on Bathsheba's farm,
finding in her manner to him "a proportionate increase of
arrogance and reserve" concomitant with her rise and his fall
in station and social influence.

Through the first dozen chapters of *Far from the Madding Crowd*, Bathsheba's self-absorption and the various in-
discretions born of it seem relatively harmless. In Chapter
XIII, however, her thoughtlessness starts in motion a train of
events destined to end in tragedy. The farm next to
Bathsheba's is owned by the prosperous bachelor Boldwood,
who is said to be immune to feminine charms. Feeling
challenged by these rumors, Bathsheba weighs sending him a
valentine, flips a coin, and decides to do so. "It was Wisdom
in the abstract facing Folly in the concrete. Folly in the
concrete blushed, and persisted in her intention. . . ." And so
Bathsheba, with the shallow, unthinking egoism that
characterizes much of her behavior in the novel's earlier
chapters, sends off the valentine which ultimately wrecks
several lives. For Boldwood is susceptible to her charms, as it
turns out, while she has no genuine interest in him beyond the
satisfaction of her own feminine vanity. The valentine
unfortunately turns Boldwood's attention toward Bathsheba;
and the narrator's comment at the end of Chapter XIII sums
up the case against her: "So very idly and unreflectingly was
this deed done. Of love as a spectacle Bathsheba had a fair
knowledge; but of love subjectively she knew nothing." Again
like Gwendolen, Bathsheba has not as yet undergone the
process of expansion inevitably involved in a genuine love
relationship. Nor does she *think,* except about herself and the
impression others may be made to have of her. And so,
naturally, she is insensible "to the possibly great issues of little
beginnings."

With Boldwood's attention at last directed her way,
Bathsheba, to her credit, finds her victory hollow. For the
first time since we have known her, she regrets something she
has done: "She resolved never again, by look or by sign, to interrupt the steady flow of this man's life. But a resolution to

avoid an evil is seldom framed till the evil is so far advanced
as to make avoidance impossible" [XVIII]. Acts have consequences. As Boldwood's attentions to her increase, her
realization of her own folly deepens. She has no feeling for
him and yet recognizes that she is to blame for his aroused interest in her: "it was but the natural conclusion of serious
reflection based on deceptive premises of her own offering."
Bathsheba's ordeal of moral education begins in earnest as
Boldwood's pursuit of her becomes serious and sustained. In
her initial apology to him she demonstrates a ready capacity
for moral expansion and the growth of self-knowledge: " ' I
know I ought never to have dreamt of sending that valentine—forgive me, sir—it was a wanton thing which no
woman with any self-respect should have done. If you will
only pardon my thoughtlessness . . .' " [XIX]. But Boldwood
refuses to accept her apology, which is genuine, and swears to
Bathsheba that he loves her, needs her, and must marry her.
Her response to his plea is entirely right: " 'O, I am wicked
to have made you suffer so!' "

Hardy makes it clear that the misery Bathsheba is caus-
ing results as much from simple thoughtlessness as from
selfishness. Her intellectual processes are not only shallow
but rash, which gives to them a certain illogic. Bathsheba, in
short, does not think deeply enough—not because she is incapable of deeper thought but because the avoidance of
deeper thought is an analogue of self-indulgence, of the desire
to eschew the labor of reasoning wherever possible. Again
like Gwendolen, Bathsheba is short on "inward strife." It is
always difficult, of course, to think of much else when one is
thinking of oneself. These things are implicit in Hardy's
acidulous assessment of his heroine's mind: "Many of her
thoughts were perfect syllogisms; unluckily they always
remained thoughts. Only a few were irrational assumptions;
but, unfortunately, they were the ones which most frequently
grew into deeds . . . With Bathsheba a hastened act was a rash
act; but, as does not always happen, time gained was
prudence ensured. It must be added, however, that time was
very seldom gained" [XX].

Bathsheba, as we have seen, is nevertheless beginning to feel the prick of conscience, which means in effect that she is taking the time and using the mental energy necessary to assess the propriety of her past conduct. What she begins to achieve in so doing is not, as yet, self-awareness; but she is at least edging toward the habit of self-scrutiny. In this new spirit of larger-mindedness she asks her old friend Oak if he thinks she has been behaving badly. When he tells her that her conduct " 'is unworthy of any thoughtful, and meek, and comely woman' " she fires him from her employ—only to order him back almost immediately to help save her stricken sheep. Oak demurs until he is asked politely to return, and at last Bathsheba begs him to help her. This small event encases a paradigm of the moral direction Bathsheba's conduct will ultimately have to take.

Boldwood renews his proposal of marriage to Bathsheba, who continues to regret the effect her thoughtlessness has had on him and yet relishes the taste of personal conquest:

> [Bathsheba's] eye was bright with the excitement of a triumph—though it was a triumph which had rather been contemplated than desired . . . To have brought all this about her ears was terrible, but after a while the situation was not without a fearful joy. The facility with which even the most timid women sometimes acquire a relish for the dreadful when that is amalgamated with a little triumph, is marvellous. (XXIII)

And so we find Bathsheba, almost halfway through the novel, still hungrily feeding her vanity. And yet, quite clearly, she has shown signs of developing a conscience born of some tentative self-examination.

While Gabriel's "tender devotion" to Bathsheba grows, she herself has become infatuated with the unscrupulous and irresponsible Sergeant Troy, whose physical beauty is only another indication that her shallow vision still perceives surfaces but not depths. Troy interests Bathsheba initially by flattering her elaborately; she is both charmed and encouraging—still a flirt in spite of herself. Her self-absorption blinds her to his real nature, which is even more selfish than hers. But there are times, says Hardy, when vain girls like Bathsheba will put up with almost any kind of behavior from a man—that is, "when they want to be praised"; and so Bathsheba's vanity overmasters her once again.

In remaining blind to the real natures of both Oak and Troy, Bathsheba of course continues to disappoint poor Boldwood, who has made the "fatal omission" of "never once [telling] her she was beautiful." Bathsheba admires men in proportion to their capacity for flattering her and in inverse proportion to their loyalty and selflessness. Like Amelia Sedley, she is the dupe of her own egoistic nature, which dotes on surfaces and posturing and shrinks from objectivity and honesty. She pretends initially to reject Troy's advances, courting them all the while. When she tells him that she never allows anyone to speak to her as he has done, he replies carelessly, and with much truth, that " 'it is not the fact but the method' " which she objects to. The more he flatters her the more she feels "a *penchant* to hear more." She flirts with him at length, feigning doubt that she is really as "fascinating" as he says she is. She makes his work ridiculously easy, pretending to derive no pleasure from his flattery while "the devil smiled from a loop-hole in Tophet." She eggs Troy on with false doubt of his sincerity, which, as a prosperous landowner if not as a beautiful woman, she ought genuinely to doubt. When he leaves her for a short time and the spell is temporarily broken, Bathsheba has a moment of glimmering truth: " 'O, what have I done! What does it mean! I wish I knew how much of it was true!' " And yet she continues to meet him alone.

Hardy now pauses in his narrative to comment explicitly upon Bathsheba's feminine nature:

> We now see the element of folly distinctly mingling with the many varying particulars which made up the character of Bathsheba Everdene . . . [I]t eventually permeated and coloured her whole constitution. Bathsheba . . . had too much womanliness to use her understanding to the best advantage. Perhaps in no minor

point does woman astonish her helpmate more than in
the strange power she possesses of believing cajoleries
that she knows to be false—except, indeed, in that of being utterly sceptical on strictures that she knows to be
true. . . . [Bathsheba] felt her impulses to be pleasanter
guides than her discretion. Her culpability lay in her
making no attempt to control feeling by subtle and
careful inquiry into consequences. . And Troy's deform-
ities lay deep down from a woman's vision, whilst his
embellishments were upon the very surface; thus contrasting with homely Oak, whose defects were patent to
the blindest, and whose virtues were as metals in a mine.
(XXIX)

"Womanliness," for Hardy, seems to have as its paramount
element a vanity which turns the mind's vision within, thus
obscuring the real nature of objective reality. "Cajoleries"
annihilate "understanding" and "impulses" annihilate
"discretion." Thus Bathsheba, whose egoism is self-blinding,
can see only surfaces; and so she admires Troy and ignores
Oak. Her shallow nature continues to eschew all "inquiry
into consequences." When Gabriel warns her, quite truly,
that Troy has " 'no conscience at all,' " she replies by eulogiz-
ing his worthiness. In a short time she trusts him entirely,
even though she catches him in a lie—his statement that he
regularly attends the parish church. Oak continues to urge
discretion upon her, but she stops listening to him when he
urges her to marry Boldwood: "she could not really forgive
him for letting his wish to marry her be eclipsed by his wish to
do her good. . . ." Bathsheba remains essentially a prisoner of
her own blinding vanity. Her new marginal self-recognition
has thus far produced little amendment in her conduct. She
does, however, at least begin to *reflect*—to regret from time
to time that her vanity has led her so far down the path of
self-indulgence. This is why, for example, she now worries
again about Oak's opinion of her and Boldwood's inevitable
disappointment and anguish. Boldwood reproaches her as
her infatuation with Troy becomes more manifest (XXXI):
" 'there was a time when I knew nothing of you, and cared
nothing for you, and yet you drew me on. And if you say you

gave me no encouragement, I cannot but contradict you. . . . Would to God you had never taken me up, since it was only to throw me down!' '' Bathsheba's response to him is an indication that she has begun to understand and regret her past folly: '' 'What you call encouragement was the childish game of an idle minute. I have bitterly repented of it—ay, bitterly, and in tears. . . . How was I to know that what is a pastime to all other men was death to you?' '' Boldwood goes on reproaching her for her "woman's folly," calls Troy a "rake," and leaves her in anger. Bathsheba sees with remorse that she has been instrumental in reducing a proud and aloof man to misery and desperation. And yet she goes on meeting the Sergeant, loving him none the less for having "penetrated [his] nature so far as to estimate his tendencies pretty accurately. . . ." Her major fear is that he will cease to love her.

Shortly thereafter Bathsheba and Troy are married secretly in Bath. Bathsheba is driven to this final step once again by selfish vanity. Shortly before their marriage Troy and Bathsheba had encountered Fanny Robin, Bathsheba's former servant and Troy's former fiancée. Troy later tells Bathsheba that he has that day seen a woman more beautiful than she; Bathsheba consents immediately to marry him to guarantee, so she thinks, his constancy. Troy, however, has never been constant in anything, unless it is mendaciousness and greed. Later, the pregnant Fanny is found on the road suffering from hunger and exposure; she and the child (Troy's) both die in childbirth shortly thereafter. Troy deliberately insults Bathsheba; he acknowledges his fatherhood, shows her the lock of Fanny's hair he always carries with him, tells her that he already repents of his marriage, and asserts that the dead woman is dearer to him than his own wife and that he would have married Fanny had not '' 'Satan . . . tempted me with that face of yours, and those cursed coquetries.' '' He leaves the house, and Bathsheba is left to the contemplation of her mad vanity and self-indulgence. Her moral education has at last reached that stage of despairing misery which is a prerequisite of self-discovery and more objective perception:

'Now, anything short of cruelty will content me. Yes! the independent and spirited Bathsheba is come to this!' . . . .She was conquered. . .Her pride was indeed brought low by despairing of her spoilation by marriage. . . . She hated herself now. . . . O, if she had never stooped to folly of this kind . . . and could only stand again. . . . [She] had not yet learnt . . . the simple lesson which Oak showed a mastery of by every turn and look he gave—that among the multitude of interests by which he was surrounded, those which affected his personal well-being were not the most absorbing and important in his eyes. Oak meditatively looked upon the horizon of circumstances without any special regard to his own standpoint in the midst. That was how she would wish to be . . . 'O God, have mercy! I am miserable at all this . . .' Bathsheba became at this moment so terrified at her own state of mind that she looked around for some sort of refuge from herself. (XLI - XLIII, *passim.*)

This is a pivotal moment in the novel's treatment of Bathsheba's ordeal of knowledge. All vestiges of her egoism are not as yet fully exorcised, as all vestiges of egoism are in Oak; but Bathsheba wishes to be like Oak, at least insofar as his selflessness and empathy are concerned. Like Gwendolen Harleth, who studied Daniel Deronda's moral perspective and attempted thereby to be like him, Bathsheba here takes as her model Oak's self-disinterestedness and wishes she could be more like him. She has, at least, chosen wisely and in a way that will help her to cultivate moral vision. The psychic reorganization going on within her is of course excruciating, bringing her pride low by means of "despairing discoveries." Self-hatred and misery as a result of the recognition of folly will help open for her the way to increased self-knowledge and sympathy. This is why, in a literal sense, she is portrayed here as attempting to seek a refuge from *self*. Self, she is finally beginning to see, is not a satisfactory end. Thus we find her, at the end of Chapter XLVI, wiping away the mud from Fanny Robin's tombstone "with the superfluous magnanimity of a woman whose narrower instincts have brought down bitterness upon her. . . ." Bathsheba's slow and painful moral expansion is gradually widening those "narrower instincts."

Troy meanwhile disappears from view, and it is reported that he has apparently been drowned while swimming: Bathsheba refuses to believe it is so. Troy's presumed death, however, encourages Boldwood to renew his suit with Bathsheba; he senses in her, as do others, a new seriousness, a new conscientiousness, a kinder disposition. Hardy chooses, in language reminiscent of *Adam Bede*, to define Bathsheba's moral evolution explicitly (XLIX): "the severe schooling she had been subjected to had made Bathsheba more considerate than she had formerly been of the feelings of others . . . . There was a substratum of good feeling in her [due in good part to] self-reproach for the injury she had thoughtlessly done [Boldwood]." Consideration of the feelings of others is precisely what Bathsheba has been lacking previously; in her emulation of the better nature so constantly near her (Oak's) her own nature has profited. Self is no longer paramount. The realization of her past selfishness has made it possible for her to eschew selfishness itself. Once again the egoist's "severe schooling" leads to anguish and increased fellow feeling.

Bathsheba's ordeal, however, is not yet over. Unknown to her, Troy is on his way home. Boldwood, meanwhile, is trying again to extract from her a promise of marriage some years hence. She sympathizes with Boldwood now because his sad plight is a constant reminder to her of her earlier folly, and she continues to wish to make reparation for it. She tells him: " 'My treatment of you was thoughtless, inexcusable, wicked! I shall eternally regret it . . .[T]here [is] nothing on earth I so [long] to do as to repair the error' " [LI]. Boldwood urges an engagement to marry him at some future date as a means of reparation, and Bathsheba, in her new contrition, is driven to serious consideration of his proposal. She talks it over with Gabriel, telling him that she now feels bound to act " 'without any consideration of my own future at all . . . . [It is] a sort of penance . . . .' " Like Gwendolen, Bathsheba has come a long way to "penance" from the earlier days of coquetry and idle vanity.

Now come the climactic events of Boldwood's Christmas party (LIII), at which Troy is planning to make his dramatic re-entrance. The scene is prepared for by the choric comments of a group of rustics clustered outside Boldwood's house, men who have heard rumors of Troy's return. One of them says of Bathsheba: " 'What a fool she must have been to have had anything to do with the man! She is so self-willed and independent too, that one is more minded to say it serves her right than pity her.' " But another man answers him: " 'No, no! I don't hold with 'ee there. She was no otherwise than a girl mind, and how could she tell what the man was made of?' " Bathsheba's mind, turned inward in its egoism, was incapable of perceiving clearly the real natures of others. Her moral growth, however, has turned her vision outward and sharpened its focus. Nevertheless, fated events take their course. Troy appears and is shot and killed by the enraged and madly jealous Boldwood, who is himself sentenced to die for the deed (the sentence is later commuted). In this crisis Bathsheba's newly strengthened nature stands in greater relief than before: "Bathsheba was astonishing all around her now, for her philosophy was her conduct, and she seldom thought practicable what she did not practise" [LIV]. One need only remember Hardy's earlier acidulous comments on the illogic of her mind and conduct to see how much she has grown. Despite her new tough-minded realism, however, Bathsheba cannot entirely escape remorse and self-blame: " 'O it is my fault—how can I live! O Heaven, how can I live!' " It is toward the answer to this question of how to live that Bathsheba's ordeal has been leading her, and in this final suffering and misery she sees the last steps just ahead of her.

Those steps are precipitated abruptly at the end of the novel when Oak announces to Bathsheba that he plans to emigrate to California. Her "chronic gloom" dissipates as she discovers how best to keep him near her, and they are married at last. Hardy makes it clear that their relationship — tried, tested, and born of experience, knowledge, and mutual sympathy—will be a happy and fruitful one. And so, like Dorothea Brooke and Gwendolen

Harleth, Bathsheba Everdene is saved by a timely fate and
her own moral growth from the consequences of self-conceit
and her own disastrous judgment—but not before she has
become worthy of that salvation, predicated on the spiritual
enlargement which is a concomitant of an education in
values. Bathsheba now knows how to live.

II

Michael Henchard's ordeal of knowledge is the result of
an egoism, like that of Gwendolen Harleth and Bathsheba
Everdene, whose chief ingredient is self-indulgent impetuosity. Henchard's temperamental, unthinking capriciousness
plunges him into grave error again and again; the results are
misery born of constant and repeated repentance as self-
knowledge grows—and, ultimately, a needlessly tragic death.
Thus in *The Mayor of Casterbridge* (1886), as in *The Ordeal of
Richard Feverel,* there is moral regeneration, but it comes too
late to reverse the process of physical decay brought on by
mental anguish.

The Mayor of Casterbridge has as its subtitle "A Story of
A Man of Character," and quite clearly Michael Henchard's
"character" is at the center of the novel, is its central subject.
Henchard constantly sinks into folly through impulsive self-
indulgence and then repents of and suffers from his
thoughtlessness. Like Bathsheba's, his selfishness results in
large part from a lack of cerebration. And his thoughtlessness
assists the malignancy of fate in the creation of tragedy.
"Character," here, is indeed fate.

The novel opens with the Man of Character selling his
wife and child to another man in a drunken fit, then repenting
of his bad temper, and finally going off to look for them.
After a lapse of twenty years, during which Henchard has
sworn off liquor, we encounter him again as a prosperous
merchant and mayor of the farming town of Casterbridge.
His unpredictable temper, however, is still manifest to all
who know him.

Henchard hires Donald Farfrae, an enterprising and likable Scot, to help run his business. Soon afterward Susan Henchard turns up with her daughter and tells her former husband that she is now widowed and poor. Henchard, the narrator tells us, is still "a man who knew no moderation in his requests and impulses . . .[a man of] introspective inflexibility . . ." [12]. This latter phrase aptly describes the handicap Henchard must struggle against throughout much of the novel. But he marries Susan and takes her and the girl he believes to be his daughter into his house. Shortly thereafter he impetuously fires Farfrae because of his jealousy of the Scot's popularity in the town, which has partially eclipsed his own. In doing so, Henchard drives his former assistant into fatal competition with himself for the hay and corn market: "loving a man or hating him, his diplomacy was as wrongheaded as a buffalo's. . . . [M]ost probably luck had little to do with it. Character is fate, said Novalis, and Farfrae's character was just the reverse of Henchard's, who might . . . be described . . . as a vehement gloomy being who had quitted the ways of vulgar men without light to guide him on a better way" [17]. "Vehemence" without "light" is clearly an ominous combination.

Henchard's self-indulgent impulsiveness continues to plague him. Immediately after Susan Henchard's death he tells Elizabeth-Jane that he and not Newson—his wife's second husband, the sailor to whom she was sold—is her father; he then opens his late wife's letter, despite her directions to wait until Elizabeth-Jane's wedding day, and discovers that he is not her father after all. Elizabeth-Jane is the daughter of Newson; Henchard's daughter died in infancy. Henchard's "inflexibility" remains unaffected by these buffetings of fortune; temperament continues to get him into trouble: "Misery had taught him nothing more than defiant endurance of it . . . He was far too self-willed to recede from a position, especially [when] it would involve humiliation" [19]. And so in his self-willed defiance he resolves to let Elizabeth-Jane go on believing that she is his daughter; and yet his own knowledge that she is not causes him to treat her badly and even to think of ways of unencumbering himself of her presence in his house.

Shortly thereafter Henchard's former mistress, having heard of the death of Susan, arrives in Casterbridge in order to be courted by the mayor. Lucetta befriends the unhappy Elizabeth-Jane and invites her to live with her, thereby unwittingly providing Henchard with a reason for staying away. While Henchard is ignoring Lucetta, Farfrae visits the two women often, ostensibly to court Elizabeth-Jane. However, he and Lucetta fall in love, and Henchard is unintentionally cut out. When Henchard discovers what has happened, he threatens Lucetta with the revelation of their past intimacy unless she marries him. His pride and self-will, rather than any love he may feel for her, demands that he triumph publicly over Farfrae—or at least that he avoid suffering a public defeat at the Scot's hands. The egoist, as always, imagines himself playing to an interested audience.

Henchard now passes abruptly from unsubtlety to undoing. A concatenation of disasters befalls him, some of which are due to bad luck but most of which grow directly and inevitably out of his "character." First, the old furmity-woman resurfaces and discloses the story of Henchard's wife-selling years before. Then, in a desperate gamble to cut Farfrae out of business competition, Henchard loses heavily in both capital and goods. The result is a general loss of confidence in him in the town. Farfrae, meanwhile, secretly marries Lucetta, and Elizabeth-Jane moves into lodgings. Henchard, finally, goes completely bankrupt, and Farfrae takes over his business and his house in addition to his old mistress. To stay alive, Henchard goes to work for Farfrae; and he starts drinking heavily again. He has come full cycle now, with this addition: he is bitterly, passionately resentful and jealous of Farfrae, whom he accuses of stealing everything he once owned. Farfrae's good luck, however, has simply been a logical concomitant of Henchard's own decline. But Henchard perseveres in his hatred.

Farfrae, unlike Henchard, is "one of those men upon whom an incident is never absolutely lost. He revised impressions from a subsequent point of view, and the impulsive judgment of the moment was not always his permanent one" [34]. The Jamesian language here contrasts sharply with that used in connection with Henchard (and with Bathsheba Everdene), who gets into trouble by acting without thinking. For Hardy cerebration will often avert disaster; impetuous reaction invites it. The major component of man's egoism for him is this unthinking self-indulgence of momentary impulses; whereas the propensity to think, to weight alternatives and advantages, to eschew "introspective inflexibility" and welcome instead "inward strife"—these things are more likely to enable the individual to avoid the snares of willfulness and self-absorption. It is, once again, the subjective versus the objective perspective that is at the crucial center of things. For Hardy, excessive subjectivity inevitably involves selfishness in that actions resulting from it, often impulsive, are usually self-satisfying only. The more objective view of things, paradoxically enough, is that view more carefully examined in advance—more carefully thought out. Self-indulgence, the indulgence of spontaneous desire, results in part from lack of thought. Objectivity comes with the clear-sighted weighing of alternatives and consequences before action. Henchard's downfall is largely the result of his propensity for succumbing to mental masturbation—to action without thought on the self-satisfying impulse of a moment. Herein lies much of the explanation for his defective sensibility; his vision of things is that of a man almost totally at the mercy of his own subjective needs.

As is often the case in Hardy's novels, everything turns out for the worst in the worst of all possible worlds. Feeling that perhaps he has been unfair to Farfrae and his wife, Henchard sends back to Lucetta letters she wrote to him years earlier, which she has been begging him to return. The letters, however, get into the hands of the Mixen Lane inhabitants before they find their way back to Lucetta, and the town buzzes with the revelation of Henchard's former liaison with Mrs. Farfrae. The result, of course, is the skimity-ride, which publicizes the affair and causes Lucetta to have an epileptic fit, as a result of which she dies shortly thereafter. Henchard is almost beside himself with remorse—even though these catastrophes have been only partly of his own making. He is "in a state of bitter anxiety and contrition. . . . He cursed himself like a less scrupulous Job. . . ." [40]. Henchard attempts to win back Farfrae's good will, but Lucetta's death and its cause have finally used up Farfrae's patience with his former employer.

And so we see Henchard, in the latter chapters of *The Mayor of Casterbridge,* living quietly and repentantly in lodgings with Elizabeth-Jane. Henchard's only joy now is in his love for his stepdaughter and in her solicitude for him (she still believes he is her real father). Thus it has now become, ironically enough, the appropriate time for the return of Newson, who survived the shipwreck of years before and is searching for his wife and daughter. Henchard at this point commits his last serious act of folly, telling Newson that both Susan and Elizabeth-Jane are dead. Henchard lies to protect himself, feeling that he will lose his stepdaughter—all he has left—if she finds out that he is not her real father and that Newson himself is still alive. His lie to Newson is, like most of his other lapses, "the impulse of a moment . . . [He spoke] like a child, in pure mockery of consequences" [41]. Newson goes away, and Henchard gives himself up to the despair of guilt: " 'Who is such a reprobate as I!' " Yet he continues in the deception, fearing that he would lose Elizabeth-Jane if she knew the truth. Had Henchard thought the matter over instead of acting like a child, he probably would have seen that Elizabeth-Jane could not have scorned or abandoned him for telling the truth. As it is, he is giving her an excellent excuse to hate him later on. But Henchard, as before, acts for the moment, "in pure mockery of consequences." It is as if, somehow, those of Hardy's characters who resist or attempt to ignore the consequences of their actions bring Nemesis more surely down upon their heads than those who, like Farfrae and Newson, accommodate themselves to whatever fate ordains. One might almost detect a Doctrine of Unobtrusiveness here.

After a decent interval, Farfrae, now mayor of Casterbridge, begins to court Elizabeth-Jane again, and Henchard
sees in this a plot to rob him of his last and only possession.
Despite this characteristic perspective, Henchard seems at
least to have learned to act less impulsively, to consider more
carefully and at greater length the actions of others as they
relate to himself: "He would often weigh and consider for
hours together the meaning of such and such a deed or phrase
of [Elizabeth-Jane's], when a blunt settling question would
formerly have been his first instinct" [42]. Henchard resolves
to control his temper and to bear almost any humiliation
necessary to retain his stepdaughter's tenderness and proximity.

The final blow, however, now looms before Henchard.
As Elizabeth-Jane's marriage to Farfrae becomes more and
more a certainty and as Henchard wonders to himself
whether or not he could live with his stepdaughter as Farfrae's dependent, Nemesis strikes once more: Newson
returns. This is too much for Henchard to bear. Unable to
confess to Elizabeth-Jane, and correctly anticipating her
angry resentment of his past dishonesty, Henchard leaves
Casterbridge. And so we see him, as in the novel's first
chapter, once again looking for work as a hay-trusser, as
lonely and miserable as a man can be and still live. But
Henchard has little desire now to live. He returns to Weydon
Priors, the scene of the wife-selling more than twenty years
earlier, and muses upon the futility of his contrition.

Henchard's egoism has been the result less of blindness
to the folly of his acts, which he was constantly regretting,
than of the inability to reason beyond subjective needs and
desires at the moment of doing or saying. For Bathsheba
Everdene a reprieve was still possible. But in *The Mayor of
Casterbridge*, written twelve years later, there is no reprieve.
Henchard's "character" is his downfall, even though he has
learned to submerge his self-willed impetuosity in a new well
of thought and feeling. His recognition of his own flaw,
though both constant and relatively early, is not sufficient of
itself to enable him to start over again in time. In terms of

final tragic value *The Mayor of Casterbridge* is not unlike *The Ordeal of Richard Feverel* or *The Portrait of A Lady*; one need only compare the endings of these three novels with those of *Jane Eyre* or *A Tale of Two Cities*, for example, to recognize the ultimate tragic intensity. For the later Hardy, character is fate; and no amount of penultimate self-recognition or contrition can finally save the essentially thoughtless character from a luckless consummation.

Henchard goes back to work briefly, resolving to return to Casterbridge for Elizabeth-Jane's wedding and ask for her forgiveness and affection. But he is defeated in these aims and dies shortly thereafter. His last statement (45) expresses the finally complete self-negation of a man who has discovered only too well his own nature amidst the harshnesses of an unforgiving world:

'MICHAEL HENCHARD'S WILL

'That Elizabeth-Jane Farfrae be not told of my death, or made to grieve on account of me.

'& that I be not bury'd in consecrated ground.

'& that no sexton be asked to toll the bell.

'& that nobody is wished to see my dead body.

'& that no murners walk behind me at my funeral.

'& that no flours be planted on my grave.

'& that no man remember me.

'To this I put my name.

MICHAEL HENCHARD'

III

In *Tess of the D'Urbervilles* (1891), Angel Clare's egoism takes the form of "introspective inflexibility" bred of intractable moral prejudices. Clare, who thinks of himself as a liberated intellectual unfettered by what he considers the narrow social codes of his time, is in fact one of the most conventional of hypocrites. It is only natural that such a man, so totally devoid of self-knowledge, should also fail to perceive accurately the true natures of others. The story of *Tess of the D'Urbervilles* is primarily Tess's story, of course; but Tess's story is also Angel's story—the story of a man who makes a tragic mistake as a result of moral shallowness, suffers for it, and ultimately discovers his own true nature by discovering that of the woman he loves. Clare ultimately sees in his misjudgment of Tess the track of his own narrow way. Once again moral blindness brings about an ordeal of education, the result of which is moral revelation.

Without "any inference of indecision" about him, Clare, the youngest son of an evangelical minister, rejects the ministry as a vocation on the grounds that the Church " 'refuses to liberate her mind from an untenable redemptive theolatry.' " A theoretical liberal who thinks he values "intellectual liberty" above everything else, Clare is publicly disdainful of "material distinctions of rank and wealth." He decides to become a dairy farmer and is learning the trade at Tolbothays when he meets Tess Durbeyfield, who is working there to avoid the clutches of her hated "cousin" and seducer, Alec D'Urberville, by whom she has had a child who died in infancy. Angel is immediately attracted to Tess; but Tess, who has heard Dairyman Crick say that Clare hates "old families" and admires simplicity of "blood," and who imagines her father to be a descendant of the ancient D'Urberville line, fears and avoids him at first. She is ashamed in his presence both of her moral "impurity" and of the supposed "purity" of her blood (both of which are non-existent). It is, of course, only the former that will repel Angel Clare, who is as conventional in practice as he considers himself to be unconventional in spirit.

Clare soon proposes marriage to Tess. He is attracted both by her simple beauty and by her obvious fitness to be the wife of a dairy farmer—but more than anything else by what he considers to be her natural and unalloyed purity as a woman. The fecundity of Tolbothays itself, Tess's own "virginal" simplicity, and Clare's philosophical self-confidence are all factors in his attraction to her. Tess, who feels that she has not the right to marry any man, retreats in the face of Clare's advances until, finally, she is so passionately in love with him that she can do so no longer. She explains her resistance to him by telling him she knows he hates the old families and that she is descended from one of them. Clare, of course, is delighted; here is a palliative to his family's expected disapproval of the marriage. Clare had told her that " ' the only pedigrees we ought to respect are those spiritual ones of the wise and virtuous.' " Now, sounding a bit less like the liberated philosopher he thinks he is, Clare tells her that " 'Society is hopelessly snobbish, and this fact of your extraction may make an appreciable difference to its acceptance of you as my wife, after I have made you the well-read woman that I mean to make you' " [4, xxx]. The fact that he places such emphasis on society's acceptance of the woman he loves is an ominous foreshadowing of things to come.

Tess, meanwhile, is troubled with the secret of her past; she wants to confess it to Clare but shrinks from doing so. She regards him as a "saint," a "seer," and glories in the "compassion of his love for her." Clare all the while is thinking of the triumph he will have in announcing Tess's lineage to his family. When she complains to him, as she does frequently, that she is not "worthy" of him, he believes that she means she is his inferior in class. His disclaimers to her make his future course of action doubly ironic: " 'Distinction does not consist in the facile use of a contemptible set of conventions, but in being numbered among those who are true, and honest, and just, and pure, and lovely, and of good report—as you are, my Tess," [4,xxxi]. Hardy meanwhile begins to prepare us for the approaching debacle of their marriage by telling us that Clare loved Tess "dearly, though perhaps rather ideally and fancifully than with the impassioned thoroughness of her feeling for him"; that Clare tends to be reckless, impractical, and sentimental; and that "Tess's lineage had more value for himself than for anybody in the world besides." Shortly before their marriage Tess attempts once again to confess her past to Clare, this time in a letter he never receives. After the ceremony, as they are departing from Tolbothays, Clare expresses to himself the noblest of sentiments (4, xxxiv): " 'Do I realize solemnly enough how utterly and irretrievably this little womanly thing is the creature of my good or bad faith and fortune? . . . And shall I ever neglect her, or hurt her, or even forget to consider her? God forbid such a crime!' " And so off they go to the old D'Urberville house—near a mill, the workings of which Clare wishes to study next—for their honeymoon, the first few hours of which are so crucial to the novel's dramatic structure.

The pivotal scene (4, xxxiv, and 5, xxxv) begins with Clare confessing to Tess that he is not a virgin. He has been afraid of telling her before for fear of losing her. He asks easily and confidently for her forgiveness. Of course she gives it, thinking that now it will be easier for Clare to forgive her as well. But Clare, who admires "spotlessness" and hates "impurity" in others, cannot forgive her. As he hears Tess's story he seems physically to "wither"; at first he cannot believe her. She asks him, finally, to forgive her as she has forgiven him. But for Angel Clare—poet, philosopher, seer, liberated intellect, unprejudiced non-conformist—" 'Forgiveness does not apply to the case! You were one person; now you are another.' " He feels that she is not the same woman he thought he loved; purity for him is something clinical rather than spiritual. Tess, shocked, asks for mercy: " 'Having begun to love you, I love you forever—in all changes, in all disgraces, because you are yourself . . . [H]ow can you . . . stop loving me?' " Clare replies: " 'the woman I have been loving is not you.' " In his blind self-righteousness, Clare adheres spontaneously to all the middle-class mores and prejudices he has always prided himself on eschewing; he does not see that Tess *is* the same woman, morally pure. His intellectual Philistinism gets the better of him; Tess becomes for him "a species of impostor; a guilty woman in the guise of an innocent one." His capacity for sympathy, for charity—apparently never very deep—now dries up completely. He reverts to a more comfortable frigidity, accusing Tess of having withheld her secret in order to entrap him in marriage. His own "impurity" is irrelevant; and so the double standard is triumphant.

Later, Clare is finally willing to say he forgives her—
'but forgiveness is not all.' " He no longer, so he thinks, can
love her. The brain has conquered the heart, and very quickly
at that. Whatever compassion and understanding he possessed have been annihilated by priggishness, hypocrisy,
and selfish vanity. He retreats into the bourgeois clichés so
abhorred by Hardy; e.g., " 'You are an unapprehending peas-
ant woman, who have never been initiated into the proportion of social things.' " Thus, says Clare, he cannot "love her
as he had loved her hitherto. . . ." Judging as society would,
the unliberated Clare finds Tess wanting and so argues
himself out of love with her. It never occurs to him that in a
spiritual, moral sense she is just as "pure" as she ever
was—that is, pure of heart, capable of loving him unselfishly
and completely. Clare, in the blind frenzy of a disappointed
egoism, cannot see this. If Tess is not all his, she is not his at
all. He has forgotten quickly enough his earlier lectures to her
on the contemptibleness of conventions and the permanence
of his love for her. He becomes polite and indifferent; his
small heart shrinks to nothing and he "smothers his affection" for his wife.

They sleep apart that first night, and the next day Clare
makes a speech. He had given up any desire he might have
had to marry a woman of "social standing" and "fortune"
and "knowledge of the world" in order to "secure rustic innocence." He has been disappointed but he will not reproach
Tess. He will not reproach her, and he will not live with her.
His injured vanity has apparently annihilated in him any
capacity for empathy. Tess's own selflessness is pointedly
contrasted with his egoism throughout. She says that she can
understand his disappointment. She feels she is "so utterly
worthless." She will kill herself if he will not kill her. Her love
for him will remain undiluted and unselfish. Clare is unmoved. For him, in the compassionless self-pity of disappointment, " 'It isn't a question of respectability, but one of
principle!' " The principle remains undefined, but apparently
it is simply the old Victorian idea that women should come to
their husbands in a state of total innocence. The husband's

past, of course, is not a factor. Clare, his proprietary impulse disappointed, remains the victim of and apologist for the very conventions he believes he despises; his concern for appearances makes true charity impossible. For Clare is not only a prig and a hypocrite; he also lacks fellow feeling. But his behavior is comprehensible, even logical, when once we understand that he is also totally lacking in self-knowledge. He has had an image of himself totally at variance with his real nature, which is conventional and patently unliberated. In his ignorance and disillusionment he also fails to see that the image is vastly preferable to the reality.

Clare's concern for appearances, for the surfaces of things rather than their substance, is underscored by his telling Tess that they must " 'stay together a little while, to avoid the scandal to you that would have resulted from our immediate parting. But you must see that it is only for form's sake' " [5, xxxvi]. The scandal, of course, would attach itself to Tess and not to him, no matter how scandalous his own behavior. Tess, meanwhile, is numbed by his hardness: "She was awe-stricken to discover such determination under such apparent flexibility. His consistency was, indeed, too cruel. She no longer expected forgiveness now" [5, xxxvi]. If foolish consistency is the hobgoblin of little minds, certainly Clare's mind is so haunted. He tells Tess that they cannot live together; their children would suffer disgrace when hers became known—and besides, she is in fact another man's wife. She is chilled by the cold judgment of his "fastidious brain." His love for her, Hardy tells us, had been more "ethereal," more "imaginative," than substantive; and so Tess becomes, for Clare, "another woman than the one who had exalted his desire." Having loved Tess "ideally and fancifully," he had loved the actual woman less than he had loved his own idea of her. (Such a phenomenon may well remind us of Dorothea Brooke, in love with her image of Mr. Casaubon; and it directly anticipates our discussion of Isabel Archer.) Thus his love for her was in large part an expression of self-love, of love of his own mind. His imagination is fundamentally self-interested and unsympathetic, as Hardy makes clear in a brief but explicit passage: Clare, he says, is a prisoner of "the will to subdue the grosser to the subtler emotion, the substance to the conception, the flesh to the spirit. Propensities, tendencies, habits, were as dead leaves upon the tyrannous wind of his imaginative ascendency" [5, xxxvi]. Clare, who tells Tess that he thinks of people more kindly when he is away from them, appalls her "by the determination revealed in the depths" of his being. For her, by way of contrast, "[s]elf-solicitude was near extinction." Tess's selflessness leaves no place for elaborate theories of moral conduct—her own or others'. Unlike Clare, she is instinctively generous and unpretentious.

Clare, meanwhile, has settled upon a course of action, based largely on the confidence he has in the power and incisiveness of his own mind: "he knew that if any intention of his, concluded overnight, did not vanish in the light of morning, it stood on a basis approximating to one of pure reason . . .[and] that it was so far, therefore, to be trusted" [5, xxxvii]. In his egoism, Clare thinks of Tess simply as "one who had practised gross deceit upon him," and so he resolves that they must separate indefinitely—or at least until Clare should make up his mind to tolerate her as his wife. So he gives her money and they part—Tess loving him no less than before, Clare attempting to exorcise the attraction she still has for him.

When we next see Clare it is several weeks later and he has decided to go to Brazil to farm. He believes he now has a "practical" knowledge of life, and yet his heart remains troubled by the loss of his lately acquired "dear possession." He thinks that perhaps he will ask Tess to join him in Brazil, where "the conventions would not be so operative which made life with her seem impracticable to him [in England]." But when Clare's father reads to him from Proverbs the chapter in praise of a virtuous wife, Clare, who does not see how well Tess fits the description of the perfect woman (" 'a working woman; not an idler; not a fine lady; but one who used her head and her heart for the good of others' "), decides that he has "utterly wrecked his career by this marriage."

Lest we somehow miss his point, Hardy pauses in his narrative to comment explicitly:

> Angel Clare [failed to perceive] the shade of his own limitations. With all his attempted independence of judgment this advanced and well-meaning young man, a sample product of the last five-and-twenty years, was yet the slave to custom and conventionality when surprised back into his early teachings. No prophet had told him, and he was not prophet enough to tell himself, that essentially this young wife of his was as deserving of the praise of King Lemuel as any other woman endowed with the same dislike of evil, her moral value having to be reckoned not by achievement but by tendency . . . In considering what Tess was not, he overlooked what she was, and forgot that the defective can be more than the entire. (5, xxxix)

The passage quite clearly underlines, among other things, Clare's major deficiency: lack of self-knowledge. He knows neither his own limitations nor how conventional his limitations make him. He has no "independence of judgment." His failure to comprehend Tess's moral value is a failure to put "tendency" over "achievement." For Hardy—unlike George Eliot, who believed that a bad act may be defined as one which has bad consequences—what is important is not actual achievement but *will*. For George Eliot, intentions are less important than results; for Hardy, a bad act is one where the *intention* is faulty—consequences for him are irrelevant, perhaps in part because most things turn out badly anyway. In such a world the individual intention becomes more important than its results. Clare fails to see that Tess, in every important way, is a pure woman of pure intentions. (Her purity, should we fail to recognize it, is insisted upon in the novel's subtitle.) Clare now has a fleeting moment of self-doubt. Has his course been wise or generous? Has he "been cruelly blinded?" He says to himself that he would have forgiven Tess had she told him her secret before they were married—another indication of how little he knows himself. Nevertheless, for the first time some misgivings about his late course of conduct are present to him.

It is at this point (5, xl) that Clare runs into Izz Huett, and invites her, with few preliminaries, to accompany him to Brazil. Such is his moral consistency. Chastity is for women, not for men. Izz agrees to go, but tells Clare that " 'nobody could love 'ee more than Tess did! . . . She would have laid down her life for 'ee.' " Clare, reconsidering, withdraws the invitation, having made the girl even more miserable by unknowingly teasing her with what she has always dreamed of. Izz's words, however, have an effect upon him. He tells her that she has saved him by her words about Tess " 'from an incredible impulse towards folly and treachery. Women may be bad, but they are not so bad as men in these things!' " Clare goes on to tell himself stubbornly, however, that "the facts had not changed. If he was right at first, he was right now." Nevertheless, he has had another moment of wavering, a moment which suggests the eventual dawning of a new consciousness.

While Clare begins the struggle with his conscience, Tess is a victim of hard times. She has given her money to her mother and is working to keep herself alive. The paramount motivating impulse of her uncomplaining life is the hope that Clare will return to her or invite her to join him. She believes in him less and less each day, but still she believes in him. She refuses to advertise the tenuous position he has left her in by asking anyone for help: "This self-effacement . . . [was] quite in consonance with her independent character of desiring nothing by way of favor or pity to which she was not entitled on a fair consideration of her deserts. She had set herself to stand of fall by her qualities . . . " [5, xliv]. The important phrase here is "self-effacement"; despite the deficiency of her formal education and her small knowledge of the world, Tess is by nature generous and without self-conceit—two qualities patently missing in her more worldly and philosophical husband. Unfortunately, in the world represented by Angel Clare, it is extremely difficult for Tess to "stand . . . by her qualities" alone.

Now Alec D'Urberville, Tess's seducer, re-enters her life. Alec, who has apparently undergone a religious conversion of sorts as a result of guilty feelings about his treatment of Tess, proposes marriage to her now. Tess tells him that she has no affection for him and that, in any case, she is already married. But Alec, seeing that she is alone, continues to pursue her, losing his tenuous "religion" bit by bit as he goes along. When Alec, again a victim of his own lust, finally declares that he can have no faith in any ethical system, Hardy puts into Tess's mouth a statement which represents both one of his own favorite ideas and one of the novel's most essential thematic expressions: " 'Why, you can have the religion of loving-kindness and purity at least, if you can't have—what do you call it—dogma' " [6, xlvii]. The religion of loving-kindness is a religion of the heart; dogma is a religion of the brain. Hardy, like George Eliot, prefers a religion of humanity, a man-centered religion based on love and sympathy for others. It is precisely this loving-kindness that the dogmatic Clare and the sensual Alec lack. Both are egoists who need the self-gratification that comes to them with the sole possession of another human being. Both lack sympathy for others; both are deficient in moral vision. Alec is to die at the apex of his blind sensualism—in Tess's bed; but Clare, as we shall see, does ultimately achieve a degree of self-knowledge which allows for moral expansion. The novel's final chapters have as their central issue Clare's spiritual re-education.

Hardy now shifts the scene briefly to South America, and we are given a glimpse into Clare's mind. During his absence from Tess, as in the case of Richard Feverel's absence from Lucy, Clare has

> mentally aged a dozen years . . . [H]e now began to dis-
> credit the old appraisements of morality. He thought
> they wanted readjusting. Who was the moral man? Still
> more pertinently, who was the moral woman? The beau-
> ty or ugliness of a character lay not only in its
> achievements, but in its aims and impulses; its true
> history lay, not among things done, but among things
> willed . . . Viewing [Tess] in these lights, a regret for his
> hasty judgment began to oppress him. (6, xlix)

Clare, who has not become rich in Brazil as he had hoped, begins now to understand that fate may sometimes thwart

one's will and that the results of a man's life may not be those
he intended. If the fault does not lie within the individual,
how can he be blamed for the results? Morality, he concludes,
lies closer to "aims" and "impulses" and "things willed" than
to "achievements." Viewing Tess in this light, he begins to
reassess her and his own treatment of her. During the trip
back to England, Clare, now "in a state of mental de-
pression," confides the story of his marriage to another
Englishman, who tells him that "what Tess had been was of
no importance beside what she could be, and . . . that he was
wrong in coming away from her." Shortly thereafter Clare's
companion dies of fever, and Tess's husband is left alone with
his anguishing thoughts. His moment of self-discovery is
sudden and complete: "His parochialism made him ashamed.
. . . His inconsistencies rushed upon him in a flood . . . [He
had allowed] himself to be influenced by general principles to
the disregard of the particular instance" [6, xlix]. Like
Elizabeth Bennet after the reading of Darcy's letter, Amelia
Sedley after discovering her dead husband's true nature, and
Richard Feverel in the German forest, Angel Clare now undergoes a moment of complete self-revelation, seeing himself
and others for the first time in his life in a light unfettered by
the shadows of egoism. In the oppressive despair of his new
awareness he grows to be Tess's advocate rather than her
critic. He understands that he has been blind to her value, to
"the dignity which must have graced her granddams." His
new "vision . . . [leaves] behind it a sense of sickness," and the
purgative anguish of his new apprehension of things drives
him speedily homeward.

Once there, Clare sets out in a mood of self-accusation to
find Tess. He asks himself (7, liii) why "His had been a love
'which alters when it alteration finds,' " why "he had not
judged Tess constructively rather than biographically, by the
will rather than by the deed?" Why had he been so pitiless?
By the time he finds her he has understood completely that it
was his own lack of charity that brought about their separation. But things have a way of happening too late in Hardy's
later novels, and it appears that Clare's new sympathy and

understanding may be belated. Tess is now "married" to Alec D'Urberville and living with him in a stylish lodging-house in Sandbourne. She has made this sacrifice for her now fatherless brothers and sisters, whom Alec has been supporting. Angel pleads with her to return to him (7, lv): " 'Can you forgive me for going away? Can't you—come to me? . . . I did not think rightly of you—I did not see you as you were! . . . I have learned to since . . . . [I] t is my fault!' " Clare's vision is now focussed; but Tess tells him that it is too late. Nevertheless, the anguish of seeing him in his new humility and compassion drive her to the frenzied killing of the predatory Alec, and she returns to Clare for the few days preceding her apprehension for the murder. Tess has committed a crime out of love for Clare much more monstrous than the one he had deserted her for, and yet Clare's moral development—the onset of "loving-kindness"—has created in him a reserve of charity and understanding. Despite Tess's crime, she finds upon her return to Clare that "Tenderness was absolutely dominant in [him] at last." Like Pip and Adam Bede, his fastidiousness has been conquered by compassion. He has acquired the religion of humanity, the sympathy and self-abnegation which are necessary prerequisites of moral vision. The extent of Clare's education in values is implicit in his statement to Tess at the end of the novel (7, lvii - lviii): " 'I will not desert you! I will protect you by every means in my power, dearest love, whatever you may have done or not have done! . . . If I lose you I lose all!' " And after Tess's execution, as if to demonstrate that his spiritual conversion has bent him unalterably toward the impulses of his newly acquired fellow feeling, Clare undertakes the care of Tess's sister 'Liza-Lu. At the last his is an open-ended commitment to the unselfishness of human sympathy.

HENRY JAMES (1843-1916)
National Portrait Gallery, London

Chapter Seven

The Portrait of A Lady

Like Jane Austen, Henry James—though not strictly speaking a "Victorian" novelist—is very much part of the same tradition. His work is remarkable not only for its impact and influence upon later writers but also for its distillation of many of the radical essences of the preceding traditions. In *The Language of Meditation: Four Studies in Nineteenth-Century Fiction* (1973), I joined the list of those who have pointed out in detail some of the things James took from earlier writers—and most especially from George Eliot, about whom he wrote more essays (nine) than about any other writer. Therefore I shall not attempt to prove again how much *The Portrait of a Lady* (1880-81) owes in both theme and technique to *Middlemarch* and *Daniel Deronda,* or to point out once more how similar James's method often is to Jane Austen's. It is the case, however, that Henry James, so often identified as the father of the modern novel, is also in fact the stepson, as it were, of the nineteenth-century novel. In virtually every novel he wrote the paramount theme is a variation of some kind on the central idea of many of the major nineteenth-century novels—that is, the expansion of the individual's moral sensibility. This is the chief concern, quite clearly, in *The American, The Princess Casamassima, What Maisie Knew, The Ambassadors,* and *The Golden Bowl,* to name just a few of James's important novels. It is *The Portrait of A Lady,* however, that most clearly and fully embodies that pattern of egoism, despair, and self-knowledge—the ordeal of moral education—which is at the heart of so much of nineteenth-century fiction.

Like Elizabeth Bennet, Emma Woodhouse, Dorothea Brooke, and Gwendolen Harleth, Isabel Archer is an intelligent young woman whose excessive confidence in her own judgment leads her to misjudge others—and most often those with whom she is in some way emotionally involved.

247

Gilbert Osmond, the antagonist of *The Portrait of A Lady,* like Wickham, Churchill, Casaubon, and Grandcourt, is not at all what he appears to be, and yet Isabel, a woman of depth and taste, chooses him over a galaxy of lovers, with any one of whom she might have had a greater chance for happiness. It is James's idea, however, that we come into life unprepared to understand it, that we learn what it is through social intercourse, and that by the time our moral education is complete it is usually too late in our lives to put to constructive use the fruits of our painfully gained understanding. Like George Eliot's, James's vision of things is essentially a tragic one. Unlike George Eliot's characters, however, James's rarely benefit from any final reprieve.

Isabel's tragedy results in part just because she is admirably independent and unconventional. Unfortunately, however, she is also self-willed and self-confident, and her admiration of her own powers of logic and understanding is the major ingredient of her egoism. Like Clara Middleton, Isabel loves liberty and independence. However, she carries these attachments of hers to the point of ignoring the good advice of others and clinging to her prejudices, no matter how dangerous they may be. She is, in sum, too enamored of having her own way in everything.

Isabel Archer is offered by her expatriate aunt the opportunity to travel in Europe. Their first stop is Gardencourt, the Touchetts' country mansion outside of London. Once he has her there, James takes great trouble to illuminate for us the texture of her mind, her own view of herself, and the more objective assessments of others. We are told, for example, that Isabel's "imagination" is "ridiculously active," that she too often sees "without judging," that "the unpleasant had been ever too absent from her knowledge," and yet that she has "an immense curiosity about life" [4]. We should by now be sufficiently conversant with the unfortunate consequences which result from an imagination unsupported by judgment, experience, or humility to be concerned for Isabel's future. Isabel's innocence is combined, as Mrs. Touchett says, with a strong conviction that she needs no introduction to the world: " 'She thinks she knows a great deal of it . . . but . . . she's ridiculously mistaken.' " We are also told that, despite "a great passion for knowledge," Isabel "will do everything she chooses" to do; ominously, " 'She doesn't take suggestions.' " Isabel describes herself to Ralph Touchett as one who is " 'said to have too many theories' " but is nevertheless " 'very fond of knowledge.' " Ralph tells her that knowledge must be preceded by suffering: " 'You must have suffered first, have suffered greatly . . . . But you haven't suffered . . . .' " Isabel's reply is offhandedly light: " 'I think people suffer too easily . . . It's not absolutely necessary to suffer; we were not made for that . . . Only, if you don't suffer they call you hard' " [5] Her egoism is comprised in an imagination, like Emma's and Gwendolen's, which overpowers objective vision, and in an inflated self-confidence which considers itself capable of discriminating social judgment. As James himself says in the preface to the novel, the story is a "history of the growth of one's imagination"; and Isabel has a great deal to learn. Her dangerous subjectivity, combined with innocence and self-conceit, is to lead her, later on, into the kind of "suffering" she now perversely considers a superfluous element of her education (though she also feels, contradictorily enough, that she is doomed to "unhappiness").

In Chapter 6, James sums up his heroine's weaknesses as a sort of preface to the rest of the novel:

> she . . . had a general idea that people were right when they treated her as if she were rather superior . . . for it seemed to her often that her mind moved more quickly than theirs . . . Isabel was probably very liable to the sin of self-esteem; she often surveyed with complacency the field of her own nature; she was in the habit of taking for granted, on scanty evidence, that she was right; she treated herself to occasions of homage. Meanwhile her errors and delusions were [frequent] . . [Her] imagination . . . played her a great many tricks. . . Altogether, with her meagre knowledge, her inflated ideals, her confidence at once innocent and dogmatic, her temper at once exacting and indulgent, her mixture

of curiosity and fastidiousness, of vivacity and indifference . . . you could have made her colour, any day
in the year, by calling her a rank egoist. She was always
planning out her development, desiring her perfection,
observing her progress . . . .

With admirable clarity James here defines the ingredients of
Isabel's "rank egoism." She is conceited, self-esteeming, and
has an "innocent and dogmatic" confidence in her own intellect despite "meagre knowledge" and "inflated ideals."
Like Gwendolen and Bathsheba, she is vain and complacent
about herself; in the absence of other "homage," she observes
herself. She is her own best audience. Her overactive imagination, like Emma's and Dorothea's, leads her frequently into
"errors and delusions" which her own self-imposed blindness
prevents her from recognizing as such. Such a young lady,
more afraid of seeming narrow-minded than of actually being
so—like Angel Clare, more concerned with the image than the
reality—such a young lady, facing the world with the egoism of
unfounded self-confidence, is likely to come in for her fair
share of suffering and experience, of painful self-knowledge.

At Gardencourt Isabel is courted overtly by Lord Warburton, a wealthy neighboring landowner, and more covertly
by her invalid cousin Ralph Touchett. Warburton accuses her
of judging things " 'only from the outside,' " while Ralph
tells her that her many "ideas," by which he means prejudices, are bound to lead her to grief. Ralph, of course, is
right, and James allows himself here to anticipate Isabel's
future disasters: " [I] f there was a great deal of folly in her
wisdom those who judge her severely may have the satisfaction of finding that, later, she became consistently wise only
at the cost of an amount of folly which will constitute almost
a direct appeal to charity" [12] . Like George Eliot, James
wants his reader to see that wisdom can come only from the
moral experience inevitably accruing from "folly"; and like
George Eliot again, he wants us to sympathize, to enlarge our
capacity for empathy as we view the tragic course of his
protagonist.

Caspar Goodwood, an old acquaintance of Isabel's from America, now appears in England along with another friend, Henrietta Stackpole, and Isabel finds herself surrounded by suitors. When Warburton formally proposes to her, she refuses him on the ground that such a marriage would interfere with "the free exploration of life" she has been looking forward to, would interfere with her worldly "education," would make things too easy for her. But she has a moment of self-doubt, in which James obviously concurs to some extent:

> Who was she, what was she, that she should hold herself superior? What view of life, what design upon fate, what conception of happiness, had she that pretended to be larger than these large, these fabulous occasions? If she wouldn't do such a thing as [marry Lord Warburton] then she must do great things, she must do something greater. (12)

In her letter to Lord Warburton, Isabel says that "we see our lives from our own point of view," and that hers does not include such an easy marriage.

Warburton, trying once more, is told by Isabel that she cannot escape her "fate," and that it is not her fate "to give up"—which would be the result of her marrying him. By giving up she means avoiding experience, separating herself " '[F]rom life. From the usual chances and dangers, from what most people know and suffer.' " Ralph accuses her of thinking " 'nothing in the world too perfect' " for her and looks forward to finding out " 'what a young lady does who won't marry Lord Warburton.' " Isabel says that she only wants to see things for herself, and Ralph resolves to find some way of enabling her to do so. He is curious; what will such an idealistic young lady do with her life?

Goodwood also renews his overtures to Isabel, and he is met with the same attitude encountered by Lord Warburton: " 'I don't need the aid of a clever man to teach me how to live. I can find it out for myself . . . If there's a thing in the world I'm fond of . . . it's my personal independence . . . I can do what I choose . . . . I try to judge things for myself;

to judge wrong, I think, is more honourable than not to judge at all . . . I wish to choose my fate and know something of human affairs . . .' " [16] . Like Hardy, James is concerned with the question of "how to live," and we are meant to admire Isabel for wanting to find the best way. We are also meant to see, however, that a tragic heroine so confident of her own intellectual powers is not likely to find out how to live easily—is, in fact, likely to make finding out unnecessarily difficult for herself. Isabel concludes her interview with Goodwood by telling him that she wishes to be free even to commit some atrocity " 'if the fancy takes me,' " and with that he gives up for the time being and goes back to America. Isabel is left with "the enjoyment she found in the exercise of her power . . . [She] yielded to the satisfaction of having refused two ardent suitors in a fortnight . . . [S]he had tasted of the delight, if not of battle, at least of victory . . ." [17]. Like Gwendolen and Bathsheba, Isabel relishes her power over men. Henrietta, always shrewdly intuitive, tells her, however, that she is " 'drifting to some great mistake.' "

Madame Merle, an old friend of Mrs. Touchett's, now arrives at Gardencourt. Despite Ralph's warning that the accomplished and clever Madame Merle is too complete, too perfect, Isabel, who as we know does not "take suggestions," admires and trusts her almost from their first meeting. While their intimacy is growing rapidly, Ralph persuades his dying father to leave Isabel a fortune—one that will enable her to be as free and independent as she wishes. He wants Isabel to be able to choose a husband freely, to remove all possible distracting obstacles from her path. His father wonders weakly if it is right " 'to make everything so easy for a person' " and fears that she " 'may fall a victim to the fortune-hunters.' " But the codicil is written.

Isabel, meanwhile, finds herself "under an influence." She likes Madame Merle "extremely," even while admitting to herself that she is more "dazzled than attracted." Madame Merle, to whom others apply such epithets as "the most brilliant woman in Europe," is obviously odious, a consummate actress who preys on her friends and is constantly plotting for social advantage. Ralph continues to warn Isabel away from her, but Isabel, as always confident in her own powers of judgment, sees only Madame Merle's glossy surface and continues to be "dazzled." In seeing only surfaces, Isabel, like Bathsheba and Angel Clare, in fact sees nothing. Still, to give Isabel her due, she is made a bit uneasy by Madame Merle's obvious unoriginality. Yet she fails to take warning from Madame Merle's subtle abuse of her hostess and old friend Mrs. Touchett or from her comments upon Ralph, whom she dislikes because he understands her so well. Madame Merle says of him at one point: " 'Fortunately he has a consumption; I say fortunately, because it gives him something to do. His consumption's his carrière; it's a kind of position.' " And Madame Merle tells Isabel " 'It's a very good thing for a girl to have refused a few good offers—so long of course as they are not the best she's likely to have.' " And yet Isabel not only fails to understand Madame Merle—she promises everlasting confidence and friendship between them. James comments: "With all her love of knowledge she had a natural shrinking from raising curtains and looking into unlighted corners. The love of knowledge co-existed in her mind with the finest capacity for ignorance" [19]. Isabel's "capacity for ignorance," her failure to "take suggestions," is an essential ingredient of her egoism. Hers is a self-confidence based on both innocence and misconception.

When old Mr. Touchett dies and it is revealed that Isabel is an heiress, Madame Merle's attentions to her young friend are redoubled. Henrietta feels that the money may be " 'a curse in disguise' " and warns Isabel that having it will give her " 'exposure on the moral side.' " Henrietta admirably sums up the dangers ahead for Isabel:

> 'The peril for you is that you live too much in the world of your own dreams. You're not enough in contact with reality—with the toiling, striving, I may even say sinning, world that surrounds you. You're too fastidious; you've too many graceful illusions. Your newly-acquired thousands will shut you up more and more to the society of a few selfish and heartless people who will be interested in keeping them up . . . [Y]ou think you

can lead a romantic life . . . . [Y] ou're too fond of admiration, you like to be thought well of. You think we
can escape disagreeable duties by taking romantic
views—that's your great illusion, my dear. But we
can't.' (20)

Henrietta here puts her finger on a great deal of what is
wrong with Isabel, whose romanticism and fondness for admiration, coupled with the extreme innocence of one who
lives in dreams rather than in reality, are too likely to lead her
into "graceful illusions." Isabel, of course, pays little attention to this incisive warning. When Ralph issues to her a
similar but more subtle one, telling her that she has " 'too
much power of thought,' " Isabel admits that she is too often
subjective: " 'I'm absorbed in myself . . . . I try to care
more about the world than about myself—but I always come
back to myself' " [21]. And yet despite this intermittent
recognition of her own egoism, Isabel continues, as James
says, to "[lose] herself in a maze of visions . . . . It was in
her disposition at all times to lose faith in the reality of absent
things . . . [O]f all liberties the one she herself found
sweetest was the liberty to forget" [21]. Isabel's particular
form of self-indulgence here is not entirely unlike that
sometimes found in Hardy's protagonists—and it is
specifically like that of Gwendolen Harleth, who in the beginning rarely thought of anything she could not see or touch.
James concludes this segment of his story by emphasizing the
"pleasure" Isabel feels at the thought that two suitors, "appreciably in debt to her," have been rejected in the interests of
maintaining her liberty.

The scene now moves to Florence, where we are introduced to Gilbert Osmond, an expatriate American
widower with a young daughter. Osmond's sole characteristic
seems to be his "style," his immaculate taste. He is an old
friend and apparently a former lover of Madame Merle, and
we now see that distinguished lady exhorting Osmond to
court Isabel, who is in Florence staying with her aunt.
Madame Merle offers to put Isabel in Osmond's way so that
he can, if possible, marry her, become a rich man, and in-

dulge his "adorable taste" to the fullest. If she is really rich, says Osmond, he is willing to make an effort—and so Madame Merle now begins her campaign. She tells Isabel of an "old friend" of hers, "one of the cleverest and most agreeable men . . . in Europe." As lie follows lie and Osmond comes to call, he and Madame Merle perform for Isabel's benefit as if they "had been on the stage"—and Isabel, still addicted to surfaces, takes it all in. Once again, before things have gone too far, Ralph issues a timely warning to his cousin. Osmond's " 'special line' " is " 'a great dread of vulgarity. . . he hasn't any other that I know of.' " Ralph also warns Isabel again against Madame Merle (23): " '[Her] merits are exaggerated . . . She's indescribably blameless; a pathless desert of virtue . . . . She's too good, too kind, too clever, too learned, too accomplished, too everything. She's too complete, in a word . . . If you wish to see the world you couldn't have a better guide . . . she's the great round world itself!' " Isabel as usual pays little attention, feeling that she knows Madame Merle well enough to judge her merits for herself. And so she goes on seeing Osmond, whose greed, selfishness, and self-conceit become more and more apparent to us the more we see and hear of him.

Isabel continues to see only surfaces, and Osmond's surface is deceptively glossy. She does feel at times that there is something beneath these new relationships that she cannot quite define, and she sees that neither simplicity nor artlessness is much in evidence in Osmond's household. The only totally natural connection Osmond seems to have is his impulsive sister the Countess Gemini, who calls him "Machiavelli" in public and says whatever comes into her mind. But Isabel continues to be charmed by him: "He resembled no one she had ever seen . . . . Her mind contained no class offering a natural place to Mr. Osmond—he was a specimen apart . . . [T]his 'new relation' would perhaps prove her very most distinguished . . . [H]e was an original without being an eccentric. She had never met a person of so fine a grain" [24]. Isabel's "capacity for ignorance," for deception and self-deception, is enormous, and Osmond and Madame Merle continue to play upon it skillfully. Madame Merle acts the straight man with finesse, and Osmond continues to impress Isabel with his "connoisseurship" and the seeming "harmony" of his life, which strikes her as "the last refinement of high culture." She feels at the same time that Osmond is too "ironical" to be "grossly conceited." In her desire to please him she unconsciously deceives him about herself, much as Dorothea unintentionally deceives Casaubon in *Middlemarch*. Osmond does not recognize her independent spirit. He believes, from her pliance and reserve with him, that she will be easily dominated as his wife; she thinks too much, perhaps, but ultimately, he is sure, she will be as docile as one of the objects in his many collections. Osmond, who has something both of Casaubon and Grandcourt in him (and perhaps a little of Sir Willoughby Patterne as well), is interested only in the self-gratification of possession. Far from being an original, he is perhaps the most conventional man Isabel has ever met. And yet she sees none of these things. Her imagination too easily transforms fact into fancy.

Madame Merle goes on telling lies, Osmond continues his performance as the agreeable man of taste, and Isabel's friends and relations persist in warning her against the pair. Madame Merle's plot is obvious to everyone except Isabel, who is too self-absorbed to see it. Even the Countess Gemini protests to Madame Merle about the "sacrifice" soon to be made. Meanwhile Mrs. Touchett enters the affair. She believes that any alliance between Osmond and her niece "would have an air of almost morbid perversity" on Isabel's part. Marriage to him, she tells Ralph, would be "folly" for Isabel; Osmond is interested only in her money, both for himself to spend and as a dowry for his daughter. Everyone sees this except, of course, Isabel herself, whose belief in Osmond's sincerity is unshakable.

As the great event approaches consummation, Madame Merle begins to draw back from " 'the abyss into which I shall have cast her,' " and Osmond exerts himself to extort the final result—his greatest purchase, the climax to his years of "collecting." He believes that Isabel has " 'too many ideas,' " but in his egoism he also believes that she will "sacrifice" them to the harmony of their marriage. He will make her "life a work of art," like his own. How little each knows the other! Osmond even warns Isabel that he is " 'convention itself' "; but of course the reality is less important to her than her own idea of it, and so she pays no heed to this, Osmond's one truthful utterance during his courtship of her. She is, as she realizes later, completely fooled by him.

Before deciding what to do about Osmond's proposal of marriage, Isabel spends several months travelling—with Madame Merle as her companion. Upon her return to Florence she considers herself "a very different person from the frivolous young woman from Albany who had begun to take the measure of Europe . . . a couple of years before. She flattered herself she had harvested wisdom and learned a great deal more of life . . . . " [31] . Isabel now considers herself "educated"; she has exercised sufficiently her yearning for "freedom," she has seen the world, and she is now ready to make some decisions about her life. Like Dickens's Pip, "The world lay before her—she could do whatever she chose." But of course Isabel has expanded her sensibilities very little indeed, prisoner as she is to her own subjectivity and self-conceit. She is still naive—and yet perhaps not quite so naive as formerly. She finally senses, for example, something not quite right in Madame Merle—"values gone wrong"—and yet this sense never leads her to conclude that the woman is corrupt or untruthful. She really knows very little of her still—surfaces only, as is the case with her "knowledge" of Osmond.

Caspar Goodwood now tries his luck once again, only to be told that Isabel is indeed going to marry Osmond. Goodwood naturally is disappointed, both for himself and for her: " 'You think [Osmond] is grand, you think he's great, though no one else thinks so,' " he tells her bluntly. Mrs. Touchett is next in line, informing Isabel that Madame Merle has engineered the engagement between herself and

Osmond and that Osmond himself is a nonentity. Isabel hotly denies these things, still believing that Madame Merle " 'has been a very good friend to me.' " And next comes Ralph, who is "shocked and humiliated" by Isabel's succumbing to a fortune hunter and by his own part in making her the prey of one. She is a dupe, he believes, of Osmond's "deep art." He tells her that she will be " 'put in a cage' " by her husband-to-be, and that he does not "trust" Osmond. Isabel replies: " 'He wants me to know everything: that's what I like him for.' " Osmond, of course, thinks she has "too many ideas" as it is. But for Isabel, Osmond's nature is noble—the noblest she has ever met, " 'the finest I know.' " Ralph, however, persists. Osmond, he tells her, is narrow and selfish; he takes himself too seriously. He has no sympathy for others. He is likely to be easily ruffled and disagreeable. He is, in sum, " 'a sterile dilettante.' " He tells her this, he says, because he loves her. Isabel, like Amelia with Dobbin and Bathsheba with Oak, forgets his past kindnesses quickly enough. Ralph to her is now just another suitor and therefore no longer "disinterested." His advice is good, as always, but Isabel, telling Ralph that he has gone too far and that he will not have her confidence after she is married, defends Osmond to him rigorously; it is the height of her self-delusion:

> 'Your talk . . . is the wildness of despair! . . . I won't promise to think of what you've said: I shall forget it as soon as possible . . . I can't enter into your idea of Mr. Osmond . . . I should like to go and kneel down by your father's grave: he did perhaps a better thing than he knew when he put it into my power to marry a poor man—a man who has borne his poverty with such dignity, with such indifference . . . [H]e has cared for no worldly prize. . . Mr. Osmond makes no mistakes! He knows everything, he understands everything, he has the kindest, gentlest, highest spirit . . . Mr. Osmond's . . . a very honest man . . . .'
>
> She was wrong, but she believed; she was deluded, but she was dismally consistent. It was wonderfully characteristic of her that, having invented a fine theory about Gilbert Osmond, she loved him not for what he

really possessed, but for his very poverties dressed out as honours. (34)

Ralph, who is the one who "put it into her power to meet the requirements of her imagination," now sees that imagination horribly triumphant. Again like Amelia, and also like Dorothea and Angel Clare, Isabel is in love with her own idea while at the same time remaining ignorant of the reality. Her attraction to Osmond is in part a pull of her egoism; it is a form of self-love—the love of one's own idea. Like Amelia, Dorothea, and Clare, Isabel succumbs to a theory she has invented herself. In defense of her delusion she promises, with characteristically stubborn willfulness, to forget what Ralph has said as soon as possible. Again like Dorothea, Isabel has been warned by her friends and relatives about the man she is about to marry, but she is too absorbed in her own faulty vision of him to pay any attention.

Osmond, meanwhile, is not so pleased with himself as to forget the duties of courtship:

> he never forgot to be graceful and tender, to wear the appearance—which presented no difficulty—of stirred senses and deep intentions . . . Madame Merle had made him a present of incalculable value . . . What could be a happier gift in a companion than a quick, fanciful mind which saved one repetitions and reflected one's thoughts on a polished, elegant surface? . . . His egotism had never taken the crude form of desiring a dull wife; this lady's intelligence was to be a silver plate, not an earthen one—a plate that he might heap up with ripe fruits, to which it would give a decorative value, so that talk might become for him a sort of served dessert. (35)

How easily Isabel is deceived! For Osmond she is simply another object to add to his collection—a good piece, though, one that will reflect and enhance his own grandeur. Like Grandcourt and Sir Willoughby Patterne, Osmond's greatest satisfaction comes from ownership. And like Sir Austin Feverel, he is likely to think that anything short of complete submission is an act of bad faith and even treason.

Osmond declares to Isabel that he is indifferent to the opposition of her relatives, secretly vowing to keep her away from them after they are married. Isabel, meanwhile, finds that "The desire for unlimited expansion had been succeeded in her soul by the sense that life was vacant without some private duty that might gather one's energies to a point" [35]. Like Dorothea, her desire for "expansion" and the satisfaction of her sense of "duty" is to be frustrated by the disaster resulting from her own blindness. James asks: "What had become of all her ardours, her aspirations, her theories, her high estimate of her independence . . . ?" What, indeed? They have become submerged in her desire for self-expression and the need to prove herself more perspicacious than her advisors. Isabel's ardors, aspirations, and theories, her desire for complete independence and unlimited expansion, issue at last in her marriage to a man who, of all the men she has met, is most likely to frustrate her desires, curb her freedom, and scorn her ideas.

When the story resumes it is three years later and we learn immediately that Osmond and his wife are very much at odds. We follow Ned Rosier on a visit to the Osmonds' home in Rome on one of their "Thursday evenings," and we find that Isabel and her husband are now entrenched in a "dark and massive structure" that seems to Rosier like a "dungeon" or "fortress," reeking with the odors "of crime and craft and violence," a cold, depressing, dour palace filled with "mutilated statues and dusty urns." We understand quickly from Isabel's manner that she is unhappy and disillusioned. She has little influence with her husband; he cares only for wealth and its appearance. When Lord Warburton arrives with the seriously ailing Ralph Touchett for a visit to Rome, Isabel remarks to Warburton that Osmond " 'has a genius for upholstery' " and that she herself has " 'no ideas. I can never propose anything.' " The young lady of large aspirations and high ardors has indeed been caged.

In a flashback we see the slow process of Isabel's disillusionment beginning to unfold. Soon after her marriage she made her first discovery about her husband; she saw that his sense of humor was defective—that he took himself very seriously and lived for appearances. His "originality" turned out to be a sham; he is in fact the most conventional of men, and decrees that his wife must conform as well. Guests of the Osmonds who knew Isabel before her marriage begin to find her changed. She has become quiet, indifferent, even at times perverse; her husband has made her into an "ornament . . . supposed to represent something." The girl who could not see below her husband's surface has now, as James returns to the present, become part of that surface itself. James gives us a sustained look at the slow process of discovery that Isabel, in her disappointment, is beginning to enter upon. Osmond, as Ralph puts it to himself and Isabel herself now begins to see,

> always had an eye to effect, and his effects were deeply calculated . . . . [T] he motive was as vulgar as the art was great. To surround his interior with a sort of invidious sanctity, to tantalise society with a sense of exclusion, to make people believe his house was different from every other, to impart to the face that he presented to the world a cold originality—this was the ingenious effort of the personage to whom Isabel had attributed a superior morality . . . . Osmond lived exclusively for the world. Far from being its master as he pretended to be, he was its very humble servant, and the degree of its attention was his only measure of success. He lived with his eye on it from morning till night, and the world was so stupid it never suspected the trick. Everything he did was pose . . . . His tastes, his studies, his accomplishments, his collections, were all for a purpose. His life . . . at Florence had been the conscious attitude of years. [It combined] many features of a mental image constantly present to him as a model of impertinence and mystification. His ambition was not to please the world, but to please himself by exciting the world's curiosity and then declining to satisfy it. It had made him feel great, ever, to play the world a trick . . . [and] the gullible world was in a manner embodied in poor Isabel, who had been mystified to the top of her bent. (39)

Osmond's overpowering desire for self-gratification and the subtlety with which he pursues it are here explicitly defined;

this is the essence of his clammy egoism. Like Mr. Dombey, he exists to sustain an image he wants "the world" to have of him. As Isabel increasingly understands these things she longs more and more for the society of Ralph.

We now see Isabel beginning to become immersed in that state of despairing misery which is both an inevitable product of egoism and a prerequisite of more complete moral vision: "there were days when the world looked black and she asked herself with some sharpness what it was that she was pretending to live for" [40]. Life has become difficult for her; and if Madame Merle had indeed had a hand in arranging her marriage, Isabel now finds little "to thank her for. As time went on there was less and less . . . . " But, Isabel says to herself, she cannot in all fairness blame Madame Merle or anyone else for the apparent catastrophe of her marriage: "It was impossible to pretend that she had not acted with her eyes open; if ever a girl was a free agent she had been. A girl in love was doubtless not a free agent; but the sole source of her mistake had been within herself. There had been no plot, no snare; she had looked and considered and chosen" [40]. Isabel's feeling that "the sole source of her mistake had been within herself" is a large step down the road toward self-discovery. She accuses herself of "grossness of vision," and begins to see how fully her own romantic ideas got into the way of truth. The growth of this new perception is now aided substantially by that famous scene in which Isabel sees Osmond and Madame Merle in conversation together and begins to understand, from the unconscious intimacy which radiates from their conference, how close they really must be.

The conference had been about Osmond's desire to marry his daughter Pansy off to Warburton. In this plan he intends to enlist his wife, who, he feels, would have great influence in bringing Warburton to the point. Isabel, "unhappy," even "suffering," looks upon this proposal at first as a welcome amusement, a diversion from despair. If Warburton wants to marry her stepdaughter and Pansy is agreeable, Isabel, in her new cynicism, will assist in Osmond's plan; she knows how a marriage may be arranged.

When Madame Merle has left, Osmond sits down to discuss the situation with his wife. He asks for her help in catching Warburton for Pansy, and Isabel tells him that she will try to act as he would like. Osmond concludes the interview by telling her that she has a great deal of influence still with her former suitor and that she can "manage" the whole business if she tries.

Isabel remains alone to meditate, and in Chapter 42 we encounter an extended interior monologue, a remarkable series of passages in which she sees, in her misery, the present realities—and therefore her past follies—almost fully revealed. Isabel's "motionlessly *seeing*," says James of this scene (in his preface to the novel), is "only a supreme illustration of the general plan"; it is "the best thing in the book." By so saying James alerts us, should we need to be alerted, to the pivotal and climactic properties of the chapter. In asserting that Isabel's extended retrospective meditation is an illustration of his general plan for the novel, James means both that the dramatic structure of the scene is a supreme example of his method as "historian" and also that the scene embodies the central moments of Isabel's "education"—the expansion of her moral sensibility and the self-revelation that follows upon the new recognition of past and present truths. It is the moment of which all that has gone before in the novel has been anticipatory. The scene thus patently lends itself in purpose and content for comparison with some of the self-discovery scenes we have already encountered in this study—particularly those revelatory passages in *Pride and Prejudice, Emma, Middlemarch,* and *Daniel Deronda.*

Isabel's "unexpected recognition" begins with a suspicion that Warburton may be interested in Pansy as part of an unconscious desire to get closer to herself, and she sees that if this is indeed the case she will have to oppose her husband's desire to marry his daughter to him. Such opposition is a terrible possiblity for her: "her soul was haunted with terrors which crowded to the foreground of thought . . . . " She thinks now of Madame Merle, sees in a flash how intimate she must be with Osmond, and wonders why she had never understood this before. And then she thinks of her husband; I must quote here at some length to give the reader a full sense of the depth of Isabel's revelation:

> her short interview with Osmond . . . was a striking example of his faculty for making everything wither that he touched, spoiling everything for her that he looked at . . . .It was as if he had the evil eye; as if his presence were a blight and his favour a misfortune. Was the fault in himself, or only in the deep mistrust she had conceived for him? This mistrust was now the clearest result of their short married life; a gulf had opened between them over which they looked at each other with eyes that were on either side a declaration of the deception suffered. It was a strange opposition, of the like of which she had never dreamed—an opposition in which the vital principle of the one was a thing of contempt to the other. It was not her fault—she had practised no deception; she had only admired and believed. She had taken all the first steps in the purest confidence, and then she had suddenly found the infinite vista of a multiplied life to be a dark, narrow alley with a dead wall at the end. Instead of leading to the high places of happiness, from which the world would seem to be below one, so that one could look down with a sense of exaltation and advantage, and judge and choose and pity, it led rather . . . to deepen the feeling of failure. It was her deep distrust of her husband—this was what darkened the world . . . Suffering, with Isabel, was an active condition; it was not a chill, a stupor . . . [T]he shadows had begun to gather; it was as if Osmond deliberately, almost malignantly, had put the lights out one by one . . . These shadows . . . were a part, they were a kind of creation and consequence, of her husband's very presence . . . He was not changed; he had not disguised himself, during the year of his courtship, any more than she. But she had seen only half his nature then, as one saw the disk of the moon when it was partly masked by the shadow of the earth. She saw the full moon now—she saw the whole man . . . . [S]he had mistaken a part for the whole. (42)

The passage contains obvious parallels to *Middlemarch* and *Daniel Deronda,* particularly in its characterization of Osmond as a blight on his wife's happiness, as a principle of opposition in everything. In this he is like Casaubon, and, even more patently, Grandcourt. Isabel, like Gwendolen, had no conception of what married life with such a man might be like—"she had never dreamed" of such "opposition" in marriage. In all three cases (Dorothea-Casaubon, Gwendolen-Grandcourt, Isabel-Osmond) there is unintentional deception on both sides due to an egoism which vitiates objective vision (there is something of this mutual deception and self-deception in the early stages of the relationship between Clara Middleton and Sir Willoughby Patterne as well). Isabel, however, is perhaps more blameable than Dorothea; for, unlike Dorothea, she had wished in her marriage to achieve a status from which she could "look down" with "exaltation." Her egoism, like Adam Bede's, had required a position from which the world could be "judged," condescended to. But her "vistas," like Dorothea's and Gwendolen's, have led nowhere; like Casaubon and Grandcourt, Osmond has put out all the lights, made the dreamed-of "high places of happiness" disappear into shadow. As in George Eliot's novels, the world appears to the heroine to be shrinking into darkness. Isabel's experience of the world, however, is less literal, less epistemological, than it is metaphorical. The exterior world here is a metaphor of a spiritual condition. In her new suffering, Isabel comes to see her husband's nature, and thus the defectiveness of her own judgment, more fully. In seeing "the whole man" for the first time, she inevitably proceeds further along the tenuous path of self-discovery. The full moon—Osmond's character—had been "partly masked by the shadow of the earth"—that is, by the projection outward upon reality of Isabel's own unenlightened self-absorption. Like the heroines of Jane Austen and George Eliot, Isabel in her egoism has *perceived* incorrectly. As her self-interest gives way to objectivity, however, the shadows on the moon begin to disappear and the full moon comes into light and focus. And so she begins to see what her husband is, and how it could have been that she venerated him. Osmond himself, like Darcy and Casaubon, has not really changed; it is that Isabel's perception, like Elizabeth's and Dorothea's, has changed.

As Isabel's meditation continues her vision becomes more and more objective and revelatory; once again I must quote at some length from Chapter 42:

> as she had wished to be charmed it was not wonderful he had succeeded . . . . [S] he had imagined a world of things that had no substance. She had had a more wondrous vision of him, fed through charmed senses and oh such a stirred fancy!—she had not read him right . . . . But for her money, as she saw to-day, [it] would never have [happened] . . . Isabel's cheek burned when she asked herself if she had really married on a factitious theory . . . . The strange thing was that she should not have suspected from the first that his own [way of looking at life] had been so different. She had thought it so large, so enlightened . . . . [But instead her] house was the house of darkness, the house of dumbness, the house of suffocation. Osmond's beautiful mind gave it neither light nor air; Osmond's beautiful mind indeed seemed to peep down from a small high window and mock at her . . . . He took himself so seriously; it was something appalling. Under all his culture, his cleverness, his amenity, under his good-nature, his facility, his knowledge of life, his egotism lay hidden like a serpent in a bank of flowers . . . . She was to think of him as he thought of himself—as the first gentleman in Europe. So it was that she had thought of him at first . . . [but] there was more in the bond than she had meant to put her name to. It implied a sovereign contempt for every one but some three or four very exalted people whom he envied, and for everything in the world but half a dozen ideas of his own . . . But this base, ignoble world, it appeared, was after all what one was to live for; one was to keep it for ever in one's eye, in order . . . to extract from it some recognition of one's own superiority . . . .

Isabel, who "had wished to be charmed," allowed her "imagination," her "fancy," to obstruct her "vision"—very much in the manner of Emma Woodhouse. Thus Isabel has "read" Osmond incorrectly. The language here emphasizes the role that self-gratification has played in Isabel's defective vision. Her theories have been "factitious." In her egoism she had unnaturally failed to perceive his; her perception of his egoism now involves the perception of her own. Far from being an original, Osmond has turned out to be the most conventional of men. The result of these discoveries, as in George Eliot's novels, is a feeling of suffocation and darkness on the part of the heroine and a shrinking away from the infinite woe of a blank future.

If Osmond were only conventional, however, Isabel's woe would not lie so heavily upon her. But Osmond's passionate concern for appearances is also personally coercive, and in the final passages of Chapter 42 Isabel reflects not only upon her disillusionment but also upon her victimization by a rigid consciousness ever watching carefully over her own. She had yearned for freedom and found constriction instead.

> [Osmond] had an immense esteem for tradition . . . though from what source he had derived his traditions she never learned . . . . The great thing was to act in accordance with them; the great thing not only for him but for her . . . [S]he too must march to the stately music that floated down from unknown periods in her husband's past; she who of old had been so free of step, so desultory, so devious, so much the reverse of processional. There were certain things they must do, a certain posture they must take, certain people they must know and not know. When she saw this rigid system close about her . . . [a] sense of darkness and suffocation . . . took possession of her; she seemed shut up with an odour of mould and decay.
>
> Then it was that her husband's personality, touched as it had never been, stepped forth and stood erect. The things she had said were answered only by his scorn . . . . The real offence, as she ultimately perceived, was her having a mind of her own at all. Her mind was to be his—attached to his own like a small garden-plot to a deer-park. He would rake the soil gently and water the flowers; he would weed the beds and gather an occasional nose-gay. It would be a pretty piece of property. It was her scorn of his assumptions . . . that made him draw himself up . . . [T]hat [his wife] should turn the hot light of her disdain upon his own conception of things . . . was a danger he had not allowed for . . . .

> She was morally certain now that his feeling of
> hatred [for her] . . . had become the occupation and
> comfort of his life . . . . What was coming—what was
> before them? . . . What would he do—what ought *she*
> to do? . . . [I]t was a horrible life . . . . Nothing was a
> pleasure to her now; how could anything be a pleasure
> to a woman who knew that she had thrown away her
> life? There was an everlasting weight on her heart—there
> was a livid light on everything.

The passage evokes eloquently the misery of Isabel's life. Her
recognition of her past self-deception suggests more objective
vision. But like all tragic protagonists, she has learned what
she has learned at a tremendous cost. Osmond's passion for
conforming respectability has lost her her valued freedom—has surrounded her with "darkness and suffocation." It is, of course, strikingly ironic that the girl who
had valued her freedom more than anything else has married
the suitor most willing and best able to deny her freedom.
Like Dorothea's later view of Casaubon, Isabel's idea of her
husband is expressed in terms of "mould and decay." And
like Jane Eyre and Clara Middleton, Isabel feels the need of
preserving a private inner life of her own away from her husband. But Osmond, like St. John and Sir Willoughby, wants
complete possession of his wife—mind as well as body. When
she denies him this he begins to hate her. And so, like Gwendolen, Isabel faces the future with blank uncertainty and
gnawing fear; for her, as for Dorothea when she views the
landscape around Lowick after her return from Rome, there
is "a livid light on everything." "What was coming—what
was before them?" What *can* be before a woman who feels
she has "thrown away her life"? Very little indeed, except
perhaps better understanding of herself and of others and a
firmer desire to help those who are in difficulty. The result of
Isabel's egoism and self-discovery—of the ordeal of her
moral education—is that this is virtually all there is left to
her. There is divorce or separation, but Isabel is to shrink
from these alternatives as vulgar declarations of private
troubles and as a self-indulgently easy way out. It is as if, for
James, the process of moral education, which is inseparable

from social intercourse, is not complete until too late to put the resultant knowledge to constructive use and thus to be happy. The necessary process of moral expansion is inevitably tragic. Isabel Archer, being an invention of Henry James rather than of Jane Austen or George Eliot, gets no reprieve; unlike Elizabeth or Emma or Dorothea or Gwendolen, she gets no second or third chance for happiness. Her initial self-absorption and innocence, no matter how painstakingly expiated, are to doom her to renunciation and unhappiness. This is the essence of James's tragic view of life.

The anguish she has suffered as a result of a manufactured marriage—and her suspicion that Warburton is not in love with Pansy—decides Isabel on unbenevolent neutrality in the Warburton-Pansy business. Isabel thereby again irks her husband, who feels she could push Warburton into a declaration if she chose. But Isabel knows that Pansy is in love with Rosier and declines further to hinder "young love struggling with adversity." She knows too well the misery of an unhappy marriage.

As we approach the novel's final climactic scenes, James brings Henrietta Stackpole, Caspar Goodwood, and the Countess Gemini—all of whom know or suspect that Isabel's marriage has been a disaster—back to Rome, and the stage is set for an explosive dénouement.

Despite her husband's furious opposition, Isabel continues to visit Ralph. She goes through the motions with Warburton but will do no more than this for Osmond, who immediately accuses her of being untrustworthy and even treacherous to his own interests. He wishes her, as Isabel now sees again, to have "no freedom of mind." He hates her now more than ever; he thinks she has been trying to humiliate him. We see their relationship disintegrating further every day—even the pretense of politeness is dropped. Isabel finally tells Osmond he can have " 'nothing to say to [her] that's worth hearing.' "

To Henrietta, Isabel confides both her wretchedness and her disinclination to "publish" her "mistake." She says: " 'One must accept one's deeds. I married him before all the world, I was perfectly free; it was impossible to do anything more deliberate' " [47] . Henrietta exhorts Isabel to leave her husband, but she will not.

Ralph, nearing his end, wants to return to Gardencourt, and Henrietta and Goodwood take him back there (Warburton has already left Rome without proposing to Pansy). As soon as they are gone from Rome, Madame Merle reappears. She accuses Isabel of sabotaging an engagement between Warburton and Pansy, and her harsh tone immediately reawakens Isabel's latent suspicions of her:

> More clearly than ever before Isabel heard a cold, mocking voice . . . in the dim void that surrounded her . . . declare that this . . . worldly woman, this incarnation of the practical, the personal, the immediate, was a powerful agent in her destiny. She was nearer to her than Isabel had yet discovered, and her nearness was not the charming accident she had so long supposed. The sense of accident indeed had died within her . . . [S]he seemed to wake from a long pernicious dream . . . [A] strange truth was filtering into her soul. Madame Merle's interest was identical with Osmond's . . . .(49)

Isabel is still making discoveries; her experience of life has taught her to be less trusting, more suspicious. Fantasy is giving way before increased objectivity. She begins to see that Osmond and Madame Merle have probably been in concert all along. This idea gains strength when Madame Merle, like Osmond, accuses her of betraying her husband in the Warburton affair. Isabel, for the first time, begins to find Madame Merle disagreeable, but that lady plunges ahead. Why didn't Warburton declare himself? Did Isabel discourage him? Osmond has a right to know. Madame Merle concludes: " 'let us have him!' " The "him" is Warburton, but it is the "us" that strikes Isabel. Dazed, she responds to Madame Merle: " 'who are you—what are you?. . . What have you to do with my husband? . . . What have you to do with me?' " " 'Everything!' " replies Madame Merle. Isabel undergoes another shuddering revelation: " 'Oh misery!' . . . It had come over her like a high-surging wave that Mrs.

Touchett was right. Madame Merle had married her" [49]. (The similarity of the language here to that in the scene in which Emma discovers that no one must marry Mr. Knightley but herself should be sufficiently striking.)

Isabel's freshly fueled retrospective meditations continue throughout the next few days during her round of visits and sightseeing with Pansy and the Countess Gemini, who is in Rome on a visit to the Osmonds. Isabel, James reminds us,

> had had no personal acquaintance with wickedness. She had desired a large acquaintance with human life, and in spite of her having flattered herself that she cultivated it with some success this elementary privilege had been denied her . . . She found herself confronted . . . with the conviction that the man in the world whom she had supposed to be the least sordid had married her, like a vulgar adventurer, for her money. Strange to say, it had never before occurred to her . . . . (49)

Isabel's self-flattery, as James insists here, has been responsible for much of her faulty vision. Self-flattery is particularly destructive when combined with both innocence and false knowledge of the world. Confidence in self has gotten in the way of objective judgment, and Isabel is paying the price. Her realization that Osmond married her for her money is a concomitant of her new understanding of her own past ignorance.

A week later a telegram arrives for Isabel from her aunt. Ralph is near death and has asked for her—will she come to Gardencourt? Osmond forbids it: " 'If you leave Rome today it will be a piece of the most deliberate, the most calculated, opposition.' " He says that his wife should not travel across Europe alone to sit at the bedside of another man—that such an action would be " 'dishonourable . . . indelicate . . . indecent.' " Isabel, he says, likes Ralph only " 'because he hates me.' " For Isabel, all of this is simply another "refinement of egotism" on the part of her husband—"the observance of a magnificent form. They were as perfectly apart in feeling as . . . ever . . . ." But Isabel realizes that they have come to a crisis. Will she disobey him? She feels the spirit of independence within her slowly disintegrating: "action had been suddenly changed to slow renunciation, transformed by the blight of Osmond's touch." Isabel returns to her room in an uncertain frame of mind and is there accosted by the Countess, whose sympathy brings out Isabel's own sense of entrapment, self-pity, and defeat: "It seemed to her that only now she fully measured the great undertaking of matrimony . . . . [M]arriage meant that a woman should cleave to the the altar" [51] .

Seeing Isabel in this state of near-collapse, the Countess gives her a weapon with which to fight her husband's opposition. Telling Isabel that her mind is a " 'beastly poor' " one, the Countess reveals to her the real story of Osmond's past. Pansy is the illegitimate daughter of Osmond and Madame Merle; Madame Merle was his mistress for a half-dozen years. The Countess is amazed at Isabel's "ignorance" and "innocence"—it is almost "unbelievable" that she should have had no suspicions, no ideas at all on the subject. Madame Merle, the Countess goes on to say, has renounced all visible ties with Pansy for the girl's own social good. She and Osmond were lovers before Osmond's first wife and Madame Merle's husband were dead, yet the pair worshipped and continue to worship "appearances" intensely. These facts filter slowly into Isabel's consciousness. Madame Merle arranged her marriage with Osmond, the Countess tells her, because Isabel was rich and would probably be good to Pansy—would give her a *dot*. Osmond, conversely, would not marry Madame Merle because she had no money. Madame Merle, for her part, was waiting to marry the first great man she could catch. They have been afraid to be too much together lest people should see a resemblance between Pansy and Madame Merle and figure out the rest.

Isabel "has been made use of" by these two plotters, all right, but she has not understood this completely until now. Her reading of Madame Merle, only recently encumbered with suspicions, had been clouded by stubborn self-confidence. She had ignored the advice of friends and thought of herself as one who could assess others accurately. She sees now how completely in error she has been.

The Countess's revelations determine Isabel to defy her husband and make the journey to England. Before leaving, however, she stops to visit Pansy, who has been locked up in a convent by her father—Osmond suspects that she might defy him and run off with Rosier. There Isabel encounters Madame Merle, also visiting. Madame Merle begins her usual sort of performance, 'but this time "not one of [her words] was lost upon Isabel's ear." Like Michael Henchard, Isabel, tragically enough, has finally acquired the power of understanding others; her new humility has unblocked her perceptions. Seeing Madame Merle in these surroundings, Isabel perceives, "in the crude light of that revelation which had already become a part of experience and to which the very frailty of the vessel in which it had been offered her only gave an intrinsic price, the dry staring fact that she had been an applied handled hung-up tool, as senseless and convenient as mere shaped wood and iron. All the bitterness of this knowledge surged into her soul. . ."[52]. James here typically expresses Isabel's enlightenment in terms of a sharpening of vision ("saw," "light," "staring," "senseless"). Isabel's revelation, described in language remarkably similar to that used by George Eliot in a famous passage in *Daniel Deronda* ("frailty of the vessel"), has made her feel dishonored, and she is eager to be rid of Madame Merle. She rushes off to see Pansy, who begs her not to abandon her to her father. Pansy has been vanquished; she can bear to give Rosier up if only Isabel will be at home when she leaves the convent. Isabel tells her: " 'I won't desert you. . .I'll come back.' " On her way out she again meets Madame Merle, who has waited for her. There is another revelation at hand for Isabel. Madame Merle, seeing that Isabel finally understands everything about her marriage, tells her that it was Ralph who made her a rich woman, that it is he whom she has to thank for her " 'brilliant match.' " Isabel allows herself one moment of bitter recrimination: " 'I believed it was you I had to thank. . . .I think I should never like to see you again.' "[52]

During the trip to England, which seems to Isabel to present only "a perpetual dreariness of winter," she has time to
consider what has happened to her and what her past egoism
has made of her future:

> Now that she was in the secret, now that she knew
> something that so much concerned her and the eclipse of
> which had made life resemble an attempt to play whist
> with an imperfect deck of cards, the truth of things, their
> mutual relations, their meaning, and for the most part
> their horror, rose before her with a kind of architectural
> vastness . . . Not only the time of her folly, but the time
> of her repentance was far . . . She saw herself, in the
> distant years, still in the attitude of a woman who had
> her life to live . . . . Deep was the sense that life would
> be her business for a long time to come . . . . [T]here
> was something inspiring, almost enlivening, in the con-
> viction. It was a proof of strength . . . . It couldn't be
> she was to live only to suffer . . . .(53)

The "secret" Isabel is now "in" is more than merely the secret
of her husband's shabby dealings with her; it is the secret of
"life," of life's intricacies and deceptions and disappointments. She now has the cards she needs to play the game
of life—the question is whether or not for her the game is still
going on. Her suffering has been complete, she feels—what
could be worse than the game she has already lost? Thus, we
are also told, she envies Ralph his dying. Her "folly" has
been so comprehensive and its consequences so annihilating
that she is past regret, past "repentance." Her whole married
life has been a repentance. For her, as for Gwendolen, the
future can only be a form of penance. But out of the tragic
consequences of her ignorance Isabel is able to draw at least
some new inner "strength." It may be, as is so often the case
in James's novels, that this new strength, this new understanding both of herself and of others, has come too late to
palliate the disaster her life has become. For, as Isabel also
says to herself, the finer one is the more he will probably suffer; and perhaps therefore she will never escape unhappiness.
But at least her new knowledge has given her a chance, has
given her a new and a full deck with which to play. And thus
she feels a final sense of "inspiration"—a sense less sanc-

tifying, it may be, than that in the final sections of Dickens's and George Eliot's novels, but nevertheless one that suggests a perspective upon the world that will be more humane in the future than it has been in the past.

With these conflicting thoughts Isabel arrives in London and is met by Henrietta, who immediately starts in on her; she must never return to Rome. But Isabel is adamant. She has promised Pansy Osmond to come back, and come back she must—even though Osmond will undoubtedly make life more unpleasant for her because she has disobeyed him: " 'It won't be the scene of a moment; it will be a scene of the rest of my life,' " Isabel sadly admits. But she must go back.

Isabel goes down to Gardencourt, barely in time to have a last, moving interview with her dying cousin. Isabel's new capacity for empathy enables her, finally, to communicate fully with the one person who has loved her generously and completely throughout: " 'What have I done for you—what can I do to-day? I would die if you could live. But I don't wish to live; I would die myself not to lose you' " [54]. Like Michael Henchard's, Isabel's ultimate statement is one of self-abnegation. Isabel wants Ralph to understand how much she appreciates his generosity in having made her a rich woman, how right he had been to warn her against Osmond—and also that the tragedy of her life has been her own fault. " 'I never thanked you—I never spoke—I never was what I should be!' Isabel went on. She felt a passionate need to cry out and accuse herself, to let her sorrow possess her . . . 'What must you have thought of me! Yet how could I know? I never knew, and I only know today because there are people less stupid than I' " [54] . When Ralph tells her that she is too young to suffer long, Isabel replies: " 'I feel very old.' " Morally, of course, she has aged considerably; like Richard Feverel's, her ordeal has rendered her both sadder and wiser. As Ralph had told her early in their acquaintance, one must suffer in order to understand.

Ralph dies, and Isabel, who feels that it is not possible for her to suffer much more, must now think about returning to Rome. Before her departure, however, the ubiquitous Mr. Goodwood reappears once again, urging Isabel with a kind of violence we have not seen in him before to abandon her husband and go off with him. The tenacity of his passion makes Isabel understand that "she had never been loved before. She had believed it, but this was different . . . . " Goodwood tells her that nothing and no one can interfere with them; they can do as they please: " 'Were we born to rot in our misery—were we born to be afraid? . . . The world's all before us . . . . ' " The world had once before been "all before" her, but then Isabel had had the power of choice. Now she has a final moment of wavering: "The world, in truth, had never seemed so large; it seemed to open out, all round her . . . ." Goodwood kisses her, violently, but this only breaks the momentary spell: "She had not known where to turn; but she knew now. There was a very straight path."

And so Isabel returns to Rome, to her suffering and her obligations. Like Dorothea Brooke, the "determining acts" of whose life, George Eliot tells us, "were the mixed result of young and noble impulse struggling amidst the conditions of an imperfect social state," Isabel Archer, according to James, has been "ground in the very mill of the conventional" [*Notebooks,* n.d., probably 1880]. And yet *The Portrait of A Lady* is not simply a tragedy of circumstances. Isabel's decision, which may perhaps seem foolish and even masochistic to some readers, is for James the correct one. He tells us in the preface to *The Spoils of Poynton,* in the conclusion of *The Ambassadors,* and in many other places in his work, that renunciation can be the noblest of human actions. In Isabel Archer's case this final act of self-denial is particularly appropriate, for it is our ultimate evidence that the "general plan" of the novel, which is the story of Isabel's moral education, has been consistent and fulfilled. The last vestiges of egoism have been drained from James's "frail vessel," to be replaced by selflessness and moral responsibility—no matter how painful or constricting. It is only in self-sacrifice, tragically enough—in honoring the oaths she has sworn to her husband and his daughter—that Isabel will find the comfort that Ralph Touchett and Caspar Goodwood had insisted were within her reach.

Appendix

A Bibliographical Note

It will be obvious to the reader of this book that much of the usual paraphernalia of criticism is absent from the text of these discussions of nineteenth-century novelists. The purpose of this appendix is to provide some of this paraphernalia. My premise was that I could adequately discuss the novels and novelists under examination here without the encumbrance of scholarly interruptions; this does not mean, however, that I am not conversant with the criticism of others or that I have remained uninfluenced by it. I had merely determined beforehand to put my past reading aside as I dealt with these novels, and I hasten now to fill what may seem to some an arrogantly gaping void. I shall not attempt to provide a complete bibliography of past studies of the English novel or of nineteenth-century fiction and its backgrounds. Rather, I shall sketch in the contents of a highly selective working bibliography, a listing of those books and essays that have been particularly helpful to me in the course of writing this book and assessing these novels.

I should probably say at the beginning of this discussion of matters bibliographical that much of my major indebtedness is expressed in the notes of a previous work of my own. This is *The Language of Meditation: Four Studies in Nineteenth-Century Fiction* (1973), which deals with the descriptive language of human psychology, and with resulting narrative structures, in novels by Jane Austen, George Eliot, George Meredith, and Henry James. The movement from egoism to self-discovery is a concern there, but not necessarily the primary one—and in any case that book deals with a number of different novels and fewer novelists and is generally more narrowly focussed than the present study. But the notes there are fairly comprehensive, and many of the secondary sources consulted are the same in both books.

I shall begin with brief mention of some general studies of the novel and the nineteenth century, and then list selectively some of the important contributions to my own understanding of the work of the particular authors discussed in the course of this book.

I

Several works in particular have deeply influenced my approach and reactions to fiction. Chief among these is the criticism of Ortega y Gasset, particularly *The Dehumanization of Art and Notes on the Novel* (1925). I have also read carefully and admired greatly Erich Auerbach's *Mimesis: The Representation of Reality in Western Literature* (1946), David Lodge's *Language of Fiction: Essays in Criticism and Verbal Analysis of the English Novel* (1966), and Mark Schorer's essay "Fiction and the 'Matrix of Analogy' " (first published in the *Kenyon Review* in 1949 and reprinted widely since). What characterizes each of these writers is a meticulously close examination of novelistic structure and the language which creates that structure, and I am grateful to have had their examples before me. György Lukács's *The Theory of the Novel* (1914-15), E. M. Forster's *Aspects of the Novel* (1927), Alain Robbe-Grillet's *For A New Novel* (1963), W. J. Harvey's *Character and the Novel* (1965), Alan Friedman's *The Turn of the Novel* (1966), Frank Kermode's *The Sense of An Ending: Studies in the Theory of Fiction* (1967), and Paul de Man's *Blindness and Insight: Essays in the Rhetoric of Contemporary Criticism* (1971) are books that should provide provocative stimulus to thought for any student of fiction. And Wayne Booth's *The Rhetoric of Fiction* (1961) has been helpful to me both for its definition and discussion of useful novelistic terminology and for the mental exercise it has evoked in me as a result of my almost continuous disagreement with its critical judgments. Two other books which also provide useful definitions and discussions of complex novelistic phenomena, in this case primarily phenomena relating to narrative structure, are Robert Humphrey's *Stream of Consciousness in the Modern Novel* (1954) and J. Hillis Miller's *The Form of Victorian Fiction* (1968).

Among more general studies of the novel I have found useful there is, first and foremost, Ernest Baker's classic and monumental work, *The History of the English Novel* (9 vols., 1924-1938). Other shorter but also informative surveys include Arnold Kettle's *An Introduction to the English Novel* (2 vols., 1951), and Walter Allen's *The English Novel: A Short Critical History* (1954). Ian Watt's *The Rise of the Novel; Studies in Defoe, Richardson, and Fielding* (1957) is an excellent account of the origins of English fiction. Q. D. Leavis's *Fiction and Reading Public* (1932) is an invaluable study of the relationship between fiction and fiction-readers during the novel's formative years. Another extremely useful volume along these lines, one whose emphasis falls on the nineteenth century, is R. D. Altick's *The English Common Reader* (1957). Among the more specifically theme-oriented studies of the novel, my listing of which could easily be several pages long, I should choose particularly to mention eight works. First must be F. R. Leavis's *The Great Tradition* (1948), which remains today one of the most interesting and provocative of all studies of the novel. It seems to me to be a book alternately brilliant and wrong-headed; but as a stimulus to reflection and argument it is consistently effective. I have been particularly influenced by Leavis's argument (one of the first) that *The Portrait of A Lady* is a distillation of George Eliot. Similarly, I have found Dorothy Van Ghent's *The English Novel: Form and Function* (1953) a continuing source of interest, though her literary judgments, excluding her work on Dickens, often seem to me to be arbitrarily subjective. Other illuminating studies of nineteenth-century fiction are John Halloway's *The Victorian Sage: Studies in Argument* (1953), Mario Praz's *The Hero in Eclipse in Victorian Fiction* (1956), U. C. Knoepflmacher's *Religious Humanism and the Victorian Novel* (1965)—and three studies of American literature: R.W.B. Lewis's *The American Adam: Innocence, Tragedy, and Tradition in the Nineteenth Century*

(1955), Richard Chase's *The American Novel and Its Tradition* (1957), and Leslie A. Fiedler's *Love and Death in the American Novel* (1960).

Four books which seem to me to be invaluable to any student of nineteenth-century fiction are Richard Stang's *The Theory of the Novel in England 1850-1870* (1959), Keith Hollingworth's *The Newgate Novel 1830-1847* (1963), Kenneth Graham's *English Criticism of the Novel 1865-1900* (1965), and Guinevere L. Griest's *Mudie's Circulating Library and the Victorian Novel* (1970). I am grateful to their authors for the insights into literary background provided therein.

The nineteenth-century intellectual and social background itself has not entered very much into my own study, so I shall not attempt here to provide the reader with a comprehensive listing of any kind. I would recommend to the student by way of introduction to this background, however, six books of very different perspective and construction: G. M. Young's *Victorian England: Portrait of An Age* (1936), Jerome Hamilton Buckley's *The Victorian Temper: A Study in Literary Culture* (1951), Walter E. Houghton's *The Victorian Frame of Mind, 1830-1870* (1957), Asa Briggs's *The Age of Improvement* (1959), J. Hillis Miller's *The Disappearance of God: Five Nineteenth-Century Writers* (1963), and Raymond Chapman's *The Victorian Debate: English Literature and Society 1832-1901* (1968).

Finally, it is difficult to imagine any study of the Victorian novelists whose author could not benefit from a reading of *Victorian Fiction: A Guide to Research,* edited by Lionel Stevenson (1964).

I would emphasize once again that the titles mentioned here represent a tiny percentage of what is available on the novel and the nineteenth century. They constitute only a highly selective and abbreviated list of those books I have found particularly helpful.

II

In the final section of this bibliographical note I shall list, again selectively and briefly, works dealing specifically with the authors whose novels have been examined in the course of this study. Once again I shall limit the listing to those titles I have found to be the most illuminating and helpful.

No student of Jane Austen can fail to be indebted to the work of R. W. Chapman, Jane Austen's foremost biographer and editor. It is largely due to him that her novels are now widely available in virtually variorum texts. Chapman has also edited *Jane Austen's Letters* (1932). Early reactions to Jane Austen's novels may be found in *Jane Austen: The Critical Heritage,* edited by B. C. Southam (1968). Among the good critical studies of Jane Austen, of which there are only a few, I am chiefly indebted to A. Walton Litz's *Jane Austen: A Study of Her Artistic Development* (1965), which I believe to be the best book on Jane Austen in print today. Next, three essays seem to me particularly distinguished, especially in their recognition both of Jane Austen's sophisticated perspective upon and treatment of human psychology and the many ways in which she anticipates some of the later and more celebrated "psychological" novelists. These essays are Virginia Woolf's "Jane Austen at Sixty," originally published in the *Nation* (December 15, 1923); Ian Watt's "Realism and the later tradition: a note," in *The Rise of the Novel: Studies in Defoe, Richardson, and Fielding* (1957); and Irène Simon's "Jane Austen and *The Art of the Novel*" (*ES*, 1962). Mary Lascelles, in *Jane Austen and Her Art* (1939), was one of the first of Jane Austen's readers after G. H. Lewes and Richard Simpson to recognize the subtle complexity of the novelist's style, and I believe her book has been unfairly consigned to oblivion in recent years. Two other excellent studies are Lionel Trilling's *"Mansfield Park,"* originally published in *The Opposing Self* (1955), and Howard Babb's *Jane Austen's Novels: The Fabric of Dialogue* (1962). A provocative, interesting, incisive, and unfortunately much-maligned study is Marvin Mudrick's *Jane Austen: Irony as Defense and Discovery* (1952), which approaches the novels from an unsympathetic perspective upon the novelist and the conclusions of which, admittedly, are sometimes distorted by prejudice. An excellent recent study is Darrel Mansell's *The Novels of Jane Austen: An Interpretation* (1973). And finally, I should direct the reader to my own *Language of Meditation: Four Studies in Nineteenth-Century Fiction* (1973), which includes a long essay on narrative structure and the language of indirect discourse in several of Jane Austen's novels.

There is surprisingly little in print about Thackeray beyond what has been done by Gordon N. Ray. Among Mr. Ray's many important writings on Thackeray the most brilliant and inimitable are the two volumes of critical biography—*Thackeray: The Uses of Adversity: 1811-1846* (1955) and *Thackeray: The Age of Wisdom: 1847-1863* (1958). Mr. Ray has also provided us with four fascinating volumes of *The Letters and Private Papers of William Makepeace Thackeray* (1945-6). Another important Ray volume is *Buried Life: A Study of the Relation Between Thackeray's Fiction and His Personal History* (1952). Outside of Mr. Ray's work, the best full-length studies of Thackeray are Geoffrey Tillotson's *Thackeray the Novelist* (1954), John Loofbourow's *Thackeray and the Form of Fiction* (1964), and Barbara Hardy's *The Exposure of Luxury: Radical Themes in Thackeray* (1972). Two provocative essays on *Vanity Fair* have been contributed by Dorothy Van Ghent in *The English Novel: Form and Function* (1953) and Kathleen Tillotson in *Novels of the Eighteen-Forties* (1954), which together provide an interesting contrast in attitudes toward Thackeray's use of direct authorial commentary. Earlier reactions to Thackeray's work may be found in *Thackeray: The Critical Heritage* edited by Geoffrey Tillotson and Donald Hawes (1968).

Fortunately, somewhat more critical material is available on Charlotte Brontë. Extremely valuable biographical information may be found in two nineteenth-century studies—Mrs. Gaskell's two-volume *Life of Charlotte Brontë* (1857) and Clement Shorter's *Charlotte Brontë and Her Circle* (1896). Fanny E. Ratchford's *The Brontës Web of Childhood* (1941) attempts to trace childhood influences upon the Brontës' early work, and Winifred Gerin's *Charlotte*

Brontë: The Evolution of Genius (1967) is a more recent comprehensive biographical study. By far the best full-length
critical study of Charlotte Brontë's fiction is Robert Bernard
Martin's *Charlotte Brontë's Novels: The Accents of Persuasion*
(1966), which has greatly influenced my own reading of the
novelist. Finally, there are a number of excellent essays, of
which the most distinguished in my view are Richard Chase's
"The Brontës, or Myth Domesticated," originally published
in *Forms of Modern Fiction,* edited by William Van O'Connor
(1948); Kathleen Tillotson's discussion of *Jane Eyre* in *Novels
of the Eighteen-Forties* (1954); and Robert B. Heilman's
"Charlotte Brontë's 'New' Gothic," originally published in
From Jane Austen to Joseph Conrad, edited by R. C.
Rathburn and Martin Steinmann, Jr. (1958), and now
reprinted widely.

Remarkably little has been written about Trollope. The
best sources of information about his life and his attitude
toward his art remain his own *Autobiography*, originally
published in two volumes in 1883, and Bradford A. Booth's
edition of *The Letters of Anthony Trollope* (1951). *Trollope:
The Critical Heritage*, edited by Donald Smalley (1969), gives
a good cross-section of contemporary Trollope criticism.
There are only four really distinguished full-length studies of
Trollope: Michael Sadleir's *Trollope: A Commentary* (1927),
which is rather whimsical in its biographical sections but
penetrating in its criticism; A. O. J. Cockshut's *Anthony
Trollope: A Critical Study* (1955), which is alternately naive
and incisive; Booth's *Anthony Trollope: Aspects of His Life
and Art* (1958); and Robert M. Polhemus's *The Changing
World of Anthony Trollope* (1968). James Pope Hennessy's
critical biography, *Anthony Trollope* (1971), is inert and
generally tells us little beyond the early biography of the
novelist by T. H. S. Escott *(Anthony Trollope*, 1913). Among
shorter pieces on Trollope, two brilliant essays should repay
the reader's attention—Henry James's "Anthony Trollope,"
originally published in *Century Magazine* in July 1883 and
reprinted thereafter in *Partial Portraits* (1888) and elsewhere,
and Gordon N. Ray's "Trollope at Full Length," published

in the *Huntington Library Quarterly* between 1967 and 1969.

There is of course a tremendous amount of available material on Dickens. Here once again I shall confine myself to a highly selective listing of items I have found particularly useful and interesting. John Forster, in *The Life of Charles Dickens,* published in three volumes between 1872 and 1874, and Edgar Johnson, in *Charles Dickens: His Tragedy and Triumph,* published in two volumes in 1952, have provided us with fascinating and comprehensive biographies, though Forster deliberately ignored or was unacquainted with a good deal of information available to Mr. Johnson and other later Dickens scholars. Ada Nisbet's *Dickens and Ellen Ternan* (1952) provides a fascinating account of the novelist and his lately discovered mistress. Until the complete Pilgrim Edition of Dickens's letters is in print (three volumes, taking us through 1842, have thus far appeared), the most comprehensive collection remains *The Letters of Charles Dickens,* edited by Walter Dexter as part of the Nonesuch Edition of the complete works (23 volumes, 1937-1938). Humphry House's *The Dickens World* (1941) is an invaluable companion-piece to the reading of Dickens's novels, and John Butt and Kathleen Tillotson, in *Dickens at Work* (1957), provide an interesting insight into the ways in which Dickens's novels were actually written. George Ford, in *Dickens and His Readers* (1955), furnishes invaluable publishing histories of Dickens's novels and some of the stories. An excellent selection of early criticism is provided by Philip Collins in *Dickens: The Critical Heritage* (1971). There are of course many excellent full-length critical studies of Dickens's fiction. I would especially recommend six: K. J. Fielding's *Charles Dickens: A Critical Introduction* (1958), a good general study of Dickens's novels; J. Hillis Miller's *Charles Dickens: The World of His Novels* (1958), a symbolist interpretation which pays particular attention to Dickens's language; Monroe Engel's *The Maturity of Dickens* (1959), an incisive assessment of the later novels; Robert Garis's *The Dickens Theater: A Reassessment of the Novels* (1965), an anti-symbolist and generally unsympathetic study which nevertheless assesses brilliantly the narrative structures of the novels; Stephen Marcus's *Dickens: From Pickwick to Dombey* (1965), which is the most level-headed Freudian study of Dickens in print; and Barbara Hardy's *The Moral Art of Dickens* (1970), which emphasizes, at times in a way somewhat similar to my own, the process of moral growth in Dickens's characters. There are many first-rate essays on Dickens, of which I wish to mention five: Edmund Wilson's "Dickens: The Two Scrooges," originally published in *The Wound and the Bow* (1947), is widely credited for having started the Dickens revival after World War II—whether or not this is true, Mr. Wilson's essay remains one of the best discussions of Dickens I know of, due particularly to his illuminating treatment of the growing complexity of Dickens's fiction as the novelist matured; Dorothy Van Ghent's "The Dickens World: The View from Todgers's," originally published in *The Sewanee Review* in 1950, remains to my mind, despite its ostensible discussion of *Martin Chuzzlewit,* still the most brilliant general assessment of the meaning and generating forces of Dickens's characteristic metaphorical language; Mrs. Van Ghent's essay on *Great Expectations* in *The English Novel: Form and Function* (1953) pursues the same subject; Kathleen Tillotson's discussion of *Dombey and Son* in *Novels of the Eighteen-Forties* (1954) is one of the very few essays in the Dickens canon which shares my belief that the ending of *Dombey and Son* is totally appropriate artistically and thematically; and Robert Garis's "Dickens Criticism" (*VS,* 1964) is an interesting though subjective account of critical trends. Finally, much of the very best Dickens criticism over the past one-hundred and more years has been collected by George Ford and Lauriat Lane, Jr., in *The Dickens Critics* (1961).

Fortunately, many useful and enlightening volumes on George Eliot are likewise available. To begin with, there is Gordon S. Haight's monumental *George Eliot: A Biography* (1968), and his edition of *The George Eliot Letters,* published in seven volumes (1954-55). An earlier and fascinating but incomplete biographical document is J. W. Cross's *George Eliot's Life as Related in Her Letters and Journals,* published in three volumes in 1885. Thomas Pinney has edited a useful volume of *Essays of George Eliot* (1963). Some of the early George Eliot criticism has been collected by David Carroll in *George Eliot: The Critical Heritage* (1971). Among the many full-length critical studies, four seem to me to stand above the rest. These are Barbara Hardy's *The Novels of George Eliot: A Study in Form* (1959), which emphasizes patterns of tragedy in the novels (there is room for some doubt here, but Mrs. Hardy is eminently convincing on other matters); Reva Stump's *Movement and Vision in George Eliot's Novels* (1959), which concentrates brilliantly upon the connections between theme and metaphor in several of the novels; W. J. Harvey's *The Art of George Eliot* (1961), which emphasizes the mimetic qualities of her art, particularly in her conception and treatment of character; and Bernard J. Paris's *Experiments in Life: George Eliot's Quest for Values* (1965), which traces her intellectual development and the progress of the various philosophical influences that helped to shape it. I have been particularly influenced by Mr. Paris's discussion of the stages of moral development George Eliot's protagonists usually traverse. The availability of some excellent collections of essays on various aspects of George Eliot's fiction should also be noted (several volumes on *Middlemarch,* for example). Collected or not, however, there are a number of shorter pieces that I would recommend first. F. R. Leavis's controversial essay on George Eliot in *The Great Tradition* (1948) helped rescue the novels from the oblivion to which they had been consigned from the turn of the twentieth century onward. Leavis's assessments of *Middlemarch* and *Daniel Deronda* and their influence on Henry James provoked a number of other critics, including his wife, to response. Q. D. Leavis's "A Note on Literary Indebtedness: Dickens, George Eliot, Henry James" was published in the *Hudson Review* in 1955, Oscar Cargill's " 'The Portrait of A Lady': A Critical Reappraisal" appeared in *Modern Fiction Studies* in 1957, and George Levine's "Isabel, Gwendolen, and Dorothea" followed in *ELH* in 1963. Mr. Leavis had appended to *The Great Tradition* James's *"Daniel Deronda:* A Conversation," which first appeared in the *Atlantic Monthly* in 1876, and James himself is an excellent source of information for the assessment of his debt to George Eliot (see also, for example, his famous review of *Middlemarch,* first published in *The Galaxy* in March 1873, and my own discussion of the subject in *The Language of Meditation*[1973], which also includes a long essay on George Eliot). Some other important and interesting shorter pieces on George Eliot are Alice R. Kaminsky's "George Eliot, George Henry Lewes, and the Novel" (*PMLA,* 1955); Richard Stang's "The Literary Criticism of George Eliot" (*PMLA,* 1957); George Levine's "Determinism and Responsibility in the Works of George Eliot" (*PMLA,* 1962); Dorothy Van Ghent's essay on *Adam Bede* in *The English Novel: Form and Function* (1953); U. C. Knoepflmacher's essays on George Eliot in *Religious Humanism and the Victorian Novel* (1956); and Calvin Bedient's discussion in *Architects of the Self: George Eliot, D. H. Lawrence, E. M. Forster* (1972).

There is remarkably little available on Meredith. Siegfried Sassoon's biography, *Meredith* (1948), is interesting but more subjective than scholarly. However, Lionel Stevenson's *The Ordeal of George Meredith* (1953) is a first-rate and fascinating account of the writer's life. There is also a good three-volume collection of Meredith's letters edited by C. L. Cline (1970). *Meredith: The Critical Heritage,* edited by Ian Williams (1971), provides an interesting selection of early critical reactions. Among the few full-length studies of Meredith's work the three best are Walter F. Wright's *Art and Substance in George Meredith* (1953), Norman Kelvin's *A Troubled Eden: Nature and Society in the Works of George Meredith* (1961), and V. S. Pritchett's *George Meredith and English Comedy* (1969). Several good shorter pieces on Meredith are Ramon Fernandez's essay in *Messages,* first published in 1927 and reprinted in 1964; Virginia Woolf's unsympathetic essay, "The Novels of George Meredith," written in 1928 but not published until 1932 in *The Second Common Reader;* Donald David Stone's discussion in *Novelists in A Changing World* (1972); and three excellent articles by Irving H. Buchen: "The Importance of Minor Characters in *The Ordeal of Richard Feverel"* (*Boston University Studies in English*, 1961); "*The Ordeal of Richard Feverel:* Science Versus Nature" (*ELH,* 1962); and "The Egoists in *The Egoist*: the Sensualists and the Ascetics" (*NCF*, 1964). There is also an essay on *The Egoist* in *The Language of Meditation* (1973).

Of the surprisingly moderate number of books and articles on Hardy's fiction, only a handful will repay the reader's attention. Carl J. Weber's biography, *Hardy of Wessex* (1940; revised 1965), is interesting but not comprehensive. A fascinating document is the second Mrs. Hardy's *Life of Thomas Hardy: 1840-1928* (1962; first published in two parts as *The Early Life* [1928] and *The Later Years* [1930]), fascinating because Hardy wrote or dictated most of it himself. Among the earliest critical studies of Hardy, Lascelles Abercrombie's *Thomas Hardy: A Critical Study* (1912) and Joseph Warren Beach's *The Technique of Thomas Hardy* (1922) remain the most penetrating. An excellent and now widely reprinted shorter piece is Donald Davidson's "The Traditional Basis of Thomas Hardy's Fiction" (*Southern Review,* 1940). Albert J. Guerard's *Thomas Hardy: The Novels and Stories* (1949) is brief and intermittently brilliant. In *The Victorian Sage: Studies in Argument* (1953), John Holloway includes among other things a provocative discussion of Hardy's conception and use of physical nature, a subject that has of course interested a number of Hardy's readers. Mrs. Van Ghent's essay on *Tess of the D'Urbervilles* in *The English Novel: Form and Function* (1953) is an excellent discussion of Hardy's characteristic fictional mode. The best recent critical studies of Hardy include Harvey Curtis Webster's *On A Darkling Plain: The Art and Thought of Thomas Hardy* (1964), Irving Howe's *Thomas Hardy* (1967), and Jean Brooks's *Thomas Hardy: The Poetic Structure* (1971). Perhaps the best book on Hardy now in print is J. Hillis Miller's *Thomas Hardy: Distance and Desire* (1970), which followed on the heels of a series of brilliant articles on Hardy (see, for example, Mr. Miller's " 'Wessex Heights':

The Persistence of the Past in Hardy's Poetry" [*Critical Quarterly,* 1968] and "Thomas Hardy: Sketch for a Portrait" in *Hommages A Marcel Raymond* [1969].

When we come to Henry James, there are a great many excellent items to choose among. A helpful survey of criticism is provided by Robert E. Spiller in *Eight American Authors: A Review of Research and Criticism,* edited by Floyd Stovall (first published in 1956; revised in 1963 and again in 1971). *Henry James: The Critical Heritage,* edited by Roger Gard (1968), reproduces much early criticism of James's work. The standard biography of James is Leon Edel's monumental five-volume work: *The Untried Years, 1843-1870* (1953); *The Conquest of London. 1870-1883* (1962); *The Middle Years, 1882-1895* (1962); *The Treacherous Years, 1895-1901* (1969); and *The Master, 1901-1916* (1972). F. W. Dupee's *Henry James* (1951), a brief critical biography, remains one of the soundest shorter volumes on James, and F. O. Matthiessen's *The James Family* (1947) also provides some fascinating biographical information. Until Mr. Edel's projected edition appears, there is still no complete edition of James's letters; a large slice of them, however, is given in a number of different selections—two of the best of which are Percy Lubbock's *The Letters of Henry James,* published in two volumes in 1920, and Edel's *Selected Letters of Henry James* (1956). James's Notebooks have been published under the editorship of Matthiessen and Kenneth B. Murdock (*The Notebooks of Henry James,* 1947). And of course more complete autobiographical information may be found in the three volumes of James's unfinished and frequently digressive memoirs—*A Small Boy and Others* (1913), *Notes of A Son and Brother* (1914), and the posthumous *The Middle Years* (1917). Most of James's essays and prefaces are available in a number of editions. Among full-length critical studies of James, there is, as I have said, a great deal to choose from; I shall list only those items which seem to me particularly illuminating. Rebecca West's *Henry James* (1916) was the first critical appreciation to suggest James's rightful place among the novelists. Another early and brilliant study is Joseph Warren Beach's *The Method of Henry James,* first published in 1918 and later revised and republished in 1954. Percy Lubbock's *The Craft of Fiction,* originally published in 1921, is still a classic of theoretical Jamesian novel-criticism, and as such tells us a great deal about James's own views on the novel. Another early and still excellent assessment of James as critic is Morris Roberts's *Henry James's Criticism* (1929). In 1944, Matthiessen published *Henry James: The Major Phase,* one of the first vindications of the novels of James's later period and today still one of the best critical studies of these novels. Harold McCarthy's *Henry James: The Creative Process* (1958) provides interesting insights into James's actual compositional methods. Alexander Holder-Barell's *The Development of Imagery and Its Functional Significance in Henry James's Novels* (1959) is an excellent study of the metaphorical language of James's fiction. Two first-rate surveys of James's early novels and stories are Richard Poirier's *The Comic Sense of Henry James* (1960) and Cornelia Pulsifer Kelley's *The Early Development of Henry James* (1965). In 1962 Dorothea Krook published her brilliant volume *The Ordeal of Consciousness in Henry James,* which remains today the best critical study of James in print. It concentrates mostly upon the later novels, but the principles it identifies are applicable by and large throughout the James canon. Another excellent study of James's novels, with particular reference to the later ones, is Sallie Sears's *The Negative Imagination: Form and Perspective in the Novels of Henry James* (1968). Among shorter pieces on James, T. S. Eliot's famous essay, "Henry James," originally published in *The Little Review* in August 1918 and reprinted widely thereafter, was instrumental in awakening earlier readers to James's pre-eminent position among writers of fiction. In the same issue of *The Little Review* Ezra Pound echoed Eliot's assessment in his own "Henry James." Stephen Spender, in an essay in *The Destructive Element* (1936), was one of the first to discuss the poetic imagery of James's later novels. In *The Great Tradition* (1948), F. R. Leavis placed James among the greatest novelists of the nineteenth century.

Leavis's discussion of *The Portrait of A Lady* is particularly interesting, and in the course of it, as noted earlier, he emphasizes James's debt to George Eliot. As I have also noted, there are essays of a similar thrust by Q. D. Leavis ("A Note on Literary Indebtedness: Dickens, George Eliot, Henry James," *Hudson Review*, 1955), Oscar Cargill (" 'The Portrait of A Lady': A Critical Reappraisal," *Modern Fiction Studies,* 1957), George Levine ("Isabel, Gwendolen, and Dorothea," *ELH,* 1963), and myself (in *The Language of Meditation,* which also discusses some of James's characteristic metaphorical language). Another excellent essay on *The Portrait of A Lady* was published in 1957 by Richard Chase in *The American Novel and Its Tradition.* Two essays ostensibly on *The Ambassadors* but nevertheless excellent general studies of James's characteristic use of language are Ian Watt's "The First Paragraph of *The Ambassadors:* An explication" (*Essays in Criticism,* 1960), and David Lodge's "Strether by the River" in his *Language of Fiction: Essays in Criticism and Verbal Analysis of the English Novel* (1966). Charles R. Anderson's "Person, Place and Thing in James's *The Portrait of A Lady"* (*Essays on American Literature,* edited by Clarence Gohdes, 1967) is a fascinating account of the dynamics of perception in that novel. In the Afterword to an edition of *The Golden Bowl* (Meridian Books, 1972; reprinted oy the Popular Library, 1973), I discuss the same subject in the context of James's last completed novel. And in "Henry James and the Morality of Fiction" (*AL* 1967), R. J. Reilly writes interestingly of the seeming absence of dogma and polemic in James's moral philosophy.

I have intended here only to suggest a few major avenues of approach to some of these pre-eminent nineteenth-century novelists. This informal bibliography, I would emphasize again, is therefore in no way definitive or complete. I have included it both to provide some hopefully helpful suggestions for further reading and to supply some critical context in which to place the discussions of novels and novelists which appear in this study.

Index of Primary Titles Cited

293

Index of Primary Titles Cited